Born in Southampton in 1971, Tim has lived in South London for the last twenty years and is married to Katie with a son Felix. A first-time book writer, Tim is a full-time communications manager and has played field hockey all his life. His eyes and heart have been opened by his health struggle with cystic fibrosis which has been a huge factor in his life, but not one that defines it.

HOW HAVE I CHEATED DEATH?

A SHORT AND MERRY LIFE WITH CYSTIC FIBROSIS

For my parents Margaret and Douglas, brothers Chris and Jez, wife Katie and son Felix.

Tim Wotton

HOW HAVE I CHEATED DEATH?

A SHORT AND MERRY LIFE WITH CYSTIC FIBROSIS

AUSTIN MACAULEY
PUBLISHERS LTD.

A CIP catalogue record for this title is available from the British Library.

ISBN 978 184963 719 0

www.austinmacauley.com

First Published (2014)
Austin Macauley Publishers Ltd.
25 Canada Square
Canary Wharf
London
E14 5LB

Printed and bound in Great Britain

Acknowledgments

I want to thank Ailsa Herd for meeting with me for that coffee in September 2010, clearing up my tears and pointing me in the right direction to share my story.

I also want to thank Gus Griffin for his bravery that day and his note that verified that my decision to open up was the right one.

I want to extend my appreciation to the authors Rupert Brow and Jonathan Trigell for their wise counsel and to Paul Allen and Stuart Harley for their unstinting guidance and support for my aspirations.

I have appreciated all the advice from family and friends, the help with the design of my blog and the persistent encouragement to carry on sharing.

Foreword

I was touched to be asked by Tim Wotton to write an introduction to his book. He writes beautifully with such honesty, clarity and humour. His blogs marking the year leading to his 40th birthday have had a huge following. For those affected by cystic fibrosis (CF) he gives hope, and for those who don't know about CF his words are inspirational, making us aware how much we can achieve and enjoy whatever problems arise.

I first knew about CF 34 years ago when my niece Rachel was diagnosed with the disease. We discovered that my brother Jonathan and sister-in-law Caroline were both carriers of the CF gene. Rachel was their first child and it took a few months of tests to discover why she was not thriving and putting on weight as she should have been. It was a very worrying time. We were unaware of anyone in the family having CF so knew nothing about it, and were shocked to hear that Rachel had a genetic, life-threatening disease. Back then, few children with the condition survived into their teens.

I was living in the United States whilst Rachel was growing up, and was unaware of the day-to-day routine that Caroline and Jonathan went through to maintain Rachel's health. The daily physiotherapy, the mountain of pills, the constant nagging fear that a cold or flu or some virus that affected the lungs would take hold and reduce her ability to breathe. I have vivid memories of her long stretch in hospital when she was about nine years old (for someone with CF, going to hospital is hardly ever for a short period of time.) Rachel had a terror of needles so the intravenous medication was a nightmare for her. I am filled with admiration for the way that Jonathan and Caroline encompassed all that was necessary to keep Rachel healthy and still managed to maintain a normal family life. Rachel was followed by a brother and another daughter, neither of which have CF.

Watching Rachel grow up, it was obvious that being a teenager with CF was a huge burden and responsibility. Just when a young person wants to fit in with their peers and be accepted they have to acknowledge their frailty, take masses of medication and spend time doing physiotherapy to make sure that they are keeping their lungs as fit as possible. Motivating teenagers is not an easy task, so imagine trying to persuade a fifteen year old to get up early so that they can do a regime of exercise, take a cocktail of drugs, have their breakfast and then go off to school. Once home in the evening, homework has to be done, and there's no time to watch TV as more physiotherapy needs to be done. And this is not for a short period of time; this regime is necessary every day, for life. It's never-ending and relentless.

This all happens against a backdrop of misunderstanding about CF as it's not that well known to the general public. Anyone with the condition constantly has to interpret their symptoms to strangers – coughing fits in the public domain have to be explained, often using humour to dissolve difficult predicaments: "Yes sorry about the cough, it will be the death of me!"

Only half of those with CF will make it beyond thirty, so a 40th birthday is an enormous milestone. For most of us, it is impossible to understand what it must be like when you can't take life for granted. I gained some level of insight when I starred in the film 'Logan's Run', which portrayed a twenty third century world where no one was allowed to live beyond the age of thirty. Of course, it's real life that is perpetually put in doubt for the likes of my niece Rachel, and Tim, who have been told that they were unlikely to reach twenty, thirty or even forty years of age.

Reading this book brings us closer to understanding how precious each day is. Rather than looking too far into the future for our hopes, it's crucial to enjoy the here and now because life can so easily be cut short.

Tim Wotton's brilliant book follows his personal struggle with CF; the day-to-day frustrations and anxieties, alongside his survival strategies, all underpinned by the absolute joy of defying the odds and living life to the full. For anyone affected by CF or facing any form of life challenge this is a compelling and heartening story. For everyone it offers hope and inspiration. I celebrate with Tim his unlikely but triumphant 40th birthday and wish him all the best for the next forty years!

Jenny Agutter
Cystic Fibrosis UK Patron

Preface

At birth in March 1971, I was diagnosed with the life-threatening illness cystic fibrosis (CF) and not expected to live much past my teens.

CF is a serious genetic disorder with reduced life expectancy. It is caused by mutations in the cystic fibrosis trans-membrane conductance regulator (CFTR) gene, which regulates the production of mucus, sweat and digestive enzymes. For a person to have CF, both his or her parents have to be carriers of this mutated CFTR gene. The name cystic fibrosis refers to the characteristic scarring (fibrosis) and cyst formation within the pancreas, first recognized in the 1930s.

It is one of the UK's most common life threatening inherited diseases, affecting over 9,000 people. In the United States, approximately 30,000 people have CF. Around 1,000 new cases of CF are diagnosed each year.

Not such a long time ago, the diagnosis of CF meant an early death. Germanic folklore has a saying: "A child who tastes like salt when kissed on the forehead will soon die." Before the 1950s, the prognosis on CF was so negative that doctors hardly believed that a child with this condition could live beyond seven years of age. The life expectancy of CF patients has been increasing over the past 40 years.

The condition affects the internal organs, especially the lungs and digestive system, by clogging them with thick, sticky mucus. This makes it hard to breathe and digest food. Difficulty breathing is the most serious symptom and results from frequent lung infections that are treated with, though not cured by, antibiotics and other medications. A multitude of other symptoms, including sinus infections, poor growth, diarrhoea, and infertility result from the effects of CF on other parts of the body.

Each week in the UK, five babies are born with the condition; however, each week, three young lives are also lost to it. Vast improvements in treatment have increased the life expectancy of patients, but currently there's no cure for CF.

As my longevity in this world was perpetually in doubt, it had a dramatic effect on what I did, how I felt and my priorities in life.

This book depicts the countdown to my landmark 40th year in diary format with the clock ticking from the day I turned 39 to the day I reach 40, as I unpick how I've cheated death for so long and lay out my formula for survival. This is the first book written by anyone with CF who has reached this significant age milestone.

When people look at me, they see a married man with a gorgeous wife and son, working full-time in London and playing regular sports. What they don't see is my chronic illness, which clogs up my lungs and digestive system with a thick, sticky mucus. It makes it hard to breathe, exercise and digest food.

All my life – every day – has been a battle to defy the odds around my life expectancy, currently set at 42 years – though for a long time it was fixed at 30. I knew that life was likely to be short, and having my own property, wife and child seemed unattainable. My very existence has always seemed held in an hourglass with the grains of sand running out fast. Every hour of every day is important as I never know when my hourglass will run out of time.

I undertake heavy and demoralising daily medication which brings regular dark, sad and fraught moments. I cannot afford to let up or cut any corners medically, as any big lapse could be my undoing. It is relentless – like having a heavy chest cold every day of your life – and unforgiving, killing many sufferers early. Throughout my life, I've had the misfortune to see many of my contemporary fellow sufferers pass away in adulthood, teens or early twenties.

To compound the problems of my life, CF is not that well known, understood, and cannot be easily seen or ever properly imagined by most people. It's like a form of 'locked-in syndrome' as all the damage is on the inside and not very obvious to the naked eye.

Historically, I tended to suppress all my emotions about CF and be very guarded about disclosing it to strangers. I never wanted to be viewed as the 'ill person' and be defined by my condition and I certainly never wanted anyone to feel sorry for me or pity me. But after so many years of secrecy and protection, there was a huge amount of unresolved sadness and emotion under the surface.

As I defied the odds to approach this milestone, I had an epiphany that surviving CF has been the biggest achievement in my life, but it was hidden away and I wasn't talking about it or using it for my own or others' benefit. The addition of diabetes to my medical regime reinforced the feeling that my survival was something to be celebrated and shared. Now I wanted to speak up...

I decided to take the lid off of my own Pandora's Box and keep a diary in the year leading to my 40th to properly reflect, for the first time on my life – past, present and future – my trials and tribulations, happy times and what it has taken for me to survive this chronic illness for 40 years. I chose not to look back in anger but to look forward with positivity.

As I stirred my conscience, I began a journey of discovery that awakened my soul to the overriding desire to share my hard-fought but enriching life-lessons of hope as a form of cathartic process for myself and also to help others. At the same time, I wanted to increase the awareness and understanding of CF and share my bigger picture of life perspective, perseverance and optimism with a wider audience. One prime driver was to inspire people that even at your lowest ebb with the odds stacked against you, that there is usually a way to overcome.

There's a saying that 'what can't be cured, needs to be endured'. By enduring all my life, I realised I had some extraordinary stories to share and some unique life insights. I wanted to highlight the approach I have honed over the years that keeps me alive and kicking, where CF does not define me but is just something I have to 'get on with' to lead my busy life.

Each chapter is a diary extract which covers the full spectrum of my daily life with flashbacks to my past and survival secrets – how have I cheated death?

Tim Wotton

1. Living the Dream

Early March 2010

I've been having the same recurring dream for nearly 40 years. Actually, it feels more like a nightmare than a dream. It's pretty damn frightening and I wouldn't wish it on my worst enemy.

In this ever-repeating dream, I'm held prisoner in my own version of Groundhog Day where it appears I have such a ferocious illness that I have to be taking a multitude of medication from the instant I wake to the moment I put my head down at night. I am always coughing and it feels like having the effects of a heavy chest cold every single day, so it must be some form of lung condition that never goes away.

In my dream, as soon as I wake up, I reach into my bedside drawer, which is like a mini chemist's shop, and I pick up the first of many drugs. The drugs don't seem to be recreational. I really seem to need them. Where a smoker's initial instinct on waking is to grab their packet of cigarettes, mine is to start taking a colourful mix of antibiotics-all different shapes and sizes.

Before I even make myself a cup of tea in the morning I've taken 15 tablets. Then I have to use a whirring nebulizer device containing a medicine. This produces a fine mist through a mouthpiece which I breathe in for 10 minutes.

Following this activity I lie back down on my bed. Not for a rest but so that I can pat my chest with my hands to bring up mucus which seems to be waiting to be coughed up – it's always lurking there, just waiting to come up.

It's pretty disgusting really to be producing such phlegm so early each morning but in my dream it seems perfectly normal to me. Curiously, I get the feeling that I've never smoked one cigarette in my life so this lung-related condition has not been brought on by my own actions – it's just there, is part of me and my DNA.

Occasionally, I cough so hard that I'm sick on myself, mainly just liquid but nonetheless pretty awful and a grim start to my day. Imagine it... you wake up and within 20 minutes you're sick on yourself – not an inspiring thought really and an utterly depressing opening to anyone's day.

Both up and down my house there are drawers and areas full of drugs and medical equipment – some are stashed away and some are on show for ease of use. Like an alcoholic with secret stashes of vodka dotted around the house, I have medication hiding places spread everywhere. Maybe I live in a show home for a pharmaceutical company and I'm their medication guinea pig?

I'm still not finished with this crazy clinical schedule as next up I'm pricking my finger with a sharp lancet in order to check my blood sugar levels via this little gadget. This gives me a score that I need to take time to register and jot down in a notebook.

At last, I can have some breakfast but that is accompanied by even more tablets and an insulin injection into my stomach, which tends to be a bit painful if I get the angle of the needle wrong. Sometimes when I withdraw the needle, I bleed from the point of injection which if not wiped up invariably ends up on my clothing. The drama never ceases with this condition...

On the worst mornings, I've been both sick and bled on myself and I've not even got showered, changed or even left my house yet. Managing this illness is non-stop and I seem to need the most amazing patience not to get wound up or annoyed by the whole thing. I seem to do all this so systematically as if it is a chore like brushing one's teeth.

This dream carries on throughout my day where there's a similarly rigorous routine at lunchtime and in the evening. At work, I usually conceal my medication – blood test, pills and injection – from those around me as I don't want to draw too much attention to the whole process.

In the evening, the patting on my chest takes longer and I have even more secretions to cough up. Also, over the years, there have been many people (male and female) who have helped me with this evening physiotherapy – for the last decade, it's been my wife who feels functional and not at all romantic. Annoyingly, this task often means that the food we are cooking that night is over-cooked or burnt and we eat later than we would like.

Before I know it, I'm back at my bedside popping pills from my chemist's drawer before I turn the light out. Most days are completely exhausting as a result of the continuous coughing.

I have a sense that I want to be more spontaneous and break free from this serial drug-taking but my conscience won't let me forget any of my treatments and the regime is adhered to religiously, like clock-work every day. I'm on some kind of crazy medical merry-go-round and there's no way to climb off.

Then I wake up from my dream…

The realisation dawns on me that this is not actually a dream, but it is in fact my harsh reality living with and coping with cystic fibrosis (CF) and CF-related type 1 diabetes. It's always been thus.

I am quite literally 'living my dream'.

My Groundhog Day starts and ends with pills and I can only survive by being utterly committed to this punishing daily routine. In essence, my existence on this planet is governed by the necessity of a cocktail of around 40 tablets each day, intravenous treatments for three weeks at a time (the CF version of chemotherapy), nebulisers, long physiotherapy sessions, asthma inhalers and regular visits to hospitals and the pharmacist.

A knock-on effect of a lifetime of medication is that nearly half of my drugs regime is needed to counter the side effects of the antibiotics and 20 years of steroids has led to the development of my diabetes and osteoporosis.

For the first time in my life I feel the desire to take stock. It got me thinking about my overall intake of drugs during my life, so I got a pen and paper and started to work out the CF numbers.

As a rough calculation over just the last 25 years, I have swallowed **280** tablets every week, which equates to **14,560** a year and **364,000** for the whole period.

So it's clear I'm very good at taking pills and I've got my technique all locked down. Indeed, I might well be a human rattle. I wonder what the world record is for the number of tablets taken in one mouthful. It's probably held by one of us CF guys. OK, I know it's not something that I can add to my CV, but if there's an English team for pill popping, my name would be in that squad.

I do have to bite my tongue not to laugh when people tell me that they suffered taking a few tablets in a day or when they struggle to remember their one tablet a day of prescribed medication. The most illuminating are those that choose not to use antibiotics as they want their body to fight the infection. What luxury it is that they can be so dogmatic.

Do I think about anything when I'm taking my medication? Not really, I just do it. I've had to put aside any ethical barriers, though I will question and challenge my doctor and I won't add to my regime without good reason.

Also during this time, I have had **10,000** nebuliser sessions, **18,200** physiotherapy sessions, over **50** IV treatments, **600** visits to my chemist and **250** appointments at Frimley Park hospital.

CRICKEY! When I look at my CF in plain numbers, it's shockingly daunting and surreal. Have I really taken all those tablets? Have I had that many physiotherapies, IVs and trips to medical centres? Was that all me? I expect for someone who doesn't visit a doctor or take a pill that often, those rare occasions are quite memorable and challenging… and worth griping about.

As I've spent so many hours of my life cocooned in this CF hell, only the really shocking moments stand out. I think by default, I block out the majority of my suffering as a way of protection from the daily grind of it all. I think if I dwelled upon every moment where my illness has to take centre stage in my life, I would come undone very quickly.

All this merely maintains my current state of health as there is no cure yet for CF. I cannot afford to let up on it or cut any corners medically, as any big lapse could be the end for me. This condition is completely unforgiving and relentless – like an incoming tide battering against a sandcastle.

Trapped by treatment just to stay alive, I'm quite literally trapped in my own Groundhog Day. I've not had a day off from this illness in nearly 40 years – fitting in my life, work, family, sport around this daunting and incessant routine. By sticking to this endless regime, I'm just about staying afloat – constantly treading water – I daren't stop swimming for a second in case I go under the surface, never to return.

While thinking about the relentless nature of my illness, I had the most shocking thought based on the CF version of the film 'Two Weeks' Notice' – what would happen to me if I stopped my treatments for just two weeks? How ill would I become? Even when I miss the odd treatment the effect on my health is pretty noticeable. I'm pretty sure that after two weeks of living without due diligence, I'd be in hospital and really struggling.

With such a condition to contend with, in every way, I firmly believe that I'm only as healthy as my last treatment.

It is against this daily backdrop that I survive each day, battling against the odds that this horrible illness heaps on me. People across the world aspire and strive to 'live the dream'. Unfortunately I'm living mine! I can only hope that one day when my morning alarm goes off, that something would have changed and the nightmare Groundhog Day spell will have been broken; and I can live a normal life untouched by medication and clinical regime.

Until that day arrives, on hearing that alarm, I'll keep reaching into my bedside drugs drawer…

2. Countdown Begins

Wednesday 17 March 2010

It's my 39th birthday today. I took the day off work to have an excursion with Katie in London. It was one of those lovely and rare days out together now that we are parents. We enjoyed a pleasant walk whilst holding hands in St. James Park, remembering again what being a couple is all about. This was followed by watching the pelicans flirt with tourists while eating our picnic on a park bench.

The highlight of the day was the matinee performance of 'Les Miserables' at a Shaftsbury Avenue theatre – my first time and I loved it, like so many before me. After clapping to a standstill at the finale, Katie and I made our way out of the theatre into a bustling Piccadilly Circus with the curious delight of an evening stretching ahead with no need to rush. An aperitif at the Opera Bar in Covent Garden preceded a delicious Thai meal. What a lovely day – a perfect day.

I also made a phone call to my twin brother, Jez, with whom I share my special day. Obviously, this is the person I've known all my life since we first met 39 years ago across a crowded womb! My twin looks nothing like me – he is tall, dark and handsome and looks more like my elder brother Chris. So what happened to me? I'm short and blonde! If I wasn't a twin there might be some serious questions to be asked! I do bear a resemblance to my mum's father so I know I'm safe in that respect...

Most people view their birthdays as special and enjoy the attention that they bring from family and friends. I'm no different in this respect. My birthdays mean a great deal to me as each one signifies a glorious achievement. Each one celebrates the simple fact that I'm still here.

All my life – every day – has been a battle to stay alive and keep defying the odds around my life expectancy (currently set at late thirties for CF sufferers, although for a long time it was fixed at thirty).

How does that feel to have one's very existence always in doubt? Consider one's life expectancy being held in an hourglass. Now imagine that the grains of sand in your glass appear to be running out very quickly... How would that feel? What would you do differently or prioritise before *your* sand ran out?

In my twenties I saw only a hopeless end. An early death seemed inevitable. I made the most of today because tomorrow might never have arrived.

This always reminded me of the 1976 film 'Logan's Run' which depicts a future society in which the population is maintained in equilibrium by requiring the death of everyone reaching a particular age. When the palm flower crystal embedded in the palm of everyone's right hand changes colour from red to black, people have reached the '*Lastday*' and are executed.

In my real-life version of the film, how long can I keep running away from the CF grim reaper?

For most of my life, thirty seemed unachievable and forty felt an impossible age to reach. This concern and fixation over my life expectancy was exacerbated after the sad deaths of certain CF friends leading up to my 30th birthday. With each departure, I questioned why I was still alive when they were not.

How had I cheated death? How many more birthdays would I have? Would I ever live long enough to feel over the hill rather than six feet under it?

When I finally made it to thirty, it felt as if I'd reached the Holy Grail. It was certainly a tipping point in my life. I wanted to carry with me the spirit of my friends who had died, and make my longer life count for something. When so much of a CF life is not at all normal, living beyond thirty was extremely fulfilling. It's something that my healthy peers took for granted but for me it was breaking the CF boundaries.

There are not too many people with CF that I know in the UK who are over forty and it always felt inspirational when anyone reached this significant milestone.

Due to my life-long battle for survival, I am hugely sentimental and I particularly want to do something memorable on my birthday. I want to make each one count for me and those around me.

I see each birthday as a time of celebration for my family, friends, medical staff and complementary therapists who have supported me and have been such a valuable part of my prolonged existence.

As I look ahead to my 40th birthday, it feels natural to also look back and reflect on my previous birthdays and the journey I've been on.

One milestone that feels like a watershed was my 17th birthday when I was feeling unwell and undergoing a heavy intravenous treatment. This meant that I couldn't go out to party with Jez and our mutual best friends. Every fibre of my body was screaming with anger and frustration about the apparent unfairness of staying in while my friends partied. I vowed never to miss out on future birthdays.

My birthdays could never be just another day. Each one was going to be a celebration of my life – a life worth living and well-lived.

Rather fortuitously, my birthday, 17 March, coincides with the Irish national holiday St. Patrick's Day – a day to be jovial and to let one's hair down. For many of my birthday evenings, I have tried to out-drink the Irish… but it should be noted that I've always failed miserably.

As well as organising activities during the day, Jez and I have always been inclined to organise a party for the majority of our birthdays with extra big venues and wider invites for the key milestone ages of eighteen, twenty one, twenty five, thirty and thirty five. There's a saying that 'if you book them, they will come' and my friends have fed off my infectious desire to celebrate life to the full and have as much fun as possible.

When I invite them, people have tended to flock. I am fortunate to have very faithful and reliable friends.

I'd like to think that an abiding memory for most of my friends will be of me taking centre stage with a pint in one hand and a rum and coke in the other laughing and enjoying myself-literally squeezing every drop out of life!

There have been occasions when I've gone too far with my 'partying'. On my 24th birthday, I was so drunk that I was physically carried shoulder high by my flatmates out of a pub in Putney to a cacophony of hysterical cheers from the Irish throng. This was definitely an example of triumph of the spirit – unfortunately it was a pint of different spirits that did for me that night!

To make matters worse, I threw up in the taxi on the way home and was in a horrible state the next day when I played hockey in Maidenhead. I was still being sick during the pre-match team talk which consisted of the sound advice: "Don't pass the ball to Tim!" Having somehow got through the game, back in the opposition clubhouse canteen, I sat on my own meticulously eating a bowl of soup while the rest of the players cheered on England in a Five Nations rugby game next door.

Another time, following a drink-fuelled birthday bash on reaching twenty nine, I got extremely emotional and melancholic outside a Putney nightclub with Sasha, a hockey friend. Perhaps this could be attributed to the underlying sadness I felt that the 'unachievable' age of thirty was looming which could hasten my potential demise.

But as I approach the forty year milestone, in March 2011, something has changed in me... I have flipped my mindset from a fear of dying to a desire to live for much longer as there is so much I still want to see and do. This was immeasurably magnified when I became a husband to Katie in 2003 and a father to Felix in 2007.

I now view the future in a different way – welcoming each year. I mentally project and expect a longer life with my own family to live it with. I firmly believe that the best birthdays of all are those that haven't happened yet.

I see reaching forty as a celebration of my life to date and what it has taken for me to survive; but I also view it as a launchpad for the rest of my life – with my hourglass half full rather than half empty. I would certainly want to celebrate my 40th milestone with the mother of all parties.

If getting to forty was the equivalent of climbing Mount Everest then I'm on the ascent with the summit in sight – almost mystical through the clouds. But will I make it to the top?

For each of us, transitioning to a new decade is a reason for jubilation. For me, it is achieving the impossible. The countdown to my 40th officially begins and I've got to make it, especially now that I've started this journal!

3. Sixty Five Roses

Friday 19 March 2010

It's uncanny in life how one situation leads directly to another. At a client meeting at work today, I had to deal with the classic CF scenario and its knock-on dilemmas.

Someone made a comment about my cough...

It was a fairly innocuous remark from this work client who didn't know me that well. We were in a meeting room together discussing a particular project plan when I felt the need to clear my throat. Awkwardly, it sounded pretty loud and then triggered a sustained coughing stint.

"Cough any harder and you'll get a gold watch," was the cliché comment from the client.

In my experience, this is quite a common phrase when someone hears a hacking cough. He wasn't being malicious and may have been surprised by the tenacity of my coughing. By cracking a joke he was probably looking to make light of the situation.

What do I say in return? Do I ignore it or tackle it there and then? What's the likelihood he would have ever heard of my illness anyway? My eternal dilemma...

This got me thinking: What's with the CF cough and why is the condition so difficult to explain to strangers?

For most people with CF the need to cough (to help clear secretions) is the most consistent irritation. This does vary for every sufferer as there is not a one-size-fits-all version of CF. In fact there are over 1000 variations of the condition, some a lot more severe than others.

The problem is that I can't always predict when a throat tickle will turn into a full-blown coughing attack.

Imagine the start-up coughs as tremors and the big coughing fit that inevitably follows as the actual earthquake with a similar Richter scale of severity. Once the main eruption has occurred, that's not the end of it as there could be hours of mini after-shocks.

When I'm coughing, I'm sure the general public in my vicinity, whether it be on public transport, in the office or on a sports pitch, think that I'm annoying and possibly callous to be out with such an awful infection – surely I should be at home tucked up in bed when I sound so awful? Some might even despise me thinking that I could be infectious and spreading my germs near them.

More ironically, there could be some people who even think that I have caused this myself and the noise they hear is a smoker's cough – which couldn't be further from the truth. You are more likely to catch a vegan munching on a bacon sandwich than me smoking a cigarette!

Sometimes after some sustained coughing, my larynx can be tight and painful which causes each subsequent cough to come out in a high-pitched tone. People can often confuse this noise with a sneeze so with each cough I get "Bless you!" from the nearest person to me. I'm sure their kindness runs out after my umpteenth 'sneeze' as they stop saying anything after a while and probably sit there wondering why on earth I don't sort it out!

The single act of coughing for someone with CF can at times be a reflex subconscious act. I will use a single cough to sense-check how my chest and lungs feel at any given moment – like revving the engine of a car. If it's a dry cough, then I can relax; if it sounds chesty then I can prepare myself for the need to go to the toilet to clear my secretions.

Similar to how newborn babies have their own distinctive cry that only their mums can hear from afar, CF sufferers tend to have their own signature cough. Indeed, it is the predominant sight and sound of my illness. If I was being mischievous, I would place a large bet that there are no burglars in this world with CF!

I can be heard by my wife, son, family and close friends before they even see me.

"I knew where you were, I could hear your cough."

It's not all bad and it can be handy. My wife Katie listens out for my cough in public places to track me down if I've gone AWOL. In a supermarket, she knows which aisle I'm on when I've gone off the beaten track – usually finding me in the sweets and biscuits section where I join other diabetics who pilgrimage to reminisce about a bygone era.

When taking an exam at university, a good friend recounted afterwards that he got so frustrated with his inability to answer the questions that to stave off boredom, he counted my coughs on his notepad. I was glad to be of help to the poor chap!

There are certain public places where it really is a pain for a coughing fit to start. Venues where silence is a pre-requisite are the worst. Cinemas, theatres and libraries are some of the places where a 'CF earthquake' has caused me and those around me much annoyance.

A coughing session can feel like holding one's breath when swimming in an underwater tunnel – no one can help me get through it – only I can get to the other end, which in my case is to get beyond the extended hack and breathe normally again.

I can be prone to coughing so hard at times that my head feels like the inside of a church bell when it's clanging. Though luckily my head is still in place at the end of it!

It can't be nice for others to listen to this infernal noise but when I'm in mid hack, to be honest, I couldn't care too much if I'm upsetting anyone else. They only have to hear my cough for a few seconds. I'm now approaching 40 years of living with it. I know which one I'd rather deal with...

Strangely enough, I've never asked anyone to find out their feelings on it, but this public coughing must be worse for CF females as it's not exactly feminine and sexy.

I tend to cough or clear my throat during the course of most days and this is inflamed by exercise but particularly by cold and damp weather. Some days are manageable and I don't cough too much. But other days, often frustratingly for no obvious reason, my lungs are absolute shockers and play up like naughty children. In some ways, CF coughing days are like Forrest Gump's proverbial box of chocolates – *"You never know what you're gonna get next!"*

This coughing malarkey is not just a day activity. I have had the odd night where I wake up coughing so hard that I'm scared that I'll choke to death and I keep myself awake petrified beyond belief that if I fall asleep, I won't be alive in the morning. In those very dark moments, it's not lost on me that the words 'coughing' and 'coffin' sound the same.

When I wake up in the morning, there is a palpable sense of relief and euphoria that I'm still alive. But after a bad night or any health set-back, I feel small, insignificant and my self-esteem is low. I want to be invisible.

So back to my dilemma of how to respond to my work client's remark: *"Cough any harder and you'll get a gold watch."*

Do you know that if I had a pound for each time I have heard this, whether out and about or playing sport, I would have enough money to buy… that gold watch!

By default, I'm usually pretty guarded about disclosing my condition to strangers and normally only mention my CF on a need to know basis in professional situations. My mind is scrambled by what I would like to tell them to firmly put them in the picture versus glossing over it and keeping it at an elementary level. After so many years handling this scenario, I have got a fairly good sense for what the person in front of me can actually comprehend or sometimes more importantly what they want to take on board. In this respect, some people exude warmth and others just don't – I refer to the cold ones as the *"I'm alright Jack"* people. Either way, I tend to gravitate to whatever level they're at in relation to what I choose to reveal about my illness.

Socially, I have always felt at odds with introducing myself and my illness in the same breath, so I tend to wait for people to get to know me first; and when I feel it is appropriate I give them the low-down without making too much fuss over it. Just occasionally, people I tell have got a current or past connection to CF and are reasonably knowledgeable. Sometimes they know a CF person from school or university –

more often than not, they regretfully inform me that their friend is no longer with us.

The worst scenario following my CF explanation to a stranger is when I am met by silence – maybe they are stunned that I have it, don't know enough to comment or couldn't care less and want to ignore it – as I feel inclined to fill the silent gap and end up prattling on and saying too much. No, in this case, silence is not golden.

In life, one is prone to storing up a certain response if anyone says something inflammatory to you on a certain subject BUT the situation never arises so your witty retort lies dormant. Well, if someone ever said to me: *"You're coughing badly,"* I would be tempted to reply in jest: *"I'm surprised to hear you say that I'm coughing badly, as I have been practising all day!"*

So today, I ended up saying to this client: *"Excuse my coughing; I've got a pretty severe lung condition. Not sure if you have heard of it. It's called cystic fibrosis."*

And thus the second dilemma is created. Cystic what?

Despite its severity and prevalence, the words 'cystic' and 'fibrosis' do not mean much outside of the medical fraternity, the sufferers themselves, their family and close friends. In fairness, the two words don't really resonate and are hard to say – one young patient couldn't pronounce it and settled for calling her illness 'sixty five roses', which sounds near enough.

In my experience, CF is like a form of 'locked-in syndrome' as all the damage is on the inside and not very obvious to the naked eye – all the ruin is happening on the inside and is not visible.

My heavy daily medication regime manages a condition that is not well understood, cannot be easily seen or ever properly imagined by most people. The life of a CF person can be described, BUT it cannot be easily imagined for the majority of people.

All this for the blank look I receive when revealing my condition to most strangers – that look where they nod their heads but are thinking *"You lost me at cystic but I better keep looking like I understand and care."* By the time I get to saying 'fibrosis', most people's eyes have already glazed over. That look punctuates the entire life of someone with CF.

I find it sadly ironic that I follow my daily regime with military precision just to stay alive and practically no-one has a clue! If I'm honest, I'm not surprised that most people have little or no idea about the condition but after 40 years it does get frustrating.

People don't realise how serious the condition is and that it's a killer and takes people in their youth. Often they recognise the name and possibly know that it's related to lungs or needs physiotherapy, but not much beyond that.

To the untrained eye, I don't look sick. In fact I can appear so well on the outside that even close friends can forget I have one of the most common life-threatening inherited diseases. There's an odd dichotomy here as I want to look well but also want people to know that I am ill underneath my skin and what it takes for me to survive.

It would be great for my condition – the one that I fight so hard to survive every day of my life – to be more universally understood and recognized. It's tough to keep giving your all to a cause that receives a blank look from the majority of folk.

Ultimately I wanted to educate people about what it's like to live with this disease and that it's no fluke I'm still around. I've had to fight bloody hard to stay alive.

Maybe in the future, after reading this, you'll remember 'sixty five roses' and know a little bit more…

4. For Once in My Life

Tuesday 30 March 2010

I'm driving to an early morning outpatient appointment at Frimley Park hospital in Surrey. It's just a routine check-up, so hopefully nothing to get too worried about.

There's been an accident on the M25 motorway, so I've decided to try a different route based on advice from a doctor who drives this journey every day. But, I've got a bit lost and didn't take the correct junction turn off and continued along the A3 when I should have gone down a well-known local road called the Hog's Back. I've just pulled into a petrol station to ask for directions and I'm now madly back-tracking to get to Frimley.

This has caused me to be running late and I'm getting steadily more annoyed – with myself, the heavy rush hour traffic and the hassle of fitting in another hospital appointment into my busy life. I've got so much on at work today that I can't afford this to take up too much of my morning.

Another damn medical appointment. More of my time doing something I'd rather not.

I sit at the steering wheel of my car in a queue just outside of Farnborough and I begin to feel agitated. The famous 'red mist' drifts over me, like the fog coming to land in the film of the same name. I start talking out loudly to an audience of one and do the classic in-car road rage, getting myself all worked up – in my own frustrating bubble of annoyance.

Come on traffic, move! Don't you all know I've got a ruddy hospital appointment and I'm running late? Why am I even bothering with yet another hospital trip? No one else I know has to put up with this.

To compound my level of angst, I decide to count up how many times I have been through this rigmarole to Frimley and how many visits I have made to hospitals in my lifetime...

I've probably been to Frimley hospital over 250 times in the last 25 years. Outside of this I have had a similar number of visits and in-patient stays in Southampton General hospital as a paediatric and the Royal Brompton in London when I was a student.

I would have spent an average of four hours at each of these 500 plus appointments over my lifetime. That's over 2000 hours of my life in hospitals and that doesn't include the in-patient stays. It may surprise people that have been fortunate enough to barely need medical interventions, but it's rarely a simple case of turning up and walking straight into see the doctor at the allotted time.

I have spent a fair bit of my life just sitting – hanging around – festering in hospitals. I've waited for doctors, for X-rays, for scans, for bloods, for physiotherapists, for nutrition experts, for diabetic nurses, for drug dispensing at the pharmacy. The list goes on and on... the lost hours waiting around stack up and up.

The patience and persistence needed to continually deal with this amount of inactivity is immense. The irony is not lost on me that as a patient, I need to be... patient. I've learned over the years to get myself in a Zen-like state of calm to bear the tedium of waiting; plus I bring something to distract me – a book, client work, iPod.

Over the years, I have heard many frivolous comments like: "I don't like hospitals!" "I cannot stand needles!" or "I don't want to see the quack!" These same 'moaners' should climb into my shoes for just one of my CF hospital days and they can see for themselves what it takes to cope and how it makes me so agitated.

No surprises here but I also don't like hospitals, needles or want to see the doctor, *but* I've got no choice. So I just have to get on with it and make the best of a harsh situation.

When you have a life-threatening condition such as CF you don't have the good fortune to sporadically pick and choose your medical soirees. They have become part and parcel of my everyday life.

Good health is the most precious and greatest gift a human could ever have. Through my lens on this world, I've noticed that very few people with few real heath concerns have any concept of how lucky they are.

I'm still in this traffic jam a couple of miles away from the hospital with the actual appointment start time creeping up on me.

I now start losing my patience and feel the fury building up inside me. Even I have my tipping point where I'm prone to boiling over – where my fortitude runs out and I need to let off steam. It's like a tidal wave of pent-up anger and frustration at my ceaseless plight. I cannot get one day off from this horrible illness. I imagine that this has been building for a long time as I've kept my anger buried away under the surface and not let it out for a long while. Today's the day to let it all out.

This is my 'Falling Down' moment. I'm a real-life Michael Douglas struggling to find any logic in my crippling physical and emotional situation. It's been so long since I cried about my health, I don't know whether to actually cry or laugh out loud with the sheer ridiculousness of my existence.

I'm about to burst – like the Incredible Hulk – go berserk, rip off my clothes and transition from the red mist to green all over. However, this is going green with envy for a 'normal' life; a healthy and spontaneous life that I've never known in 39 years but insatiably pine for.

I park my car near the hospital and sprint-walk to the CF unit where I arrive over 20 minutes to late, looking and feeling dishevelled. After the habitual weight and blood level examinations, I return to the reception area.

"The doctor is running about an hour late", the nurse dutifully informs the room of patients.

I look around the waiting room, taking in all these other poor people having to endure this monotony. I close my eyes. The earlier rage has been replaced by a calmer, dream-like state. My perfect storms don't tend to last that long. I can only remain angry for a short while – it's infinitely more tiring being upset than happy.

As I meditate on the stress of the journey and my 'hulk' moment, I start to daydream. We are all prone to say or think "What I wouldn't give…" or "For just one day I want…" at different times in our lives. But I dream of that day – the perfect day – where I can be spontaneous and take a holiday from my illness. For just one day in my life...

I would wake up and not cough like a 40-a-day smoker.

I would go and make a cup of tea after getting up rather than taking my first instalment of drugs.

I would not need to prick my finger and check my blood sugar levels.

I would not need to nebulise some medication and then clean my nebuliser pieces.

I would not need to lie back on my bed and 'pat my chest' to force a coughing spasm.

I would not be sick on myself as a result of coughing too violently.

I would not inject insulin into my stomach after breakfast.

I would go off to work without needing to find 30 extra minutes for treatment and taking 20 tablets.

I would get to work early and leave late without having to factor in any medication whatsoever.

I would be on hot public transport or a small meeting room without sweating profusely through my face and having to wipe my brow repeatedly.

I would eat lunch with colleagues without having to surreptitiously take tablets when they're not looking.

I would eat whatever I wanted to eat, unconstrained by the need for carbohydrates and diabetic-friendly foods.

I would return to my desk and not need to inject myself with insulin or bleed onto my work shirt.

I would go for a run and not need to stop regularly to cough. And not for one second would I worry how my coughing would appear to the public passing by.

I would be spontaneous with my activity, food and drink.

I would not worry about bringing on a diabetic hypo.

I would go through the day oblivious to the threat of a coughing fit and having to continually suppress it. I would speak without fear of wheezing or fret when a cough would rear its ugly head.

I would go through the day without receiving a call from a healthcare professional or have to visit a pharmacist, GP or hospital.

I would take the flight of stairs rather than the lift to prevent being out of breath.

I would get caught in the rain and not care at all about catching a chill.

I could be carefree that I have no need for an umbrella because it doesn't matter if I get wet.

I would have all the energy I need to work and play. In fact, I wouldn't even think about preserving my energy levels.

I could have a relaxing evening without the need for my wife to do my physiotherapy.

We could eat when we wanted to because I wouldn't have to fit my treatments in.

I would not need to do two more insulin injections and one final nebuliser.

I would go to bed at the end of the day without worrying how my coughing might wake up my wife and my son.

What I wouldn't give for just one day off. For once in my life.

My wish is unlikely to ever come true…

5. Playing to Live

Saturday 3 April 2010

I am playing field hockey this afternoon in Surrey for my club, London Edwardians. This is one of the final games of my 24th consecutive league hockey season and it's a run I don't want to end while I am still able to get on that pitch and make a contribution.

It's a hard fought game against Purley who are above us in the league. We need to get at least a point from the match so that we don't fall into the relegation zone. We end up drawing 2-2 and I play at right back for over half the game, substituting on and off as is allowed in hockey. I do reasonably well and am competitive without being one of the stars on the pitch. It's vitally important to still be playing as sport is one of the key differentiators in my survival.

Without a shadow of a doubt, a large part of my longevity in my battle to defy CF can be credited to the amount of sport I have played throughout my life; mainly hockey, basketball, tennis, rugby, football and cricket. I have always preferred to get my exercise while running around after a ball!

Exercise is not actually straightforward for most CF sufferers as the build-up of mucous in the lungs means that less oxygen is available which causes problems with breathing and general fitness. It is also an extremely exhausting condition – just think how tiring it is to cough for five minutes non-stop. I find it quite literally knocks the wind out of my sails.

In my experience, I have found that regular exercise has become a necessity to keep my lungs 'tuned' and it impacts on me both physically and mentally. I strongly believe that any activity that exercises the lungs of someone with CF is hugely beneficial.

I've never been one for gyms, partly due to the feeling that I would be in 'competition' with healthier people therein, but predominantly because if I needed to cough hard or clear my lungs, a gym is not terribly conducive or discreet. I'd hate the idea of drawing too much attention to my disability.

It's fortunate that I come from a sporty family – my dad and both brothers play hockey and my mum is a useful tennis player.

I have played hockey for countless teams and at many levels. In lots of ways it has defined who I am and it's what I'm well-known for. As well as playing for club, county and for my region, I was also selected for an England Juniors team and toured Germany back in the 1980s. I was playing first team hockey till I was 32 and I now play a reasonably competitive level for the Edwardians third team, though this is ad hoc depending on my health and parental duties.

Representing England Juniors, like my brother Chris before me, was the pinnacle of my sporting life. The immense pride I felt during those national anthems on a foreign field is something that can never be taken away from me.

In my playing prime, I had to think hard after a game to remember any mistakes I had made. In my youth, when my lung function was still reasonably unaffected, I could do whatever I wanted on a hockey pitch and would often make the difference between winning or losing for a lot of the teams I played in. Being a pretty skilful player who read the flow of the game well, I helped to influence the result of a lot of matches. I can comfortably say that I was good.

During some games, I felt sublime – like no one could touch me and with that came a confidence – arrogance at times – that I could play at any level and compete. Like most good sportsmen, I would back myself one hundred per cent that I was good enough and could help my team to win. That sort of attitude dissipates any fear of the opposition and of achieving what you wanted on the pitch. Sometimes, I would find it almost too easy playing and I could read the game quicker than most which always gave me an advantage over others. This all sounds big-headed now but it was the reality back then.

I hang on to these memories as playing now is so laboured and anything but easy. My lungs and body won't let me do what I want them to do.

Unfortunately, the unavoidable demise of my lung function and a hectic university life took its toll and at just 20 I had to come to terms with the harsh realisation that I would never be able to fulfil my obvious hockey talent.

In my late teens and early twenties I struggled with managing my health and fitness so much that I would look for any ways to deceive my unwanted reality. Like some kind of bulimic sportsman, I would take myself off to the changing room toilet prior to a game to cough so hard and for long enough that I'd be sick. This enabled me to start the game with as little sputum in my lungs as possible and allow me perform at a fair level early on in the game. Ahead of one summer cup final for Southampton Hockey club, with all my family and friends watching, I was so desperate to hide my demise that I walked into the nearby woods to do my pre-game hack and vomit. We won the game so it worked on that occasion. Looking back, it's amazing that I thought vomiting before a game was conducive to playing well, but I was young and naive.

At university I initially tried to carry on as normal, playing for the college team, Old Kingstonians Hockey Club and for Surrey but it was too much and caused my health to falter badly. Towards the end of my first term, following a tip-off from my brother Chris, I discovered that my diminishing health due to excessive hockey was causing a rift between my parents. My dad was encouraging me to keep playing for all these teams as I was able to before I went away and my mum was concerned about the effect on my body.

This forced me to make one of the hardest decisions I have ever had to make – stop playing for the club and county and concentrate purely on college hockey, where I had more of a chance of maintaining my health and fitness. This in effect halted any aspirations I ever had to reach the highest level in the sport as any sporting prospect would need to be playing for both club and county to climb up the ladder. I remember the phone call as if it was yesterday. I went to a secluded phone box in the college campus and rang my parents in Southampton at a time when I knew they would both be in. I told them of my decision and explained that it was for the best – for my health and their harmony. We all knew it was the right thing to do; no matter that it signalled the end of my high-performance hockey career.

I was given a real health boost in 1994 by a drug called Pulmozyme, which I still nebulise daily. This really has been a miracle medication for me – before it I was only working part-time and was struggling to play lower league club hockey. After it, I had the health and vitality to work full-time and play first team hockey again. It quite literally gave me a new lease of life, breathing new vibrancy into my lungs.

For most of my twenties and early thirties I played hockey both Saturday and Sunday and would go on summer tours around the UK and Europe. This made me feel 'normal' as I was competing and socialising with relatively healthy and fit people. It was through this hockey social scene that I met my now wife Katie. Note to self: partying hard does pay!

Over the years I have matured in my approach to exercise and finessed my appreciation of how my body and lungs feel and the appropriate times to exercise. To supplement my hockey, I joined a local tennis club; had some coaching and play quite regularly. With my hockey, the good news is that I've not lost my pace as I never had any in the first place. I've learnt to pass the ball better and let the ball do the work.

When I'm struggling on the pitch, the chaps (who know about my CF) ask me if I'm OK, but the opposition jokingly check if I had a night on the town or have a bad cold. It's especially tough in this country with the inclement weather. I often jog early in the evening or in a secluded park so when I need to cough, I can be more discreet. This has been magnified with my recent diagnosis as a type 1 diabetic. Now just getting on the pitch or court, let alone actually playing, takes more and more effort.

I won't be taking part in an Iron Man competition any time soon, as any exercise is relative to your fitness levels. But my hockey, tennis and jogging keep me going, feeling as if I'm conducting a relatively normal life. It all helps me to defy the ravages of my illness.

For me, still playing sport, running and competing is the best barometer for how my health is. It also serves as an indication for others, not least my dad, to know that if I'm still able to play, that CF can't be winning the battle. Indeed, my dad will always ask "How's your wobble son?" and most old friends tend to lead conversations with "Are you still playing hockey?"

At times, I feel the weight of their hope and expectations on my shoulders. What would they think should I ever reply: "Actually, I've had to pack it in as it became too much for me!"

I play on for my own health but also for the positive lift it gives to others. I now feel a tremendous sense of elation on completing any sport as it feels like 'my Everest' moment. It's hard and I do have to get pretty psyched up these days before most exercise. It's still important for me to compete against relatively healthy and fit people as it serves as my health benchmark.

My lungs do definitely benefit from exercise, even small jogs and I feel more vibrant and alive afterwards. I wouldn't say the exercise is always enjoyable, but the rewards and positive sensation drive me on. It's only after I've pushed myself during a hockey or tennis match that I feel really 'alive'.

I have had to consistently find the motivation to keep going with my hockey. Few 39 year olds I know are still partaking in competitive sport and they all have their reasons not to – it's easier not to be active once you have a busy work and family life. Some people need a goal to get running again – something to aim for, like a 10K charity run, marathon or triathlon. I have my hockey.

I am desperate to still be playing sport at 40. Fighting CF gives me the encouragement that few can harness. It's more than feeling that I have to do exercise, it's lighting my own internal touchpaper to force myself to 'want' to do it, which creates my own intrinsic motivation. I focus on both the mental and physical aspects of this desire. Physically, I think what's more of a benefit to me – running (and enduring a short-term discomfort) or not running (and letting the effects of CF build up). Mentally, exercise is my two finger salute to CF, defiantly declaring "I won't be beaten. I can do this. I will do this. Just watch me!"

It's a simple equation for me to keep playing sport. If I exercise and keep as fit as possible, it's likely that I will stay one step ahead of the grim reaper. In fact, I would go as far as stating that it's a matter of my life or death.

They say you are a long time retired from sport. To still be playing competitive hockey at 39 is better than I could ever have hoped for, considering I wasn't expected to live beyond my teens. If I make it, being able to play at 40 will feel gargantuan. Winning used to be everything, it's now a nice to have – just being there on the pitch or court feels amazing and is worth celebrating.

Who knows? Down the line, like father like son, I look forward to coaching my son Felix how to play. Who can tell at this early stage of Felix's life whether he will take up hockey or any other sport? But he's lightening quick, always running and he seems very robust. Cats are prone to mad five minute spells where they fly around the place or chasing their own tail. Well, Felix, appropriately named, is permanently like that cat! I won't push him towards any particular sport as I'm convinced he'll be drawn to the one that suits him best but I do want to be around to support him in whatever way I can. I know the enjoyment and pride my dad would have had coaching us when we were young. I'm ready for that same involvement.

I might not be able to fully make a difference to the result of the game anymore as I could in my younger playing days. Plus my coughing at times can be pretty shocking for those on the pitch. But while there's breath in this body of mine, I'll keep playing on for I know it makes a difference to the outcome of my health and my sustained battle with CF.

I used to live to play sport… now I play sport to live!

6. Business Unusual

Thursday 8 April 2010

I had a busy and eventful day at work in my role as an internal communications consultant juggling meetings and deliverables for two separate clients.

The morning was spent with a telecommunications client at their office in Warren Street, London. Barely had the meeting got underway than the building alarm went off and everyone had to evacuate to a nearby muster point.

In these situations, one is supposed to leave all belongings and follow a colleague down the stairs and out onto the street. I took a quick look outside before leaving my floor and as the weather looked a bit inclement, I grabbed my small umbrella from my laptop bag.

This proved to be a justified decision as it started to rain as soon as we left the building and I followed the mass of fellow evacuees to the designated meeting point which turned out to be a good five minute walk away from the office. Even though the rain was not much more than a fine drizzle, I was glad that I could cover myself with my umbrella. I had no intention of getting damp and potentially risk my health during the thirty minutes we had to wait in that congregation area before finally returning to complete the meeting. I was one of the few that took such a precaution.

This afternoon I was back in the Soho office of my consultancy, The Fifth Business, where I had some actions from the morning meeting followed by a mad flurry of deliverables for another client request that came in out of the blue. It's on days like these that the thirty minutes lost due to the earlier evacuation was precious time and had a knock-on effect for the rest of my day. It also meant that I had to work later than I wanted to.

In turn this caused me to arrive home so late that I missed my dear Felix's bedtime. This is one of those frustrating moments as a dad. A tough day at work can be instantly wiped from my memory by just a few minutes with my son. Today it was not to be...

My work career has been centred on working with people and efficiently communicating to them. Previously I was a company training manager and since 2002 I have been an employee engagement manager both in-house and agency side, where I currently reside. Being a people person I've always been an intuitive communicator and appreciate the different needs of the multitude of audiences within any organisation.

However, I've not always had a typical business career. My health upon leaving university was in a pretty dire state and due to a lack of energy and lung function I struggled to work more than part-time. Actually planning a career too far into the future and setting up a pension seemed a million miles away. With my reduced life expectancy as a backdrop, I preferred to work to live rather than live to work.

As I've mentioned previously, this all changed in 1994 with the arrival of the nebulised drug Pulmozyme which helped to thin the mucous in my lungs, making it easier to cough up. This wondrous medication quite literally transformed my life – both work, social and sport – improving my lung capacity and restoring pretty decent energy levels. It allowed me to increase my working hours to full-time which gave me more money and life autonomy.

This independence has been crucial in my fight to live as normal a life as possible and to keep defying the CF odds. Working gives my life extra direction and purpose, acting as another crucial element of CF not defining me.

Going to work and being at work is a useful distraction from the burden of a life-long condition. It's extremely hard keeping up in the business world but it takes my mind off the CF struggle as opposed to being at home and potentially dwelling on my illness too much. This could likely trap me inside a harmful bubble, convinced that I'm not fit and well enough to go to work.

I have never wanted to use my CF as an excuse for not delivering whether at school, university and now in business. I certainly didn't want any extra attention, special dispensation or to just sign myself off sick and never work. Instead, I'm resolute that CF isn't going to knock me down and I can make a difference and prove my worth.

And yet...

For anyone suffering the daily grind of a life-threatening illness, there's no such thing as a normal working day. There are some significant challenges with managing CF and diabetes in the workplace. Every day while at work, there's a multitude of 'moments' unseen by those around me that I just have to get through and endure, usually in silence.

Obviously there is the daily medical regime to fit in during the working day from taking tablets to diabetic injections at lunchtime, or if really busy, in-between meetings. The mornings when my lungs are fragile are so horrendous and debilitating that I feel as if I've done a day's work by the time I get into the office. It's on those trying days when I have to put on a brave face and cover up my inner turmoil.

I've made the decision to mainly keep it under wraps at work, only telling people about my health on a need-to-know basis. As much as possible I'm keen to stand out for my professional abilities and performance rather than for my condition.

On numerous occasions, a work colleague, probably assuming I'm a disgusting smoker who deserves all I get, enquires if I'm OK after hearing one of my coughing fits.

"Yes, I'm fine thanks!" I retort in full cover-up mode.

Little do they know and where would I begin trying to tell total strangers that this earthy cough of mine is 39 years old and is never going away.

Embarrassingly, on hearing my uncontrollable hacking, other concerned parties have asked me whether I'm contagious. I tend to brush it off as befits the spin I have to put on these comments, "No, you couldn't catch this from me!" I reply with a hint of sarcasm.

There are some days when I'm feeling flat and excruciatingly tired that I seriously question why I put myself through this rigmarole. At such times, I'd love to shout out loud in the office, vent my anger and frustration – put people in the picture about what it takes every day for me to be at the office – how gruelling and unfair it all is for me to be 'competing' with healthy, energetic colleagues. As a business consultant often embedded in a company, even more so, I'm not expected to show my emotion or reference my private life.

One very distinct memory was of an internal interview away from home while working for the energy company British Gas. I was getting over the effects of a cold which led to my lungs being full of extra phlegm. Just when I needed to get a good night's sleep in the hotel room in preparation for the early morning interview, I endured an all-night coughing fit which left me shattered, my throat sore and my voice hoarse. Somehow I pulled myself together, got through the interview and was delighted by being offered the role.

One person who has to be aware of my health issues and requirements is my direct line manager. I've experienced the full spectrum of management abilities in handling my health predicament.

I have sadly been made to feel less capable and worthy due to my condition but luckily that was a rarity. The managers and clients who stand out in my memory were the ones who were able to see past the condition and hone in on getting the best out of me. They showed the required flexibility and compassion I needed for ad-hoc hospital appointments and my prolonged IV absences. They have enabled me to keep working, delivering and succeeding while keeping the tiller on my health boat moving forward.

Another key challenge I encounter concerns business travel, particularly flying and staying in hotels. As well as my work clothes and laptop bag, I have to fly with all the medical paraphernalia that I would normally keep at home and fit in all my physiotherapy, nebulisers and injections around busy non-stop work schedules.

It's also not been realistic and possible to work in another country to progress my career like so many of my friends have done. As well as the high cost of the drugs which may not be funded if I moved country, I need to maintain proximity to my doctor and expert CF knowledge which may be lacking abroad.

I do try to keep up with healthy people in the business world; marvelling and envying them for their energy levels, constitution to work long hours without seriously damaging their health and their restorative powers. Of course most of these fellow work associates can just focus on the job at hand. They don't have my medical regime to fit in before they leave the house, throughout the day and as soon as they arrive back home.

From my work experience, when I've worked long hours flat out for too long a period, my CF treatments have often been compromised and my lungs have had to come second best in order to keep up. It's a tricky balancing act getting it right and not becoming overtly tired and too run down. When exhausted or overly stressed, my lungs will quickly deteriorate and I'll cough repeatedly through the day.

As much as I give it my all, I don't always feel energized enough to really go the extra mile. Having seen my health damaged before, I'm sceptical about taking on more than I can handle and undermining my health. I've learnt on many occasions that I need to be very careful going for new jobs or assignments that could potentially push me over the edge and lead to irreversible damage to my lungs.

If I misjudge this workload balancing act, it could be the straw that breaks the camel's back – an idiom that stems from an Arabic proverb about how a camel is loaded (by one single straw) beyond its capacity to move or stand, causing cataclysmic results.

I try to be as professional as possible despite my situation. As so few people really understand CF, I have encountered many tricky situations born out of selfishness and ignorance.

In the late nineties when smoking was still commonplace in restaurants I was alienated at certain team night out and dinners or would have to suffer the second-hand smoke of others in order to be part of the team. Back then, I spotted that the smoking room was usually the place for the company movers and shakers and not being in these venues could be limiting for one's career.

People's lack of understanding about CF can count against me in other ways which have proven problematic for both me and the employer or client. I imagine it's confusing at times for them that I might be struggling with my lungs and fatigue as outwardly I look fairly well. I fear that at times my lack of size and youthful demeanour give me potentially less business gravitas and I'm prone to being taken less seriously, especially in start-up meetings with strangers.

The ultimate dilemma comes during any final interview for a new job. When exactly to tell that potential employer about my condition as no one likes surprises in business. There are no real guidelines about how and when to mention my CF. Unfortunately it's a sad fact and an even harsher reality that I've never been offered a job when I've mentioned my CF in the interview process.

I know it can be daunting for those trying to get work, especially if they are feeling particularly unwell. From my own experiences, I think once you are offered a job, that you should then reference your condition and help to coach the employer about CF on a need-to-know basis.

I have found that employers and clients do need coaching about the condition but once I've proven myself, they have accepted my need for the odd break for IVs. By seeing me deliver, they are then more open and obliging with any medical time off.

I'm proud that I haven't taken a non-IV related sick day for over 10 years! I have only had time off for IVs and am determined not to take other days off if at all possible. When I'm in work I want to prove myself and not seen to be taking advantage of my illness in order to have an extended time off unless it's a real necessity.

When I do require that time away for IV treatment I have learned the hard way not to work at the same time as managing these powerful drugs. Previously, the effect of the medication was severely negated when I tried to keep on working. After all, no one thanks you any more for being a martyr at work. Bitter experience has taught me to sign myself off for the two to three weeks needed to improve my health. My current employer wants me back only when I'm ready for duty. Additionally, I feel that these IV sessions away from the hustle and bustle of work don't really lend themselves to the continuity and flow of a fruitful career. It's an unfortunate aspect of working with an ongoing health condition that as much as these IVs keep me alive, they are more than likely the death knell of my long-term career aspirations.

Battling this horrid condition day in, day out uses up the majority of the serious side of my nature; so I inherently try to have fun in the workplace, injecting light and humour into my interactions with others to compensate. I would categorically say that I struggle with being too serious but knuckle down when needed.

At the same time I choose not to define myself as a person by my job. Life feels too short to make work become all-encompassing and my raison d'être. There's more to my life than my work. I've got to enjoy living while I'm still around. I most definitely see the need to make a difference while I still can and while I'm physically still able to work. I would like my work legacy to be meaningful.

Having said that, I do want to make every day count and be memorable. That includes my days in the office. I have a catalogue of achievement at work, won excellence awards and been part of teams that have been nominated for industry distinctions.

My illnesses do keep me feeling pretty grounded most of the time. I tend not to get too ahead of myself as my daily health challenges keep me in check. At work I'm like a swan – calm on surface and paddling like crazy underneath. However,

I want people to recognise me for doing a good job and delivering, rather than pity me for my health.

In the parallel work universe that I inhabit, working with CF is more business unusual than business as usual. But I can deliver for myself and for others and that makes it all worthwhile.

7. The Good, the Bad and the Ugly

Wednesday 14 April 2010

"All you need to do, Mr Wotton, is add one more injection into your daily regime and that will make a big difference to your health."

Those were the words ringing in my ears as I left the office of a Diabetic Consultant in St Helier hospital, Surrey.

Just one more injection to add.

No problem for the doctor to recommend this. They're just words to a doctor. It's a different story for the patient who has to do the injecting. The drug in question was the long-lasting insulin drug called Levemir which I had to add to my bedtime regime. No problem. Brush my teeth, wash my face, shove a needle into my stomach, read my book, turn off the light – simple!

I had been diagnosed with CF-related type 1 diabetes the previous July after a glucose fasting blood test which was part of my annual CF appraisal. I found out the news after a long day at work when I came home to open the following letter from my doctor:

<u>30 July 2009</u>

Dear Tim,

Your glucose tolerance test shows that you are in fact diabetic now.

We need to teach you how to take your blood sugar and also show you how you can administer some insulin. I suggest that you start with Novorapid insulin 4 units with small meal and 6 to 8 units with large meals... so that your blood sugar level before the next meal is running between 5 and 7.

This should make you feel a great deal better with more energy and will improve the infection in your lungs.

For the preceding six months, going to work on the London underground, I'd religiously buy a bottle of lemon Lucozade, which I immediately downed as if my life depended on it. I had put it down to the tiredness of working hard and early parenting. The diabetes diagnosis did help to explain why I had been feeling consistently tired and why the summer jog in the local park had been like running through treacle.

Cystic fibrosis-related diabetes (CFRD) is a unique type of diabetes that only people with CF can get. The build-up of thick secretions in my pancreas eventually damaged the hormone-producing cells, causing insulin deficiency. This variation combines the characteristics of both type 1 and type 2 diabetes, making the sufferer 'insulin-dependent'.

When I was first warned by mum in my twenties that diabetes was a common side-effect of CF, I got angry and informed her that if I had to deal with CF *and* diabetes, I would probably want to end my life. This form of diabetes was always likely as the pancreas is affected by my CF but even so I was not expecting any diagnosis when I took that fasting blood test.

This was bad news. I was numb. It felt cruel and amazingly surreal. I seemed to be at a crossroads in my life. For the first time in 38 years I had a serious condition that I knew little about. I certainly didn't know how to manage it physically and mentally. I was completely out of my health comfort zone, conscious incompetent, and that scared me.

Would it all be too much for me to handle? Could I deal with two major health conditions at the same time? Was it more than I could bear? Would this act as the tipping point that might send me on a downwards spiral? *Or* would I be able to draw a line in the sand, step up to the plate and rise to this fresh medical challenge?

I handed the letter to Katie and dramatically exclaimed, "I now have bloody diabetes as well." Katie, typical of her nursing profession, went straight into medical mode and was the perfect mix of calm, practical, encouraging and caring. Indeed, it had an effect on our relationship because all our petty squabbles were temporarily laid to rest as we focused on this very real and daunting situation together.

As it turned out, the diagnosis proved to be one of the most decisive and defining moments of my life.

After a few days of feeling sorry for myself I decided to gain more knowledge and insight from expert medical teams, deciding to re-set my attitude towards having two significant afflictions.

During this time of reflection, I also re-read the diagnosis letter and I suddenly noticed the magnitude of the final sentence which came flying off the page at me.

This should make you feel a great deal better with more energy and will improve the infection in your lungs.

From that point on, I chose to focus on those words rather than get too ensconced with the 'heavy duty' treatment section of the letter. I realised that if I could get my blood sugar levels in check, I might just feel a bit better and have more energy. I needed to concentrate on the desired outcome rather than the extra treatments.

The following week I spent a morning back at the CF unit getting the low-down on the condition with a diabetic nurse who showered me with an abundance of literature and explained the preferred diet choices. She also showed me all the kit – the insulin pen, the needles and the gadget to prick my finger to test my blood glucose level. I was also instructed by the nurse about how and where on my torso and thighs to best inject myself with the insulin needle pen.

She also explained what happens when my blood glucose levels get too low which can occur due to stress, exercise, hot weather, eating too few carbohydrates and drinking excess alcohol. This Hypoglycaemia, or hypo, causes a number of symptoms such as dizziness, sweating, shaking, confusion and palpitations, which usually go away 10 to 15 minutes after eating sugar.

In our lounge that night with Katie, surrounded by all this paraphernalia, there were some truly ugly scenes with lots of swearing and tears as I endured a baptism of fire. I repeatedly pricked my finger without drawing blood and practised injecting into my stomach and thigh. Injecting oneself for the first time is very disheartening – actually taking a needle and sticking it into my abdomen or leg. It's luckily an extremely thin and fine needle that's attached to a pen which contains the insulin. People often talk about hating needles and having a phobia. Well, I had no choice and had to bury any such worries very quickly. I had never injected myself before but I had to jolly well get on with it! It was all pretty fraught and I was filled with oodles of self-doubt that I could ever manage this new regime.

The next day was a Friday and as I didn't need to be working from my client's office I went to my consultancy premises in Soho. Getting out of Oxford Circus tube on my first proper day as a diabetic, I felt strange, as if everyone knew my secret and was looking at me... but of course they weren't. In keeping with my secrecy about my CF, only my line manager was in the know about my diabetes and I chose not to mention it to my co-workers. It was my first opportunity of 'managing' my new blood test and injection in an office environment without drawing attention to myself. We had a briefing session over lunch and I had to excuse myself to go to the gent's toilet to conduct my insulin injection. All went reasonably well and no one was aware of what I was up to.

Later that day, I was extremely tempted to mention it to a colleague but I still kept it to myself. The potential moment occurred when our creative designer asked to meet in private to discuss a recent unsuccessful client bid with me. As she spoke about her frustration and annoyance that her design proposal was not chosen by the client, she began to cry. There I was, consoling this poor girl, while all the time thinking, "If only you knew about my diabetes – that's something worth crying over!"

It was trial and error during the months that followed my diagnosis as I grew accustomed to handling the condition, understanding how my body was responding and fitting diabetes into my social, work and sporting life. Every day I'm learning more and more about how my body works for and against me.

I soon discovered at work that it was foolish to have a long delay between injecting my lunchtime insulin and actually eating. In my first proper week as a diabetic, this led me to have a huge hypo in my client office during a conference call, which involved sweating profusely and feeling mildly drunk while trying to talk business.

I discovered that any form of physical activity will drop my blood sugar levels so I had to have some glucose to counteract the effect. When I played hockey, I had to prick my finger before, during and after the game to monitor my levels and pre-empt any potential hypos. Rather amusingly, I remember rejoicing at the end of the first half of one game when a rough tackle had cut my finger. *Great,* I thought, *I've got some ready-made blood to test my levels at half time and I don't need to prick my finger!*

It's strange but it did open my eyes to those around me who might also be diabetic. It's similar to learner drivers. You don't really notice them, but once you start to learn yourself, you see them everywhere. I carry my glucose tablets around with me like I'm some kind of diabetic guardian angel. One time, a young chap in the opposition was carried off the hockey pitch suffering from a severe hypo and I was at hand with my glucose tablets and chocolate bar to help rejuvenate him. Another time, on the London underground, my glucose tablets revived a lady who was slumped over on the side of the platform when passers-by didn't know what to do.

Diabetes meant that certain food luxuries had to be reduced or removed completely from my diet. I absolutely loved sweets and was initially gutted to have to limit my intake of them. I went to Boots and bought their bespoke diabetic sweets but they tasted awful. I would visit the sweet aisle of the local supermarket wistfully bemoaning all the goodies that I was now denied. Occasionally I would 'fall off the wagon' and indulge myself with predictable results that my sugar levels went sky high. I have learnt over time that there is a balance to be found where I can still enjoy some of my favourite sweets or a chocolate bar as long as it's accompanied by some insulin. What causes problems is to have a cake or doughnut mid-afternoon without any insulin.

Interestingly, out of the dispiriting diabetic transition has come some good. A positive result out of a negative situation, you could say.

I have become quite obsessed and competitive with having stable blood sugar levels, making the insulin work to my advantage. Indeed, I have had more energy and fewer lung infections which enabled me to go without my usual February IV session in 2010 and feel capable of pushing on.

I decided not to dwell on the negative consequences of the condition; what could go wrong with possible diabetic comas, loss of feeling in my extremities, amputations and issues with vital organs. Instead I adopted the mindset of 'Just tell me what I've got to do and I'll add it to my on-going medical regime!' I realised that inheriting CF at birth made it slightly easier to adapt to the harsh realities of diabetes as I had already knuckled down into a treatment regime. I've witnessed that those who develop diabetes later in life after a period of good health will likely struggle more with the mental and physical adjustment that is required.

I also understood that it was easier for me to come to terms with being diagnosed with the condition in my late thirties rather than succumbing to it in my teens or twenties when I would have struggled with the loss of spontaneity around drinking excess alcohol and carefree partying. Other CF sufferers are diagnosed with diabetes at an earlier age. I found it hard enough to accept aged 38, but for small children and teenagers, it must be incredibly difficult for them and their parents.

Furthermore, being forced out of my comfort zone by the diagnosis galvanised me into looking at my propensity to see the negative spin rather than focus on the possible positives. I now work hard every day to maintain my positive thinking, turning the majority of my negative thoughts into positive ones.

As ever with me, there's always room for humour. I do joke that at last I now have a condition (with diabetes) that people have actually heard of! CF is not well understood and people are more concerned about my diabetes than my CF, usually because they know more about diabetes. I politely inform them that CF is more likely to finish me off first. Also when explaining to people about my diabetes, I joke that it's my reward for defying the odds with CF and staying alive.

The healthier body and mindset was the good that came as a result of the bad diagnosis news and going through some ugly experiences while getting used to a new regime. The Good, the Bad and the Ugly.

My diabetes is just one more thing to add. No problem...

8. Windows 7

Saturday 17 / Sunday 18 April 2010

We enjoyed a busy social weekend. Katie and I went to the London Wayfarers hockey club's twentieth anniversary black tie ball in Clapham on Saturday evening and followed it up the next day with the London Strollers mixed hockey festival in local Surrey. Wayfarers were Katie's hockey club. I also knew them well socially and Strollers was the mixed hockey team where Katie and I met back in the mid-1990s.

For a lot of my adult life, I was never happier than when my weekends were crammed full.

'Windows 7' was my phrase to describe these ideal weekends. Essentially, there are seven windows of social opportunity during any given weekend – Friday evening, Saturday morning, afternoon and evening and Sunday morning, afternoon and evening. It I could 'fill' all these slots with some activity – sport, lunch, dinner, shopping, cinema, family, partying – then, in my mind, I was savouring every moment and living the life I wanted to live.

In my social heyday, Friday night would consist of work drinks or dinner with friends; Saturday morning and afternoon would be filled with a league hockey game and possibly umpiring another game on the same pitch or nearby; Saturday evening would be spent at a multitude of hockey club socials, birthday parties, clubbing in London or at the cinema; Sunday morning consisted of Strollers mixed hockey; Sunday afternoon was when I crashed with house mates to watch a football or rugby game on TV and this was all rounded off on Sunday evening with a meal out with college friends. Sounds tiring? Well, yes it was, but just the sort of activity that I thrived on for more than a decade.

This full-on lifestyle which spanned my late teens, University, all my twenties and early thirties, was driven by the likelihood that I was unlikely to make it much beyond 30 years old. When time is likely to be short with the life-clock ticking loudly and the sand emptying from my hourglass, I always felt there was so much to do but with so little time to achieve it. I'm also convinced that this was a way of channelling my anger and bitterness about my condition and that some of my behaviour back then was rebellious and self-destructive. This in turn drove my thirst for life and an insatiable appetite to meet people, have fun and make my time and life count. Forget minutes, I wanted to make every second matter and I felt I couldn't afford to waste any time.

To quote Jim Carrey from 'The Mask' film – P A R T Why? Because I had to!

In truth, I wanted to fill my potentially short life with substantial memories and have no social regrets. I hated to feel as if I was missing out on anything social. In my youth I was quite immature about a lot of things that others were serious about. I felt the seriousness of CF and my daily grind of treatment was enough for me and everything else should be as fun as possible. To this day I still feel the same way. After all, tomorrow may never come.

But I did push things to the extreme. If there were more than one social opportunity on any given night, as long as it was commutable, I'd often try to do the lot. At certain times of the year, like Christmas and the end of the hockey season in April and May, it was not unusual for me to attend more than three parties a night. I would carefully plan how I would map out the whole night – which engagement to start at and the best one to finish with (normally dictated by where there would be the most number of women!). As I said, I didn't like to miss out on anything.

To make sure that my Windows 7 mantra was adhered to, whatever time I got back home in the small hours of Sunday morning, I would make sure I was up early, sometimes after only a few hours' sleep, and be ready to play hockey around South London the next morning. For a long period of my life sleep was not important as it got in the way of actual living. Indeed, I used to joke with friends and family that I'd get all the sleep I needed when I'm dead. This mindset suited my frenetic lifestyle back then, but it caught me out from my mid-thirties when I became a dad and I suddenly needed to re-educate my sub-conscious that sleep was important and I needed more than I was getting!

I think my record for attendance on a Saturday night was five separate parties, starting in Battersea before moving to Soho where the other four events were conveniently spaced so I could stage-gate the night to perfection.

There are countless examples of when I pushed myself to the brink of extinction. A huge school house party on a Friday night in 1988, where I was shockingly drunk and sick, was followed by waking up very sheepishly the next morning to watch on TV the Seoul Olympic hockey final which the Great Britain team won. I then played a few hours later for Southampton hockey club versus a strong Guildford side. For the first 10 minutes of the game I was all at sea before slowly but surely coming good and having a strong game. I'm sure I only woke up during the post-match shower!

On Christmas Eve, like a lot of school friends who have left home, I would reconvene with my old chums in certain Southampton hot spots in the evening for a night of raucous festivity prior to Christmas Day itself. There were two local pubs five minutes from each other that held the majority of my old school friends on this particular evening. Not wishing to miss out, I would toggle between the two venues for the whole night, often consuming a beverage at each. Towards midnight, I would make the decision which of the two would be best positioned to enjoy the most fun. Those nights were an annual fixture in my busy calendar for a long time and I remember them with much fondness.

For more than four years I attended our university summer black tie ball, where I would stay up all night until daylight; then sneak home for a brief four hour siesta before getting up to play a game of tennis with other friends. The concept of 'pushing on through the night' at certain events wholeheartedly appealed to my sleeping is cheating life edict and perfectly suited my need to squeeze every last drop out of my socialising.

Many nights out during my decade of defiance would be unnecessarily elongated by ending up in a nightclub where I would shine brightly in the bar and dance floor for about two hours before crashing and burning on a comfy couch. Those who know me well from this era would have witnessed this phenomenon, knowing that I would often get better sleep in a noisy night club than in the quiet surroundings of a bedroom. Indeed, I became pretty well known for my ability to fall asleep in clubs. I was bestowed by one hockey tour team with the nick-name of 'hamster' as I would be found sleeping in the corner of clubs.

On one notable occasion in a club in Wandsworth, it was the loud bass speaker that served as a pillow and jolly comfortable it proved to be.

In my defence, this all happened in the days before the advent of Red Bull so by about one in the morning in these places, I was surviving on energy fumes. Like the Duracell bunny, I would keep going until my batteries went flat and needed recharging.

Even on the pre-Christmas Wayfarers hockey club party in Battersea which was where Katie and I got together for the first time in December 2000, I had already been to two parties up town, including a Polish vodka bar, before I hailed a black cab from Holborn to Battersea – which proved to be an inspired decision based on my eventual marriage to Katie!

In keeping with my social raison d'être, in my twenties, I had very few evenings at home and I didn't give myself a chance to relax, much to the chagrin of my family and friends, who felt I wasn't always putting my health first with my kamikaze approach to socialising. Nicknamed 'Tiles Tim' by my dad (in reference to a late 'night out on the tiles'), I would regularly go two to three weeks at a time without a night in.

As most people put social engagements on their calendar, I used to put the rare nights at home in mine and in the end I used to really look forward to those monastic nights in as much as others look forward to nights out!

Partying and playing sport took my mind off CF and made me feel normal amongst my peers. My bloody-minded attitude to living life decreed that if I could out-party and out-exercise my friends, then all was fine...

I did draw the line with smoking cigarettes and taking illegal drugs. With a lung disease, that would have been like signing my own death certificate. Along with my thirst for life was a thirst for alcohol – my only proper vice and my anaesthetic from the effects of CF. Despite my size, I was actually a reasonable drinker and my favourite tipple was dark rum and coke.

However, as hard as I socialised, I still tried my utmost not to miss my treatments and medication, knowing that my medication should not be sidelined. I could just about keep my health reasonably balanced by not cutting any corners on my treatments (even when hung-over!). This mindset was instilled and embedded by my parents and has served me well all my life.

It's stating the obvious but smoke is not terribly helpful to my lungs and general well-being. For the majority of my youth, if I wanted to socialise in bars, clubs and restaurants, I had no choice but to suffer the second-hand smoke of others. After visiting some ridiculously smoky places, I felt like a dragon, with smoke coming out of my nostrils. The effect on my lungs the next morning was noticeable. Not only with the awful smell of smoke clinging to my clothes and hair, but the way the smoke would horribly stir up my lungs for the next few days. Bizarrely I found that alcohol was medicinal as it masked the effect of smoke and took my attention away from how damaging the smoke was to my lungs.

Of course, I could have stayed at home and lived a monk-like existence between the age of 15 and 35 but what kind of life would that have been? There's a tricky balance to be found between being sociable and enjoying your life versus being a recluse in order to maintain your health. I did try to dodge the smoke if at all possible when out, drinking in pub gardens, drinking in non-smoking areas and generally socialising with people who were non-smokers. This led me to be rather selfish with where we went out and who I socialised with but sometimes I couldn't avoid the smoke of others and I had to quite literally 'suck it up'.

However, over the years I did socialise in hundreds of different establishments that were smoky and they would, without a shadow of a doubt, have contributed to diminishing my lung function.

Now that the law is in place in the UK which has banned smoking in public places, I can go out without any concern for how my lungs will be affected. It's come too late to be honest as all my craziest partying days are behind me but it's welcome nonetheless. I just wonder how much healthier I would be today if I hadn't endured over 20 years of second-hand smoke.

Nowadays, like most people with a busy job and young family, I enjoy a quieter existence and my Windows 7 has been reduced to Windows 3 or 4; though at certain times, I still enjoy trying to fill all those weekend windows.

This weekend was one of those where I was flat out from start to finish, playing and partying with the best of them.

I am more likely to stay in far more during the working week and I can only physically play hockey on one of the weekend days, rather than on both. Doing both would seriously wear me out. These days, I look forward to the odd night out as much as I used to look forward to those rare nights in during my twenties.

If I make it to 40 next March, I think it will only be appropriate to celebrate in style and have a full-on Windows 7!

9. Body Whisperer

Thursday 22 April 2010

I have a kinesiology appointment today in Surrey with the fabulous Vera Peiffer. I've arrived early – a rare occurrence – and sit in my car in front of her driveway and ponder on why I add this to my already full medical agenda and why it is worth paying for such help.

Take it from me, when you have suffered from a condition every day of your life, you'll jump at anything that might improve your health. I often joke that I would stand on my head for an hour if I was told it would make a difference!

The early seeds were sown from university onwards when my parents had to let me take more ownership of my treatment. Up to the age of 18 I lived at home with my parents and brothers and had been looked after and reasonably cosseted. At university in London, the management of my health was all down to me pretty much. I had no choice but step up to the plate and work things out for myself. This empowered me to take personal responsibility for my health, hospital appointments and the daily medical decision making. Looking back now, I thank my parents for giving me that autonomy and ability to think on my own two feet. I learned many valuable lessons over those years and began to instinctively do the right thing for my medical regime more often than not.

By taking more accountability for my health I set free internal whispers in my head and started to use feedback from within my body as much as the advice from doctors. My condition involves perpetual internal dialogue. It's critical what I communicate to myself on a daily basis.

I've learnt that my body is the place where my emotions, thoughts, and memories reside. It is the container of my life story and it registers and records the events of my life in its cells. This may sound strange, but my body hears everything my mind says. Our constant internal monologue offers each and every one of us vital information on what to do or not to do in life and health situations and scenarios.

If we say yes to something while our bones are screaming "NO!" we need to be aware of what that does to the body. The tension this creates immediately releases stress hormones whether we are aware of it or not. These stress hormones engage the body's fight or flight system. And if we do this continuously – override our needs – we wear down our adrenals which then compromises the immune system. If acted upon correctly, this silent voice could be your friend or if ignored, it could be your foe.

From my mid-twenties onwards, I began to better experience the ability to hear and understand what my body was saying. What was my body trying to tell me? What were the whispers of my body instructing me to do or not do? I listened intently to the whispers circling around my body on a daily basis and interpreted what I needed to do in order to prevent my body having to scream at me to act!

I see it as deciphering my inner code. There's a health-related version of the Bletchley Park Enigma machine in my body and it works overtime to challenge and defeat its enemy – my CF and diabetes. By listening to this inner voice, my body tells me what needs enhancing from my energy levels and lung function through to my immune system. I have become a secondary doctor for myself and I'm always on call.

Indeed, my body is permanently tweeting and sending me short and punchy health update messages, both good and bad. However, it's a two-way process. As well as receiving messages from my body, I have also discovered the importance of sending whispered tweets to myself early in the morning and last thing at night. In effect, I re-set my mindset twice a day and tell my body how healthy I need and want to be. I also outline what I will achieve that day – work, sport or social – and state that this won't be affected by my health issues.

As part of taking more ownership for my illness, I also looked outside of the medical world at other more holistic ways to boost my health both physically and mentally. This comprehensive approach to the treatment of my disease examines the complete person, physically and psychologically; hence treating both the mind and the body. To paraphrase a line from JF Kennedy's inaugural speech: 'Ask not what your body can do for you, but what you can do for your body.'

By far the most important holistic approach I undertook was to explore the power of complementary therapies. The catalyst for this was my good friend from Southampton, Jessica Hyde-Brown; a lovely girl with a wonderful aura. As well as treating me with deep tissue massage and reflexology, she opened my mind to the helpful possibilities of other therapy interventions. Over the last 15 years, I have had repeated private sessions of reflexology, aromatherapy, health kinesiology and even crystal and hands-on healing.

The latter occurred at the Hale Clinic in London back in 2002 after seeing an article for hands-on healing in the Times magazine. I lay on the couch with an assortment of small crystals on my chest. Then the male practitioner, who looked like a wizard, placed his hands on my feet and his female colleague put her hands on my neck. After a while, there was a warm sensation around my feet and a cold feeling where the lady's hands were. Not only that, but the crystals did start to make crackling noises! I can't explain how they achieved this as I'm convinced they didn't move their hands to use assistance in the form of heat pads or ice cubes. The whole experience reminded me of a scene from the 'Man on the Moon' film, featuring Jim Carrey as the comedian Andy Kaufman. Seriously ill with lung cancer, he heads to the Philippines to seek a medical 'miracle', where doctors supposedly pull out infected organs from the body. On discovering the scam he laughs out loud at the irony that he thought it might work for him.

Even for me, this experience was very surreal but I'm glad I gave it a crack! After all, how do you know until you try something new? I find that the process of trying something fresh and obscure will lift my spirits.

As well as countless reflexology sessions with Jessica, usually when I'm enduring one of my intravenous treatments, the other therapy I have used the most is health kinesiology which I've been having for nearly a decade. Before my first ever kinesiology treatment in 2001, I had lunch with a college friend Ann Hirst, during which she asked me about my current health and well-being. I still remember my tragic reply, *"I'm so tired. I've not felt alive for ages."*

This long established bio-energetic approach of kinesiology combines the ancient wisdom of traditional Chinese medicine with the modern technique of muscle testing. It's guided by a principle that my body is asked what it needs to enjoy vibrant well-being, and my body actually answers back. This technique accesses my body's unique inner wisdom, to determine where imbalances lie along the body's 14 energy meridians. Armed with this information, the practitioner, Vera in my case, performs a range of corrective techniques specifically tailored to the needs of the patient. In my experience, Vera's greatest help is re-correcting my energy flow and vitality twice a year when the ravages of CF have dragged me down and I'm struggling.

As well as these therapies, I control the controllable by researching the best ways to boost my immune system through buying certain over-the-counter vitamin supplements which I add to my daily cocktail of drugs. Anything to ward off a cold is vital because a cold affects my lungs for a long time afterwards. I always make sure to have a flu jab in the autumn.

For anyone who doesn't have a chronic disease or a need to boost their health, then these therapies might seem rather bizarre. The key is to completely believe that these treatments will benefit me otherwise they are a waste of time and money. They allow me to visualise better health and 'see' a body undiminished by my illness. In some cases, it acts as a form of placebo but if it works then it's still worth doing. Even a five per cent improvement in my health would make a noticeable difference to the quality of my life.

All these complementary therapies have in different ways boosted my energy levels, immune system and provided me with a sounder, more resilient body and mind. Using a dual approach, I now physically challenge CF through my medication and exercise, while the alternative treatments help my mental prosperity.

This is not the only reason why I spend time and money with this alternative method. I have not had a new medical drug for over a decade which is long time to wait for a morale lift. In the interim, the expectation that comes with any new therapy gives me renewed hope that I can reverse my declining health... and this in itself is tremendously powerful.

The therapies make me feel as if I'm attacking back against my conditions rather than just accepting the suffering. This is crucial. It can move mountains in me, make me happy when I have no reason to be and put a spring in my step. To complete the virtuous circle, any hope of improved health reinforces the credibility of my body 'tweets' and in turn feeds my courage to keep fighting CF and diabetes.

I never underestimate the power of hope and how important it is to keep it renewed. Hope can be the difference in my life when all my motivation has drained away, when CF is beating me, when I've got nothing left to give; when I'm at the last-chance saloon. When everything is dark and depressed having some hope can offer a ray of light to guide you through to the other side. Anything that gives me hope is worth pursuing. I know that when my hope runs out, then so will I.

I decided a long time ago to not just rely on National Health Service drugs but to help myself in every way possible, leaving no stone unturned. I imagine my body as a sandcastle being battered by the incoming tide or as a fortified castle back in medieval times under constant and relentless attack. The medicine and the complementary therapies help to build stronger ramparts to defend my castles from the ravages of my conditions.

By taking an integrated approach for my health, seizing more control and having a two-way narrative with my body, I have been able to help flip my mindset from expecting to die

10. Miracles Can Happen

Saturday 1 May 2010

It's Felix's third birthday and Katie and I have taken our special boy to Bocketts Farm Park in Surrey. There were a lot of different animals inside a gigantic barn and we went around feeding them with a bag of pellets. My attention was distracted for just a few moments and as I turn around, I find Felix is tweaking the nose of one of the sheep. What a cheeky young chap my son is. Amusing moments like these make parenting so worthwhile. However, my journey to paternity and bringing this gregarious boy into the world was a long and precarious one. He could easily never have existed…

"I'll not live long enough to have a wife and child," was a statement made to my mum on Weston-Super-Mare's pleasure pier in the late 1990s. Back then, staying alive with CF and even getting to 30 was not certain, so speculating about a family was furthest from my mind. In 2000 I began dating Katie whom I already knew on the field hockey social scene for over six years. She helped me to celebrate the all-important 30th birthday. After reaching this milestone, life felt different and I had an eye on a renewed future.

Reaching the average life expectancy for a CF sufferer – as it was then – felt liberating. Aligned to this, the desperately sad deaths of my CF friends in my late twenties made me more determined to carry their spirit with me and make my longer life count for something. When so much of a CF life is not at all normal, it's fulfilling to do something that your peers take for granted and breaks the CF boundaries. Marriage to Katie in 2003 spurred me on that my destiny was going to be different than I had originally thought back on that pier with my mum.

When we married, it felt natural and normal to start a family as something was missing. I did have serious concerns about getting married and starting a family when there's no certainty of being alive for them, but I was feeling healthy enough, so marriage to Katie and starting a family seemed a natural way to keep defying my illness.

Unfortunately, due to my CF and not being able to conceive naturally, our road to paternity was not a straightforward one as we had to undergo in vitro fertilisation, or IVF, as it's commonly known. Without getting too medical, my illness meant that were we to have a child, we would need to go through IVF and a particularly intricate version called Intracytoplasmic Sperm Injection (ICSI).

We decided not to wait the standard two years before commencing with a free IVF cycle via the National Health Service, plus we had been advised to use a particular private IVF clinic in Hammersmith, London. So in 2004, we started what would turn out to be an extremely long process involving countless trips through busy London traffic to the Wolfson clinic in Hammersmith.

IVF is an extremely exacting procedure – it's drawn-out, cruel, torturous, expensive and an emotional rollercoaster. Not something I would wish on any couple to be honest, but if that's your only option, and you're not considering adoption, then you have no choice.

There's a bottom line when a couple embark on IVF treatment and it is that you both have to be one hundred and fifty per cent up for wanting a baby or the stress may be the undoing of your relationship. With IVF, you also need to be ready for the likelihood of having twins – double trouble! The pressure on the couple for it to work is intense where you can get to the point where nothing else exists. Also the emotional changes that the woman goes through are extremely exacting for everyone concerned. If the male partner is doing it to appease his other half, it could lead to problems.

For my part, I felt broody and was desperate for a child of my own and a 'plus one' for Katie and myself. We could almost touch it the desire to be parents was so tangible. Like most couples who want children, we felt that something was missing and two becoming three was an ideal worth pursuing. I know it's mainly women who start to get clucky about having kids but I had big pangs of desire to be a dad. I used to picture myself holding my own baby in my arms and when out and about I used to view children and wonder what it would be like to be a real dad. This intensified over time and after three years of the IVF process with no luck, my inner soul did start to bellow, *"Where is my baby?"*

During the IVF rollercoaster where the odds of success are less than twenty-five per cent, we hoped for the best but feared the worst. To have just one child feels unachievable so we didn't plan or dare to dream of a large family. IVF is such a strange dynamic because although one child would feel amazing, we had to be prepared for the likelihood of twins!

My hat goes off to any woman who undergoes IVF or any type of fertility intervention. In brief, Katie went through a month of injections – normally into her torso – which helped to stimulate her ovaries to produce enough eggs to mix with my sperm. For my part I had to have my sperm retrieved via an procedure called a TESA, where I experienced the sensation of an epidural and my 'swimmers' were removed by a needle and then immediately frozen ready to be thawed out when needed. Going through that painful procedure definitely cemented my commitment to becoming a parent!

There's a few days wait while the clinic confirms how many embryos have been created and what condition they are in. We then went back in at the crack of dawn for what is one of the most nerve-wracking days of our lives as the best embryos are transferred back into Katie's womb. Thus begins a two week wait which put us, but particularly Katie, through another mini hell until we find out whether any of the embryos have created a pregnancy.

Our clinic, while we were doing IVF, had a pretty harsh system where the woman would go to the clinic early on a pre-defined day to have some bloods taken. We were then given a two hour window between 12 and 2pm when we would receive the call from the clinic with either positive or negative pregnancy news. During our three years undergoing IVF, we waited by that phone on five separate occasions and let me tell you, it is one of the most nerve-shattering times of our lives.

Katie picked up the call on three occasions and I did the last two as she couldn't bear it anymore. To make matters worse, the clinic seemed to ring close to 12pm when we had good news but called us later with the bad news, which made the experience even harsher. It's all changed since then as the woman now receives a pregnancy testing kit so she can see if she has been successful or not, which is much more humane.

On our first ever IVF attempt in 2005, when that call came through, we did get the wonderful news that Katie was pregnant! The feeling of elation was amazing and we went out for a meal to celebrate. "Our first ever IVF with the odds stacked against us and we got there!" was how we were thinking. Sadly, a few weeks later disaster struck…

Katie, a nurse, was driving back from a shift and had the most enormous haemorrhage which was the miscarriage of our child. To this day, she will never forget that drive home, knowing what that blood signified. The odds of getting a successful pregnancy with IVF is about one in four depending on many facets, not least the age of the woman; so to get a pregnancy on our first go was unexpected and felt miraculous. To achieve the holy grail of pregnancy only to see it washed away not long after in a sea of blood was just so cruel. Imagine a mountaineer being able to see the summit of Mount Everest only to break his leg and never make it to the very top!

That's how it felt – absolutely devastating and crushing. We had to cling to each other to make sense of it and gather strength to raise our head above the bar to carry on. There seemed nothing to smile about for a long, long time…

We had a three month wait before Katie's body was ready to try another IVF cycle. From the off we decided to tell family and friends about our IVF process in order to be transparent and honest. It also prevented the usual barrage of the question "Are you trying for kids?" which is common for married couples to hear. Although every couple will handle this in their own way, I know of a lot of couples who keep their fertility treatment hidden away, even after their children have been born – probably due to the perceived stigma attached to it.

Everyone has their own way of dealing with it I suppose and there's no right or wrong way.

We endured six IVF cycles over three years. When a cycle hadn't worked, we entered into an abyss where our spirits were very low. But we worked hard at being happy for others who already had children or those falling pregnant, strongly believing that what goes around comes around. There was still room for humour. At one point while I was having one of my IV treatments and Katie was in the early stages of an IVF cycle, we were both lying on our bed injecting ourselves. I've got to admit that it doesn't get much more romantic than that!

Our reaction to each cycle that hadn't worked was one of utter dejection. I would try to be as sympathetic for Katie as possible. I would also find some time for myself to register my disappointment and re-establish my hope for future attempts. This would often occur in our back garden; sitting on the bench and praying hard.

One of the most challenging times of my life occurred around the 2006 Easter weekend. Our female cat had been sadly run over a few weeks before the fifth cycle of IVF had been unsuccessful and the two combined made Katie and I nosedive into a unique depth of despair. As well as making time for sharing the anguish together, I knew that the individual partners needed to grieve on their own and in a way that suited them. On the Easter Monday, the day before starting my new job as a communications consultant at Royal Dutch Shell, Katie was outside gardening and I decided to watch one of my favourite films 'Chariots of Fire'. I have always found this film emotionally charged and it wasn't long before the tears were flowing. Typical of most men, I am not prone to crying that often but subconsciously I probably knew I needed a release for my built-up feelings and this film allowed me to cry away my sadness at our very cruel double loss.

During our sixth IVF cycle in July 2006 when the desire for a positive outcome was almost unbearable, I decided to change my routine while Katie was undergoing the embryo transfer under sedation. In the past, it was always at these moments in the process that I would feel most unable to help. With my CF medication, I'm always able to help myself and take control, but with this, there was nothing I could do that would make a difference. As well as going for a long walk in the nearby park I also sat in the hospital chapel for 20 minutes praying for Katie and the right result – effectively handing it over to God. This at least helped me to believe that I was doing something to help and it helped to calm me down.

When I received that dreaded phone call from the clinic a few weeks later 'Sixth time lucky' became our new catchphrase. Katie was miraculously pregnant and in May 2007 we had our miracle boy Felix. The name means 'happy' in Greek and 'lucky' in Latin. Like me, he will be 'happy-go-lucky'.

After three difficult and torturous years we had finally reached the holy grail of parenthood and I wanted to hold Felix for an eternity. Following a 48-hour labour, on the early evening of 1st May 2007, I left Katie and Felix going up to the maternity ward together. We both felt shattered and elated at the same time. I texted our good news to our nearest and dearest. It's at that precise point that I realised how a new life positively impacts the lives of so many others. I spent that night back at home on my own, as serenely happy as I can ever remember.

The next day on visiting the maternity ward, things had changed. Felix was not feeding and was listless after his long traumatic birth which ended in a ventouse delivery in theatre. That afternoon, as a precaution he was wheeled off to the ante-natal ward where he had a gastric tube fitted and they did the standard tests on him. Our emotions were in shatters. What did this mean for our cherished boy after the arduous journey we had been through to bring him into our lives? That night I rang one of my best and most practical friends, Bo Williams, to let off some steam as I was in such a state of worry.

The following day, I arrived at the neo-natal ward, put on the gown, washed my hands and waited to be ushered to Felix. These units are very humbling with all the incubators for the tiny premature babies wrapped up in what looks like baking foil. As I sat next to Felix the nurse handed him over for me to deliver him his first bottle feed and then change his nappy. On that day, at that exact time, I'd be surprised if there was a father around the world who was more delighted to hold his son and give him some nourishment and care.

At last my beautiful boy was in my arms. It felt amazing and a little surreal that I could produce a healthy child after a lifetime of suffering. Felix does not have CF. He is a carrier but doesn't suffer in any way. In fact, I would go as far to say that he is my 'healthy clone' and as vibrant as any boy I've ever seen at his age.

Nothing can prepare you for being parents, especially making the adjustment when there are health problems to factor in. Katie bore the brunt of the early morning wake-ups and other activities to help preserve my energy levels which in turn stretched us as a couple.

Katie had to suffer and endure to get through IVF and her subsequent post-birth nerve damage. She was prepared to put her body through so much to get our plus one and the nerve damage meant she couldn't easily sit and hold him. She could only manage this by sitting on a special cushion, which she still needs to this day.

As Katie was struggling with her own health, I took Felix out a lot for walks in his pram to help him go off to sleep when he was tired and fractious. When asleep, I would find a park bench to sit down and take stock. I'd always feel proud that my boy was next to me. Having a new life to look after seemed to make the sky and horizon stretch out as if the world had opened up. I always found those moments, just my baby son and me, deeply meaningful and thought-provoking.

I initially thought that the rigours of parenting would mean that my health would only hold out to get him started in life; but now the thought of not being there for Felix feels abhorrent. This is best expressed in a World War One poem by Wilfred Owen, 'Wild with all Regrets':

"A short life and a merry one, my buck! We said we'd hate to grow dead old. But now, not to live old seems awful: Not to renew my boyhood with my boy..."

There's not any part of us becoming parents that we took for granted as IVF can be a fruitless and cruel exercise. It would be callous to say I love my son more than others love their children just because we struggled with IVF, but I definitely believe that you appreciate something more if you have had to strive to obtain it. They say that what doesn't break you makes you stronger. It feels unfair to have gone through so many storms to get our boy, but the rainbow at the other end has more than made up for it. Felix is our miracle boy and someone that I fully intend to see grow up into a man and have his own family.

I hope Felix reads this one day so that he can understand what it took to bring him into this world and what he means to us. I don't expect a thank you from him as gratitude from your child isn't always expected or forthcoming. I just want him to know that if you want something enough, miracles can happen and he's our proof.

11. About a Boy

Sunday 2 May 2010

After the fun of the farm yesterday on Felix's actual third birthday, today is his family celebration at our house where he will be joined by both sets of grandparents and also his great granddad.

Within seconds of receiving a paddling pool from one of his grandparents, Felix shot upstairs into his bedroom only to return dressed only as nature intended in his birthday suit. He then ran past all his guests out into the garden carrying his new gift. Outside on a warmish May early afternoon, we helped him to pump air into the pool, before getting the hose to fill it up with water. He then splashed around utterly naked – a happy, innocent little boy, high on life.

Watching him in action with his adoring grandparents in tow made me reflect on what had gone on behind the scenes to parent this miracle boy of ours.

There's a huge tendency to prioritise your brand new child – to put their needs ahead of one's own. For the mums, it's a natural instinct to be attentive to their child, in lioness mode as it were, protecting their fragile lion cub. During the early years of being a parent I had to put CF away in an emotional box labelled 'Only break open in an emergency'. I didn't stop any of my treatments during this time; I just never complained or talked about my condition. It just seemed less topical than the very real scenario of first-time parenting, which is all-encompassing.

This all changed back in summer 2009 following my diabetes diagnosis, when I had to crack open this metaphoric box and bring CF back into the equation. Katie and I had to get to grips with it as quickly as possible.

Nothing can prepare you for being parents, especially making the adjustment when there are health problems to factor in. Katie bore the brunt of the early morning wake-ups and other activities to help preserve my energy levels which in turn stretched us as a couple. I helped where I could. As Felix didn't get on with breast feeding, I certainly did my share of bottle feeding, winding, nappy changing and pram walks.

I am a great believer in the power of music for all generations but especially with children. I would stimulate Felix with different music when he was a baby. During the day, while holding him in my arms, I would play Michael Jackson's 'Another Part of Me' and Al Green's 'Let's Stay Together'. At his bedtime, he always relaxed to the soothing qualities of 'In Dreams' by Roy Orbison. Indeed, the 'Big O' turned into a favourite during the witching hours in the middle of the night when Felix needed to get back off to sleep. Just me, my son, Roy and a lovely long cuddle…

Being a father figure was and is at times counter-intuitive to my primary instinct to maintain my health which has been systematically built up over the years. I've found that parenting often involves situations that put my own health second. From the extra tiredness, to the increased risk of infection, to being exposed to the elements when taking Felix out. At the same time, being a parent while managing the daily CF regime of 40 tablets, nebulisers and physiotherapy is punishing and at odds with always being able to play my part in parental duties. Katie has often felt like a one-person family in my absences during medication times and especially when I go away for my intravenous treatments.

More so than most parents, I'm very aware of the risks of being too close to Felix when he has a sniffle and as harsh as it sounds, I shield myself by not kissing him at these times. I certainly do not share his eating utensils, cups and food. One example of my desire to protect myself from cross-infection is that I will never eat his ice cream as I see so many parents doing without a second's thought.

I am missing out on sharing particular life moments with him, but common sense has to prevail for me. I wouldn't be terribly happy with myself if I let my guard down and subsequently got a cold from him. I am delighted to be his dad but it comes with certain limitations. Generally, I do as much as I can and act like any normal dad running around with Felix, which I know he appreciates.

Felix is a force of nature, has a passion for life, likes to work the room and is a constant blur, socialising with anyone and everyone – the apple hasn't fallen far from the tree! My healthy clone certainly lives up to the meaning of his name – 'happy-go-lucky'. Although I know I'm biased, I'm in awe of how beautiful my son is. Indeed, a good friend tells me that my voice and face change when I talk about him.

Nicknamed 'Little Dude', we have some brilliant times together with our own handshake and our rough-and-tumble sessions. I love the way he tears around soft play areas as if he's auditioning for Total Wipeout.

Felix has been along to watch me play hockey, which I adore. At the end of the game, he will often run onto the pitch past players and spectators and jump into my arms. He has joined me on the pitch after a few of my games and I'm always full of deep and heart-bursting pride that I have a son and that he's targeted me for a hug.

Fathers of sons are not always the one that their boys run to in emergencies; but this is one time when I know there's no one else he wants but me. I feel that he's the centre of my universe and I feel like the centre of his. It's at these moments that I know how my own dad must have felt when we brothers would watch him play and then make a bee-line for him afterwards. As far as Felix and sport, he's definitely a quick runner which will help him. For now I plan to let him be a free spirit and hope one day he will take up a sport that he enjoys and excels in.

Felix is aware that I have a health concern and I don't completely hide my illness from him. He has always seen me doing my nebulisers and heard me coughing. He doesn't really ask me about it and just takes it in his stride as children do. When I'm having a dark CF moment, Felix has the knack of taking my mind off it. Recently after I coughed heavily, he patted my chest and said: *"Daddy, better, better!"*

His acts of compassion help to inspire me to keep fighting my wretched illness. He is a useful distraction, stopping me from dwelling too long on my personal health battle. Indeed, I only need to look into his eyes to see all my tomorrows.

Back in our garden, while playing with Felix in his paddling pool, my mum commented to my dad, "He reminds me of Tim at the same age." Looks may have been the only thing I had in common with Felix when I was the same age as him. It was extremely tough growing up as a boy with a serious illness, such as CF.

Apparently, due to my health difficulties and routines, I could be temperamental most of the time but my parents knew this was not always my fault. I suffered daily from a huge amount of stomach pain, because in the 1970s there were no sophisticated enzyme capsules to digest my food. Instead, I had to rely on Cotazyme powders which were sprinkled on my food, which digested the food in my stomach only partially but no further. These powders made the food taste absolutely foul but I didn't know any different. As the food was unable to be digested further down the alimentary canal, this caused major discomfort, some days worse than others. The stomach pain could make me fractious and family members were coached that sometimes my tummy was 'mighty uncomfortable'. To this day, I remember crawling into my parent's bedroom in the middle of the night, lying down on the floor to the side of them, doubled up with 'gut-rot' but not willing or wishing to wake them up. I just felt comforted by being close to them.

From diagnosis at six months I was put on a low-fat diet so that steatorrhoea wouldn't be too much of a problem. I am told that on some days flushing the toilet was difficult after I'd performed and I would become very agitated if 'it didn't flush away'! Toilet training hadn't been too troublesome but all the family knew that 'if Tim wanted to go, Tim HAD to go'.

I would never miss out on a party unless a cold or worse was rife amongst my fellow partygoers. My digestive powders would be mixed with fruit juice and poured into a covered small beaker labelled 'Tim's magic drink'. I was allegedly popular at nursery school and had frequent party invitations. Although mums were apprehensive about what to feed me, it was explained that as long as I had my beaker drink during the tea, I should be fine. This invariably worked well although there was one explosive exception, when the host's mum admitted that the birthday sponge had been filled with thick dairy cream. The horrid enzyme powders couldn't cope with that at all and the rest go down in the anals, I mean, annals of history!

Being on a low-fat diet meant I was reasonably hungry and my appetite was invariably excellent unless I had a chest infection. At about this age, I became aware that I was eating different foods compared to my brothers. My parents made up a pint of low-fat milk for me. In those days there were no cartons of skimmed-milk in supermarkets. Apparently I was not bothered that my brothers occasionally had a fried egg whilst I had boiled or poached; and ice cream, a child's staple, had to be limited in my case. If and when I was tempted by a high-fat food, my mum warned me of the consequences for my stomach and I acquiesced.

Because I started twice-daily physiotherapy sessions after my six-month diagnosis, it became so engrained that I never knew any different – treatment had to be done before breakfast and supper come what may. During hospital in and out-patient visits, I was popular with every physiotherapist which helped my cause no end. My parents introduced a colour television around this time to make lying on my physiotherapy frame more conducive and stimulating. I was even allowed to choose the channel, not that there was much choice back in 1974.

Although I was extremely active at this age, due to my poor digestion abilities, only so much food bulked me up and this led to me being very thin. I am told that despite my small stature, I made up for it with sheer determination. Typical of the bond of brothers, we played all sorts of sport and activities in and outside of the house, which became exceptionally competitive. Of course, I disliked it when Chris and Jez would beat me at anything. Keeping up with them certainly kept me energised.

In hot weather I used to sweat profusely which is a common trait of most CF sufferers. On a hot night, I would sweat so much that I would have crystals of salt on my forehead; and my pillow and covers would become quite discoloured.

What I lacked in speed or energy I made up with being incredibly funny, so I'm told. Even when I was three, I could sense the need to lighten the darkness of my situation and our collective plight by making others laugh. I've always felt that I can help reduce the burden for myself and those around me by bringing fun and laughter into most situations. Indeed, I was a good mimic and loved being the centre of attention. Even at school, when I was called 'poo poo boy' as I needed to go to the toilet more often than anyone else, I would come back with some appropriate remark to maintain my popularity. Such an experience might crush some children but it only served to spur me on.

So I look back to my darling three-year-old birthday boy still going wild in his pool. My hearty son who, luckily, doesn't have to suffer what I went through when I was his age. Felix and I have both broken the mould in our lives – me to stay in this world and live a longer, fuller life and Felix to enter it after the IVF struggles. He's the best of me, my lasting legacy, the final piece of my jigsaw. I'm determined to be a part of his life for as long as possible.

Happy birthday Felix! Today was all about a boy- our boy – a very special, much-loved and wanted boy. There were no guarantees that you would come into our lives, but in our lives you are and here you are to stay…

12. Field of Dreams

Saturday 15 May 2010

One of the highlights of my year is the meet-up with some very good friends and our weekend hockey tour somewhere in England. The touring team is called the 'Phantoms' based on the fact that we play completely in white kit – socks, shorts and top; and our badge is that of a ghoul carrying a hockey stick.

I inherited playing with this team from my dad who had played for them every Easter when we were young. In fact it's become a core part of the Wotton family as all us brothers have played for the Phantoms over the years. The baton has been passed along the generation you might say, not just for my family, but for other players in the team whose fathers played before them. For most of my early playing days we used to play over the four days of the Easter weekend in Weston-Super-Mare, West of England, and also tour other English hockey festivals throughout the years.

We had some successful tours over the years, and were winners or finalists in most tournaments we entered. Playing a lot on grass which required old-fashioned skill levels, we had a very attacking style and often missed twice as many goals as we ever scored. There were also some very memorable games, none more so than a comeback-win over the local Weston team, the Torpids, on a Saturday afternoon one Easter. Having had a disastrous first half, we huddled together at half-time, four goals down and the opposition sensing a rare win over us. We decided on having some 'Dutch courage' so everyone had a slurp from a bottle of white rum. The spirit of Bacardi did the trick for us as we went on to score five unanswered goals to win 5-4!

One other outstanding result for us came on the Monday morning of the third day of an August tournament in my home town of Southampton, in a semi-final against a strong Dutch team who were destroying other teams up to that point. On an exceedingly wet morning, we were untouchable, playing some sublime hockey to win the game 7-1 – a truly awesome result. The Dutch manager was rather shell-shocked afterwards and enquired if we were a national team on tour. His face was a picture when I remarked that we only met twice a year and had left the hotel bar at 3am that morning!

For the last decade I have been the captain and chief organiser of the team. I don't find this a chore as it means we get together and carry on the Phantoms spirit. It is as close to a band of brothers as I have ever encountered. We are now middle-aged hockey veterans who all played a good standard but now we come together once a year to enjoy a runaround followed by a quiet beer and then about 15 noisy beers! It's a recipe for success on and off the field.

This year we are playing up in Leamington Spa against a Khalsa select team and as is the norm, I drive up with my good friend Richard Sharpe. It was a very hot day and age caught up with us as we ended up losing 5-3. As I went for a warm-down jog after the game I stopped in the corner of the pitch and did some light stretching. Not that I broadcast it to anyone but this weekend also signifies the 24th anniversary of my England hockey away trip to Braunschweig, Germany back in 1986. We were the Under 15 England Team and were called the 'Rosebuds', which on reflection doesn't sound very macho.

It was a four-day and three-game tournament during which we played Germany, Holland and France. We lost to Germany and Holland and drew with France which by goal difference meant we won a bronze medal. That medal proudly sits at my parents' home where it justifiably belongs. Without their support and dedication, I would never have been healthy enough to play for my country.

Most young children tend to have a dream, an obsession, as they grow up of achieving something in particular. Mine was to play hockey to as high a standard as possible and hopefully for my country, following in the footsteps of my dad who had a full England trial and my eldest brother who played for the same England team two years before me. It was all I ever wanted to do and back then I didn't dwell too much on my CF and how that might limit me. On the whole, my lungs were pretty manageable back then, before the adverse effects of partying and related second-hand smoke. I could compete with others my age and my innate ability carried me through.

I was successfully able to shine for school, county and divisional teams which led to my selection for the junior England team. Although we came away with a medal, I have some darker memories of the trip. My lungs struggled while in Germany when looking after myself with no help and sharing a room with little privacy to do my physiotherapy properly. I played most of the games at right half and acquitted myself pretty well but I did suffer some bouts of coughing while on the pitch. I remember crying later when I recounted the tale to my parents once I'd got home. I'd achieved my dream of being picked to play for England and when I was finally achieving my goal, my lungs began to let me down. It was a sad sign of things to come...

Representing England Juniors 24 years ago, like my brother Chris before me, turned out to be the pinnacle of my sporting life. A year later I did however train at Bisham Abbey with the Great Britain Olympic team that went on to win gold at the Seoul Olympics. After the bitter disappointment of not being selected for the England Under 16 team, I was selected for an unofficial Under 17 England team but the team didn't tour. The inconvenient truth was that my health was already on the wane. I was never able to fulfil my latent talent, which will always be an itch that I can never scratch and a huge disappointment for me. Those few days in May 1986 were the beginning and the end of my international sporting career.

One life-defining moment came in the mid-1990s at the English Hockey Cup Final game. Alongside my two great hockey buddies, Stephen Banbury and Stuart Ward, we drove down to Canterbury in Kent to watch Guildford beat Canterbury in the final. The Guildford team had two ex-school friends playing for them who were younger than me and in my opinion had less natural ability than me. Seeing them compete at this very high standard and celebrating afterwards with their team brought home my acute situation. I was once a very promising hockey player and junior international when my health was still good but now at just 23 my CF was beginning to ravage me and I was struggling to play in a third team for my club.

On the long drive back to London I went into meltdown. How was I going to deal with the confirmation of my shattered dreams? If I was unable to be the player I ought to be, should I just give up? It took many years to get my head around how to make sport work best for me.

After much soul-searching, I decided to make the most of my hockey talent and life in order to deflect the sorrow of what could have been in my sporting career. The nebulised drug Pulmozyme helped me to rise from the ashes and my health improved enough that I could once again play at a reasonable level. So as well as getting back into the first team at my club, playing hockey during the official autumn and winter seasons, I took part all year round including spring and summer tours. Like the Forrest Gump film scene where he kept running, I just kept playing hockey all year round.

The hockey tour, both men's and mixed, became an extremely important part of my life and during certain summers, I would attend as many as seven separate tours. Around Europe, I played hockey in Belgium and Norway; and in England I toured to Worthing, Weston-Super-Mare, Bath, Devon, Salisbury, Basingstoke, Southampton, Reading, Chichester, East Grinstead, Cannock and Stratford-upon-Avon.

The other side of losing my dream of playing seriously at a high level allowed me to play less seriously and enjoy the partying as much as the playing. Subsequently, fellow tourists have marvelled at my perseverance during tours. Even when they were flagging, I was still there squeezing every last drop out of my body, my hockey ability and my very life force. Tours were exhausting and hedonistic experiences. I would begin each tour with a reasonable level of fitness and energy, usually having my best game on the first day. But my energy and lungs went into free-fall after the first night out. I was never going to hold back and partied hard with the best of them. At the end of most tours, I was utterly spent and my lungs were faltering. But in a strange way it felt good because I was keeping up with healthy and normal people. Another example of me defying the medical odds and looking to put CF in its place.

Bizarrely, just like me, my illustrious friends Stephen and Stuart, all met our now wives through playing for the mixed hockey club, London Strollers. I wonder if my destiny with Katie would have been different if I had played elite hockey instead of the fun touring and our paths may not have crossed.

I had made my health situation work for me and my hockey has given me prolonged and better health, barrels of laughs, the sense of teamwork, a wife and subsequent child.

I toured for more than a decade post-University and had the time of my life with memories, those that I can remember, that I will cherish for a lifetime. There's a well-known adage that 'what goes on tour, stays on tour', but here are some tour anecdotes which highlight the fun we had.

To commiserate with an ex-University friend who had just been dumped by his girlfriend, we thought it was a fantastic idea to drink beer out of his top hat during this fancy dress party in Worthing. Amazingly a top hat does hold a pint of lager pretty well and serves a purpose as a drinking vessel, though I imagine it was wrecked the next day.

In Weston-Super-Mare on the final night after three heavy days, we stayed up throughout the night in the hotel bar. We then went for a sea-front walk at 5am before going straight to breakfast. Following a quick shower and change into our kit we went out to play and win that morning. Sleeping was cheating that night!

We enjoyed the most surreal experience in Belgium where mid-afternoon we went from the rave tent and full-on dancing straight onto the pitch. It was a novel style of warm-up. It didn't help us as we were soundly beaten by a German team who were taking it a bit more seriously than us.

Other less memorable moments that I have been told about include ordering a curry from my mum at my parent's house in Southampton at 3am after a heavy night of drinking Stella Artois and nearly missing the boat home after being left in a bar toilet in Cowes, Isle of Wight.

In the corner of that pitch in Leamington Spa, lost in my own thoughts, it didn't take me long to be back on that grass pitch in Germany where I'd been 24 years ago. As I looked back at those few days in 1986, one thing I'll always remember and treasure was standing in a line with my fellow England players and the immense pride I felt during the national anthem. Proclaiming "I vow to thee my country" was very inspiring and it's something that I'll never forget and I'll take with me to my grave.

Perhaps that was my own version of General Custer's last stand on those grass pitches in Germany. Representing my beloved country even for a few days conjures up the poem 'The Soldier' by Rupert Brooke:

> *'If I should die, think only this of me:*
> *That there's some corner of a foreign field*
> *That is forever England.'*

In some ways those 24 years have gone in a heartbeat. I've played a lot of hockey since then, for my county, University, club and touring teams. Despite the deterioration of my lungs, when I walk out onto the pitch, I know I can still play my game and contribute. It's extremely hard to keep playing when competing is so tough and it does diminish my love and passion for the sport. But in my dreams, I'm still fit and able to play pretty well and that more often than not is the difference between playing on or not. The hockey pitch will always be my field of dreams.

13. Not Alone

Sunday 6 June 2010

We visited Southampton for the day to celebrate my mum's 67th birthday with a family lunch. The full complement of our close family were in attendance, my mum, dad, brothers (Chris and Jez), their partners (Lisa and Julie), and finally Katie and Felix.

A lovely main course was accompanied by the familiar family chat and laughter before Felix decided he'd had enough and left us to watch TV in the lounge. As we ate dessert, the topic of a recent CF fundraising activity was discussed. As I looked around the table, it dawned on me that my condition does underpin a lot of what we think, feel and do as a family; without it taking centre stage too much and dominating everything. I've learnt over the years that it's not just the person suffering who's affected by the diagnosis of CF but close family and friends are enveloped by it and have a crucial role to play.

My immediate family's feelings about my illness would probably be varied. They might feel some guilt. My parents might be prone to blaming themselves that their mutual genes caused me to inherit the condition in the first place. Especially as Chris was not suffering from it, they had no way of realising that they were both CF carriers when I was born. Similarly my brothers might also have felt a level of guilt that it was me and not them who suffered the affliction while they were both spared.

Their other emotions could include helplessness, sadness, worry and frustration about my daily suffering and survival regime. After all, this isn't just short-term sympathy for a loved-one with a cold or an injury. This covers nearly 40 years – a lifetime of being around an ill son and sibling. I can only imagine that this has a discernible effect on the close family and friends of anyone who suffers. I was extremely unlucky to be born with CF but very lucky to receive the support and care from my parents, brothers, family and friends. They all handled my situation with understanding and empathy but not with patronising sympathy.

My mum was a career nurse. By a quirk of fate in her early nursing career she had worked on a CF children's ward at London's famous Great Ormond Street Hospital. So when I was struggling to thrive, she saw all the likely CF 'signs' and pushed for my diagnosis at six months old. She was a pillar of strength, transferring her innate nursing skills towards caring for her sick child.

She also instilled the medical discipline to remember all my individual treatments and tablets so that over time it became second nature for me. My mum's unstinting support, understanding and knowledge is the reason I am still alive today and I owe her more than words could ever convey. Forged by many distressing times, especially during my dreaded IV treatments, our mother-son relationship is a rare and uncompromising bond.

As well as helping me herself she was driven by an unquenchable desire to leave no stone unturned in finding experts to treat my CF. Indeed, one of the most important medical interventions of her life occurred in my early teens when she tracked down the maverick CF consultant physician, Doctor Ron Knight, who has played a significant part in my survival. In the early 1980s, my health and lung function were stuttering under the care of non-CF specialists in my home town of Southampton. Mum had caught wind of Ron's expertise and sought him out. We had our first appointment with him on 6 June 1983, my mum's 40th birthday. Little could she have imagined that 27 years later I would be sitting at the dinner table, raising a toast for her birthday, with a wife and son in tow.

For near on 30 years, mum's radical move to switch my care to Ron Knight has paid off. From the first moment in his presence, Ron acted differently to other doctors. He spoke directly to me and not my parents, treated me like a young adult and involved me in decisions about my medical care which coming from the world of paediatrics was a welcome change. He has always been positive, offering a perpetual 'can do' attitude which felt like a godsend when I needed guidance and direction. Giving off an aura where anything and everything in life was possible, Ron consistently used language like *"What we need to do is…"* and *"There's no reason why you can't…"* He quite literally breathed life into my lungs and bolstered my belief.

Benefiting from a two-way interactive relationship, over the years we have worked well together challenging and finessing my care and drugs regime. I take the time to research possible new CF treatments and bring them to Ron's attention and we discuss their merits and likelihood. Within the confines of hospitals and clinics the days are long but the years are short and Ron has seen me across the full spectrum of my life – highs and lows, best and worst, upbeat and crestfallen, happy and battered. I would say Ron has a 'cup half full' approach to patient care and advice which has certainly made an impression on me.

My dad also played an enormous part in my survival. Although he kept his emotions hidden, like many men of his generation, he must have realised early on that he could play his most crucial role by helping me physically. He got me involved with all sports which exercised my lungs and kept me fitter than expected. But my hockey talent and his subsequent coaching and support were the most far-reaching gifts he ever bestowed upon me. Our primary bond was one not forged in a bar with alcohol or doing DIY together. It was one based on the love of playing and watching sport, particularly hockey which he coached all three of us brothers in our junior days. His amazing enthusiasm and devoted support for my hockey both as a coach and as a loyal spectator was immensely appreciated and will never be forgotten.

Dad was my greatest sporting fan and admirer. He would always attend my hockey games, either supporting from the side of the pitch or sometimes from a distance in his car when on a work lunch hour if I was playing for my school during the day. In the winter months, to keep out the cold, he would bring a small tumbler of sherry for me to swig at half-time. When I had divisional trials away from home, he drove me there and booked himself into a local hotel so that he could support me every step of the way. He also had a passion for curry and would often leave me some onion bhajis to supplement my 'sporting diet'.

"How's your wobble, son?" was his enduring question and catchphrase anytime he saw me. This of course related to my hockey skills rather than whether I'd had one too many alcoholic drinks.

As a parenting unit, before I was 18, mum and dad pretty much did all my physiotherapy and reminded me to take my medication. But at the same time, they instilled the right discipline in me not to miss a trick with the condition. They also were extremely involved in local CF fundraising events at different venues and their commitment has been instrumental in raising important funds to help treat CF.

From university onwards, my parents let me take more ownership of my treatment, which empowered me to take personal responsibility for my health, hospital appointments and the daily medical decision making. This did not always produce positive outcomes, but they were always there to pick up the pieces. As I'm now a parent myself, I can better appreciate that this must have been torturous at times. I'm sure that they bit their tongues when I was overdoing it, particularly when I partied too hard in smoky venues in my twenties!

They brought me up to feel that anything in life was possible – school, university, sport, socialising, marriage etc. I was empowered by them to take ownership of my treatment and believe that CF wasn't the end but the start of my life. I was free to believe that my stay on this planet wasn't going to be about merely existing with CF but it could be about living as full a life as possible and making a difference.

My own experience tells me that there's a tricky balance to be found between receiving the right level of care and being too smothered and mollycoddled. I wasn't overly wrapped up in cotton wool but my parents knew the situations and environments where my health would have been compromised. It was in this area that they showed me that I could lead a full life but I needed to understand certain constraints. Over time and through trial and error, my parents got the correct balance while engraining in me the bespoke health risks of CF so that they became second nature to me and I could be independent.

I thank them for giving me that autonomy and ability to think on my own two feet as I learnt many invaluable lessons over those university years and began to instinctively do the right thing for my health more often than not. Even though they may blame themselves for my condition, I never allowed them to torture themselves over this. In my mind, I squared it off by hoping that my illness and suffering meant that others in the family didn't have to endure any bad health themselves.

There's more to family support than just my parents. Siblings, extended family and close friends also play their part. My brothers Chris and Jez are very much enrolled into the equation and have been with me all the way on this rollercoaster journey.

Jez is my twin which is two miracles instead of one. We first met about 40 years ago across a crowded womb. He is, amazingly, a non-carrier of the CF gene. He has been a very consistent thread throughout my life, always there for me with his constant acts of kindness which is his way of sharing my health burden. He's a mutual fan of many teen comedy films and we have the same pre-university social buddies. He manages the subtle trick of engaging me about my health when needed but without being overbearing. We've always lived relatively close to each other and meet regularly. We've socialised together and always celebrated our mutual birthdays, but he's also been on hand when I've reached some very low ebbs.

When we were 17 and in our parents' kitchen after a boozy night out, I got very morose about my health and picked up a knife and put it against my wrist, exclaiming that I'd be better off dead. Jez sat with me for some time telling me all the reasons to keep alive and put the knife away. Unsurprisingly once I'd seen sense and put the knife away, we both ended up crying and hugging. More recently, seven years ago, he was in the same room as me when I read the news that Alice Martineau, the talented young English singer, had succumbed to CF. *"This is my reality!"* I uttered before throwing the news article on his lap and walking out the door. If I had my time again, I probably would have handled that differently. After all, it's not Jez's fault that I have this illness. What could he do about the death of this poor girl, and what could he possibly have said at that precise moment to make sense of it all? Sometimes there are no words for a solemn situation.

Chris, my elder brother, is a carrier of the CF gene. We have a solid bond through our mutual representative hockey playing and socialising with the same teams. We also have similar work environments. He helps companies communicate externally and I support them with their internal communications and employee engagement. He hates my suffering and I think he keeps a lot of his internal angst to himself but it comes out in little comments. *"You poor bugger!"* he'll say when he hears me coughing heavily on the hockey pitch.

Chris did rather add to my woes for a while when I was a toddler by pushing me down the stairs and breaking my leg. No real harm was done as it never slowed me down. Chris would be the one over the years that I would socially speak to the most, whether it be on the phone or face-to-face. He definitely adopted the 'big brother' approach on occasions when he must have been particularly worried about me. Memorably during my twenties when I was on a path of social self-destruction he tried to intervene with me on the way back from a black-tie party. The conversation went something like:

"I think you need to slow down Tim as you're burning the candle at too many ends."

"I'll be fine. I've got no choice. Tomorrow may never come."

"Perhaps you should stay in more and not go out to every party?"

"I thank you for your kindness and I'll think about what you have said but for now this is the life I want to lead in the time I have left."

The next day, all my weeks and months of excess caught up with me while in a supermarket and I was quite literally poleaxed and bent double by exhaustion. I had to sit down at the back of the shop for 20 minutes completely unable to move. Chris had seen the signs – he knew me better than I knew myself at times!

I imagine that my brothers have both dealt with the difficulty of explaining my CF to friends and colleagues and been faced with the habitual barrier of CF unfamiliarity – "cystic what?" Their partners, Julie and Lisa, are well aware of my predicament and daily medical regime; and they are very caring and thoughtful. As well as their 'better halves' I'm sure both Jez and Chris have been involved in hundreds of little conversations about my health that I would never be privy to. Indeed, I've noticed over the years that some people tend to ask my parents, brothers and wife how my health is rather than asking me directly.

How would I feel if it was one of my siblings who had CF and not me? Based on my life to date, I'm not so good being the carer or seeing loved ones suffer. Maybe my make-up and coping mechanisms are better suited to being the sufferer rather than the carer?

Typical of brothers, we played a lot of different sports at home, breaking each other as well as the interior and garden. On summer holidays, we would find some grassland or wet hard sand to play hockey and cricket with dad. Importantly they treated me no differently and no quarter was ever given nor taken which is exactly how I would have wanted it. Without realising it, they made me feel one of them – healthy, normal and not afflicted. Importantly, they have rallied when I'm not feeling so well and have always made the effort to visit me during each of my horrendous IV sessions; buying me little gifts, usually jelly babies. Now that I'm a diabetic, I even share some of them around!

They must be proud of all my achievements, not least to still be alive and approaching 40. Especially as they would have been gearing themselves up for my early demise for the majority of our time together. I doubt they take my longevity for granted. During the exceptionally tough times, they may have hoped for the best but feared the worst.

For the last three years, they have been loving and caring uncles to my son and I can see elements of Felix in both of them. They see the extra motivation that being a dad myself now gives me in staving off the effects of my CF and diabetes. I've already got Chris in mind to coach Felix hockey and Jez to teach him football; and they can both take him out on memorable day trips.

Back in the dining room with my family, I complete my vista around the room with the person next to me, Katie. I could write a complete book on our relationship, but suffice to say, her nursing background has helped her to not only comprehend my condition but to accept me and not be too put off by the sights and sounds of CF. In some respects, I find it's what Katie doesn't do that is as important as what she does do. Taking the constant CF grind in her stride can't be easy. If the roles were reversed I'm not sure I could cope and not be put off by it all. It takes a special type of person to marry, live with and love someone with any disability or impaired health.

I feel that all my close family and friends have a form of CF by association with me – seeing my trials, tribulations, anger and frustration; witnessing my pain, medication and IV treatments and hearing close-up my barbaric coughing.

Close family, friends and my wife have all added something to my survival mix – a complete dynamic of care and support – all showing their bespoke and instinctive acts of love. Their love and care has underpinned my on-going health. I strongly believe how a family and friends pull together is vital in determining the likely outcome for the sufferer of a long-term health condition. I am the living evidence of this and I doubt I'd be alive today without their unconditional love and support.

CF is an immense burden. Sometimes it's too much for me to handle single handily. But this burden can be shared and alleviated somewhat by one's close family and friends coming together in the right way and at the right times.

CF is and always will be part of my DNA. It's me who has to relentlessly knuckle down every day to do my medication, physiotherapy and nebulisers... but I'm definitely not alone.

14. University of Life

Saturday 10 June 2010

Katie and I are away for a rare break in Tunbridge Wells, Kent, for the 40th birthday party of my great and long-standing university friend, Ben Dascombe. Felix is being looked after at home by his grandma, so everyone's happy.

The hotel I had booked was full, so they've kindly moved us free of charge to their sister hotel which has bigger rooms and a lovely garden. After a classic English afternoon tea and scones, Katie and I take a turn around the estate, which included relaxing in the late afternoon sun by the lake. This was the calm before the storm of the evening party which also coincided with watching England's under-achieving football team in their opening game of this year's World Cup.

As I lay there enjoying the sunshine on the hotel's lawn, I thought ahead to my fellow university friends who were expected to be attending tonight's soiree. There's a real intensity about the primary friendships formed from your college days that can't really be replicated elsewhere. We obviously saw each other continuously during the core three to four college years and then stayed in close proximity living around South London for the next decade. Slowly, the group married their partners, had families and left London. We don't see each other as much now, so parties like tonight are a wonderful way to catch up, have some drinks and spin the old yarns of fun we had together.

But going to university was not a straightforward matter for me as it came with many health-related complications and considerations. Having said that, I think it can be an ordeal for the majority of people as it's a step out of one's comfort zone from the familiar surroundings of home. For someone with a major health condition, there's extra anxiety about leaving the family nest.

My university life or, to give it its other name, 'The University of Life', was at Roehampton College, close to Wimbledon Common, which was part of Surrey University. I studied the Double Honours course of Business Studies and Social Administration, and majored in Politics and Sociology during my third and final year.

As part of the preparation for my time at university, we had to find the right chemist that would be close to my campus and understand my medical needs. My mum and I took the train to Wimbledon from Southampton and walked up the hill towards Wimbledon Village. It was there that we entered the only chemist and introduced ourselves. It must have been the right move, as it's the same chemist I attend over 20 years later. I have been loyally looked after by the Patel brothers, their wives and colleagues in what has become an enduring and important relationship.

I stayed in the on-site halls of residence accommodation for the whole of my three college years, where I kept the same room for the duration. 'Roberts House Room 116', was my fun version of Prisoner Cell Block H. We made the decision to live on campus so that I could be close to the on-site GP and medical team in case of an emergency. It also meant that I could avoid living in likely cold and unhealthy 'digs' after my first year.

It was a Sunday in September 1989 when I finally attended college, placed all my belongings into a small room and hugged my parents goodbye. I can only imagine their feelings, dropping off their vulnerable CF boy to effectively fend for myself. For me, it was a great adventure and I was pretty sure that at the tender age of 18, I could look after myself and manage everything. I learned a lot about myself – good and bad – in those next three months, probably more than in the preceding 18 years.

University life back then still belonged to the bygone era before it became structured and syllabus-oriented. During my tenure, we still enjoyed the laissez faire approach to being students with a lot of independence bestowed upon us. "It's up to you whether you turn up for lectures. Make of it what you want," were the introductory words from my first lecturer. *Excellent*, we all thought as one. *So what you are telling us is that if we don't want to attend a seminar, we don't have to!*

Despite all this new-found freedom, I had a couple of academic golden rules at university:

1. Never be late for written essay and thesis deadlines,
2. Try not to write when drunk (I didn't always achieve this rule) and
3. During exam time, never try to study in halls or in the library as there was always too much noise and distraction. In the end, as I lived on campus for all three years, I discovered that the college chapel was the best place to hold up for a day of revising. This was the main reason I didn't ever need to do any summer holiday exam re-takes.

It's often said that you tend to meet your friends for life in the first few days at university. I can vouch for that. Within my first week, I was part of a group of great chaps – Ben, Bo, Bruce, Jon and Noel – and we had a brilliant time together. I was lucky that the majority of friends lived in or close to Halls during my three years there. Amazingly for me, these chaps took my condition to heart and gave me their altruistic and invaluable support. One of the main ways that they helped me was with my physiotherapy. I had some man-made wooden blocks that went under the bed to elevate it in order to help the drainage position and the boys took it in turn to pat my chest in the early evening prior to going to the campus canteen.

Even though I mainly covered up my CF while at college, the coughing and sound of my old fashioned nebuliser must have been audible at times on campus. I personally never thought too much of the CF-related noises that came from my bedroom as I put my music on and just got on with it, being self-obsessed with putting myself first. Rumours abounded over the years from students that I was ill; one rumour even had me suffering from multiple sclerosis. On reflection, it was initially very odd to be so open about my CF with these strangers and it must have been odd for them as well, but we all just got on with it. I needed the help and they wanted to help. As well as help from my friends, I booked in for professional physiotherapy once a week at Roehampton hospital with a Polish chap called George.

Time at university is often wistfully referred to as one's 'salad days'; a youthful time, accompanied by the inexperience, enthusiasm, idealism, innocence and indiscretions that one associates with young people.

It certainly was not because we ate salad, far from it! The canteen food served in the main campus restaurant Monday to Friday was just about edible but not terribly inspiring. At the weekends we made do ourselves or went home for proper food. I struggled with eating the mass-produced college food. This was exacerbated when my lungs were infected and my oxygen supply was limited, which caused my appetite to dip and only really appetising food would appeal. We did order a steady stream of pizza and Chinese takeaways to override our disinterest with college food. I was very thin for most of my duration at college and would reclaim the lost weight in the holidays. The notches on my trouser belt would alter as each term went on and I became steadily thinner. I would then put the weight back on in the holidays, when on IV medication to kick-start my health, along with my mum's lovely home cooking and extra night time snacks. Indeed, I was quite well known as this gaunt looking chap with a blond haircut like the fictional character Tintin.

To supplement the canteen food, I would cycle to the local shops in Southfields every Tuesday morning to buy extra goodies. The boys soon worked out that there was a constant supply of sweets and cake in my room, which added to my popularity. Plus, I owned a small red television so we could watch rubbish TV together!

One tends to remember songs from key times in life and university is no exception. 'Getting Away With It' by Electronic was a popular song during my first year and a metaphor for my social life at college. As ever, living for every moment was my mantra and the anecdotes of our collective revelry go on and on. The boys were on hand with my physiotherapy but they were full throttle in the bar!

As is typical of the social scene of most colleges, there were campus and local town nightclub and party options on every night of the week. We also benefited from living just outside the heaving metropolis that is London. An average week would offer the social activities of Options nightclub in Kingston on Monday; Samantha's club in Piccadilly or The Theatre in Wandsworth on Tuesdays; Wednesday night sessions in the college bars after hockey; Hammersmith Palace nightclub or Rave at Heaven nightclub on Thursdays; College disco on Fridays and finished off with a house party on the Saturday evening. Sunday was the welcome day of rest. After my second year exams I had a two-week period before working at the Wimbledon tennis tournament where I underwent a solid fortnight of partying at these daily venues. It almost put me in a coffin... but was worth every minute.

Of all these social opportunities, the one we attended every week without fail was the session on Wednesdays after playing college hockey. This involved getting a shuttle bus from our campus to the Digby Stuart site where we enjoyed 'playing away' and the sporty drinking games. When time was called at the end of the night, it was customary to line up three different colour shots at the bar – the so-called 'traffic lights' – and down them in order before finishing with a final pint. This was followed by a stagger home across Wimbledon common, detouring via a Chinese takeaway in Roehampton. If the Wednesday night sessions were standard fare for my three years of college, unfortunately so were Thursday morning lectures. My lecturers must have got pretty fed up with me sheepishly turning up late every Thursday with a can of Lucozade and no voice!

I was silly and rebellious at times pushing the envelope and testing the boundaries of my health. None more so than the time that I nebulised the lager drink Holsten Export, just to see what it tasted like! Some of what I did when I look back completely shocks me as being rather reckless, but I'll put it down to youthful brashness.

With my new-found freedom, playing hockey for club, county and college and my desire to leave no social stone unturned, it wasn't long before the wheels came off my chariot and two weeks before the end of my first term my lungs took a dramatic turn for the worse. Things had slowly been deteriorating but I was unable to see the vital signs or change my course of mass destruction. Before I knew what had happened I hit rock-bottom. The memory of the event still haunts me to this day and serves as a reminder of how my CF can destroy me if I let it get out of hand. I was taking a short walk back from the library to my halls one cold and blustery autumn evening when I got so out of breath that I had to stop and cough violently in the gutter. It was uncontrollable and lasted for what felt like 10 minutes. I entered one of those out of body experiences where I felt that I was looking from above down onto myself and saying, "What is happening to me? Will I even make it back to my room tonight? Is this it for me, sitting on my own in the leaves of this road? Who will find my body?"

Eventually, I did manage to curtail my coughing fit and stagger back to my room. This warning was loud and clear. A few days later I was on a train from Wimbledon to Frimley Park hospital in order to see my doctor and commence a course of much needed intravenous (IV) medication. Even the journey there felt like mission impossible as I was in such a terrible state. It was fortunate that the train carriage was empty of passengers because I must have looked horrendous. At one point on that journey I had to cough so ferociously that I was sick in the rubbish bin of the carriage. It was the worst I'd ever felt in my life.

"Just get me to the hospital!" I kept telling my body.

My parents came up to the hospital to pick up the pieces. They drove me and all my IV medication back to Wimbledon where I commenced my morning and evening treatments from my college room. Even then, I couldn't say no to all parties and even took my IV drugs out with me in a bag to a night in the East End of London so that they would be ready to take in the morning.

Those two defining moments – in the gutter and on the train – were awful but hugely needed episodes in my life. My downfall acted as a dramatic wake-up call which taught me valuable life lessons and helped to improve my health risk management. If ever there was any doubt, this illness was not a game, it was real and it could be the death of me. By having my very foundations shaken rigid, it was obvious that I required a new game plan to get me through my college years; one where I needed to be more rigid with my medication and not to miss a trick or cut corners with my treatments. I also learned to stay away from smoky places in between the big night out. In essence, I wanted to keep well enough to enjoy myself and not miss out on what University life had to offer. By staying healthier I was still able to party hard at times but I learned when to ease off. I would make life count each term and then have an IV in the holidays to boost my health ready for the next term. This meant that during my tenure at university, I had nine separate IV sessions.

Further social highlights from college life included the end of year black-tie balls where I stayed up through the night and pushed on until dawn; a weekend trip to Amsterdam where sleep was dispensed with in favour of heavy drinking, 'space cake' and ice skating in my trainers; a May Day celebration where at 6pm Ben had to put me in the shower to sober up, order me my favourite Chinese dish before dragging me back out that night for more partying; participating with the boys in a drinking board game called 'Pass Out' which lived up to its name and swapping clothes with my good friend, Karen, wearing her summer dress on a bus down to Wimbledon town centre during Rag Week.

My university experience was all part of my much needed independence and path to taking more ownership of my life, health and coming to terms with coping on my own. I learned more about managing my condition on my own than I ever would while being cared for at home by my parents. I also met very good friends who I consider my brothers, some of whom became my wedding day ushers. I realised the importance of friendships and the two-way kindness that those alliances bring.

By keeping up with others and pursuing a normal career path, I was defying the odds that CF had decreed at birth that I would not live long enough to even make it to university. Once there, I was going to enjoy every second of every day, with no regrets that I could have done more than I did. If I had my time at college again, I would do exactly the same thing. I've been getting away with it all my life…

15. Wish You Were Here

Tuesday 22 June 2010

Team Wotton is on its annual holiday. Just as we did the year before, we've got two weeks in Benodet, Brittany and we are living in a mobile holiday home as part of a campsite. To get here, we did that classic 'fly-drive' which involved flying from Southampton to Brest and then driving for an hour to the campsite. All pretty convenient and quick, which is handy when you have a three-year-old boy in tow who's not keen on sitting for long.

Travel and holidays always come with a back-catalogue of memories of one's previous adventures, especially trips when I was young with my parents and as an adult. Every holiday I've ever had comes with extra CF-related precautions that I need to factor in.

On the whole for my early family vacations, we tended to stay close to home in Southampton just in case I had a medical emergency and we needed to get back home urgently. The Channel Islands, Wales, Devon and the Isle of Wight were all regular destinations. We had some extremely happy times doing what young families do – days on the beach, rock-pools, ice-creams, swimming in the sea and campsite pools. Back in the 1970s and early 1980s, we tended to stay in the sort of hotels where a glass of orange juice was served as the starter. This left you with the conundrum of whether you drank it one go like a shot or took your time. These were the type of establishments where a prawn cocktail was considered an exotic delicacy. It's a world away from the assortment of food that is on offer these days.

As an adult I have been on holiday to many different continents. I've been to many parts of Europe – Spain, France, Majorca, Minorca, Italy, Sardinia and Sicily. As well as a lovely eye-opening South African holiday in 1999, I have visited America a few times. Back in 1998, I spent a fabulous time in Boston and New York celebrating a friend's wedding. Also that year, I won a free Pepsi sponsored trip to meet and watch the Spice Girls in San Diego and Phoenix, which I took my brother Chris along to. A good time was had by all although our Pepsi host was a little disappointed when I asked her if they had any Coke! I also have fond memories of a fortnight in California with Katie in 2001 on our first holiday away together. Each and every time I travel, I try to make sure I am accompanied by someone who understands my requirements just in case something drastic happens and I need support.

There is one element of these holidays that remains constant and that is my preparation before I leave so that I've got all my CF medication packed. When I prepare for any break, I tend to spend less time packing clothes into a suitcase and longer getting my medication just right. For this to be exact, I have always had a checklist and tick each item off as I get it ready. I need to bring a sizeable wash bag of drugs with me and this has to be exact with all the different drug variations – more than 20 types – and all my physiotherapy, nebuliser antibiotics and ice blocks to keep certain drugs cold while on route to the holiday destination.

For just the two weeks of this holiday in France, I painstakingly counted over 600 tablets into two separate bags. This always makes me feel rather dizzy. I have to get it right because once I'm at my holiday venue, there's little chance of finding any replacement pills. I've been caught out before and learnt some harsh lessons. I didn't always get my preparation correct and some holidays have not been without their fraught moments. On day one of that trip to New York I had to hunt around Manhattan with my friend Simon Moy for a nebuliser part. There was a significant amount of concern that my two-week holiday in America could be placed into jeopardy because I'd have to miss a key part of my medical regime. Luck was on my side that day as I found the right piece of equipment in the third pharmacy I visited.

For many years, my nebuliser compressor was this huge monstrosity and it came with tubing designed to be placed out of the window for all the mist to exit the room. Just carrying it around negated the need for me to do any weight training. It ran on mains only, which meant that I had to be fairly coordinated to plan my holiday accommodation so that I could use such an appliance. This prohibited me from holidaying in tents or in places with no electricity. Indeed I used to joke that I couldn't plug my nebuliser into a tree! With the advance of technology, I now own a nebuliser the size of a small plate that can operate with batteries. How times have changed.

The size of the bag needed for my drugs has limited me to only two weeks away at any given time – it's not much of a holiday if one's bag of medication is the biggest one you bring. Backpacking for a few months, sleeping rough or visiting countries off the beaten track were never a realistic option. With just two weeks of drugs, the bag starts out bursting at the seams and gradually reduces in size throughout the duration of the holiday, which I find strangely cathartic. Even though I'm unable to take an actual holiday from my treatments, by being thorough with my preparation and medication, I'm able to enjoy a proper break that isn't ruined by any unexpected health dilemmas.

Once packed, there are many pitfalls during the actual journey itself. Not least is going through the airport customs and security. I have learned that it is wiser to bring all my medication in my hand luggage rather than risk it being put in the hold of the aeroplane and potentially being lost in transit.

This is always a tense time as my rucksack is half-full of my medical paraphernalia (nebuliser, cooler bag with ice block and drug vials, bumper bag of drugs, insulin pens). On my person I have ready on all these trips a letter from my doctor about my CF and all the different types of medicine I am carrying. This now quite scruffy piece of paper waits patiently in my jacket pocket just in case I'm pulled to the side like some renegade drugs dealer for an interrogation. As I place my bag through the scanner, I feel like Brad Davis in the film 'Midnight Express', worried that all hell will kick-off and their x-ray machine would trigger an FBI-style body search. That level of madness has never occurred yet, though the security team have occasionally mentioned the contents of my bag but the majority of times I breeze through with no fuss.

While on the flight, particularly on long-haul journeys, I ask the flight attendant to put my Pumozyme medication in their fridge so that it is kept as cold as possible. There is also the worry of any coughing attacks disrupting the flight for the other travellers, so I do make regular trips to the toilet and I coincide the flush of the toilet with clearing any mucous from my lungs. If there is a less sexy version of the 'mile-high club' for coughing attacks, then I expect all CF flyers are gold members!

As is typical with family holidays with young children who wake up early, Katie and I take it in turn to get up with Felix while the other one has a lie-in. Today was my turn to be the early rising lark. The mobile home in the campsite was made of the type of material that makes it freezing in the morning and boiling hot during the day. These early mornings with Felix are pretty chilly affairs as we have to put the heater on in the front room and try and be as quiet as possible so as not to wake up Katie. We watched the 'Happy Feet' animated penguins film together, while we ate our Weetabix. We also engaged in a game of Connect 4 which brought out my competitive streak as I wanted to win, while my boy seemed intent on disrupting the game and knocking it over. Boys will be boys.

At 8.30am we leave the tepid mobile home to feed the horses in the nearby field using apples from the massive orchard that the campsite resides in. We then stroll down to the holiday camp shop to buy some fresh French bread for our second breakfast with Katie. The sun comes out and it's starting to warm up inside and outside our mobile home.

We decide to go on a morning excursion and drive to the picturesque walled town and fishing port of Concarneau. We take a walk around the inner ramparts, have a crêpe lunch, and enjoy the habitual holiday ice-cream before driving home thus allowing Felix to have his early afternoon siesta in the car.

For the majority of the afternoon as the heat seems to be at its height, we push Felix in his pushchair down to the local beach front. Once at the beach, we use our son quite deliberately as the homing pigeon for the spot on the sand we will hold up for a few hours. Felix walks ahead of us to locate the best spot on the beach for us to set up camp. This is because his inner GPS tracks down other single children who would enjoy playing with a similarly-aged chum. We have lots of fun with Felix in the sea and sand, build sand castles and catch our first crabs together in the rock pools. Katie and Felix have more ice-creams. As is de rigueur for Felix, he has one in each hand as if he's the Statue of Liberty.

It would be tempting to totally relax and take the foot of the pedal of my medical routine but even on holiday my CF comes along – lock, stock and barrel. After all, just because I'm taking time off, doesn't mean that my sickness follows suit. I still need to do all my treatments, but while I'm on holiday, my CF feels as relaxed as I am. However it is delightful not to have to rush my medication and be too prescriptive with my timings.

Very warm weather is good and bad for me and my health. It's good for my overall lungs and lung function and I cough a lot less than back in the damper conditions of England. The heat does however affect my diabetes, increasing the risk of having a hypo. As a young lad with my parents, we did stay in Barcelona once and I got severe heat rash and mum had to put cold flannels on me in our hotel room.

I also have to be more careful than most people about being out in the sun as I have a high risk of getting sunburnt. This is partly because I'm fair skinned but mainly due of the change in my skin pigment from decades of taking the antibiotic Doxycycline. I wear high-factor sun cream and don't spend too long out in the sun. This does tend to leave me whiter than other sun-seekers – I joke that I'm so white that when I'm swimming in the sea, I'm in danger of being harpooned!

Either way, even with great care not to overexpose myself to the sun, after a few days in warmer temperatures, I am heavily prone to vicious heat rashes on my arms.

After some delightful time down on the beach, we head back to our campsite for some fun on the water slide and splash about in the massive indoor and outdoor swimming pools. The pool is the next potential concern not least for hygiene reasons but also depending on its level of chlorine. Too much of it causes me to cough uncontrollably. When growing up, my parents had the fear of me getting too damp and developing a chill in my chest, so I was not allowed to swim in the swimming pool for too long or at certain times. One of those times was when it was raining. I have distinct memories of watching my brothers enjoy themselves swimming in the rain while I stayed under cover. It's always tough to watch your brothers partake in an activity in which you are not able to join them.

Also, I couldn't swim for long in the sea as I would get very cold and my knees would go blue. My parents would be at pains to avoid me chilling on the beach after a swim and they wrapped me up in a big towel and supplied a hot drink to warm me up.

We go back to the mobile home for Felix's tea which is now as hot as an oven. Next is his bath time which involved splashing him with a bucket of water outside on the grass as the home didn't have an actual bath. This would normally be followed by his bedtime routine which had worked for the first few nights but had been scuppered due to the prolonged daylight and campsite noise. After all, if your child can hear other young happy campers shouting and playing till 10pm, why would he be interested in going to bed earlier?

On holiday, the usual routines need to alter and you have to go with the flow, so Felix stayed up later with us, sitting at our dinner table, having a second evening meal and watching his films in the lounge as we reclined outside on the decking. Still getting our little man off to sleep had proved tough so tonight at 9.30pm I take Felix for a drive in the car around the local countryside to finally rock him off to sleep. As parents, you do anything at times to get your child to sleep. On arrival back at the home, I carry him into his box room and we settle back onto the decking with a glass of wine. I sit down and write a postcard to my parents. I reflect on the day we've just had as a family and ponder whether this is how my own parents must have felt when taking my brothers and me away for all those memorable holidays – good family time away from the rigours of work and home life with the freedom of a time away with no fixed agenda.

I start to write the postcard…

Wish you were here!

16. Grin and Bear It

Friday 25 June 2010

I unfortunately picked up a cold while out here on holiday. Sometimes it's hard to identify the time and place that a cold is caught but this time it could have been that my body was at a low ebb following some extremely busy weeks at work.

The sniffle has pretty much cleared up but as is typical of these situations, its after-effects have gone to my chest. So despite the warmer weather here in Brittany, my lungs are suffering. I'm coughing heavily at times, particularly in the latter part of the evenings, before bedtime and during the early mornings when the holiday home is at its coldest. Like an agitated wasp made angry, unreasonable and spiteful by a child looking to swat it, my CF is very much stirred up and is taking it out on me.

A night can be a long time with CF. Last night and into this morning was such a night and as torrid as any I can remember. *A night to forget*, you might say, but I can never forget how these occasions make me feel as they are indelibly burnt into my soul. The coughing commenced in the early hours and continued on and off for most of the night.

Usually with CF a cough in time saves nine follow-up coughs. However last night the timing went awry and instead of one all-encompassing cough before falling off to sleep, it seemed that all nine of those coughs rolled themselves into one seismic one. Once it was obvious to me that a coughing tsunami was breaking on my shore, I left our bedroom and de-camped into the lounge area. There I coughed into a hand towel repeatedly in order to muffle the sound for my family lying asleep next door and for those in nearby holiday homes.

Lying flat was causing the mucous in my chest to rise up my oesophagus and tickle my larynx so sleep was out the equation until I was able to contain the coughing fit. Sitting bolt upright on the couch was my only option for a couple of hours but I may well have drifted off to sleep in between coughing attacks. Some of the sleep haze coughs were so brutal that they scared the living daylights out of me. I was worried that I might even choke to death. When was it going to end? How was I ever going to get through this attack? Who could hear me make all this noise?

This in turn forced me to keep myself awake, eyes out on stalks, petrified beyond logic that if I fell asleep, I might not be alive in the morning. I began to believe that it would be better to stay awake rather than fall asleep which could possibly cause me to choke to death. It felt as if I was dramatically on Elm Street and CF was my very own Freddy Krueger! Sleep is a nice thing to have, but staying awake and protecting my survival is the most important prize on a night like this. They say that the darkest hour is just before the dawn and this felt like a very dark hour for me, sitting upright in that lounge, my mind a scrambled mess of insecurity and worry.

As the night wore on and the new day approached, I felt there was something quite symbolic about the darkness outside dissipating, and watching it being replaced with the first vestiges of light. You can't help but feel that you are the only person witnessing this virgin sunrise. As I moved back into the bedroom and got back into bed with Katie, a new day was dawning both in my life and for my lungs. I decided to draw a metaphoric line in the sand to banish what had just happened and start all over again. This allowed me to relish the purest human high of all – just being alive – and the simple act of breathing quietly in and out. I would live to breathe another day.

The tortured frown of the last few hours was superseded by a half-smile of triumph. CF hadn't taken me yet. I would get another reprieve. People talk about being 'born again'. Well, with this condition, after despicable nights like this, I've felt born again on numerous occasions.

With the calming effect of my very existence secured for the time-being, I must have drifted off into a deep sleep because I didn't hear Felix wake Katie up. I slumbered on for a few more hours. When I finally woke up in the morning, I felt a palpable sense of relief and euphoria that I was still on God's sweet earth.

But at the same time, after such a horrible night, I felt small, insignificant and my self-esteem was low. I wanted to feel strong but felt weak. It was as if I was in Marty Mcfly's disintegrating photo from the 'Back to the Future' film. My mind was awash with a mass of negativity. How can I respond to this? What's there to be excited about? How can I conceal these negative feelings? And then...

As I stagger back into the lounge – the scene of my nightmare a few hours ago – I see Felix out on our decking playing noisily with his toys, blissfully unaware of the torment I've just endured. It's strange how a song can spring into your head at times of crisis. The song I heard at that very moment was 'Don't worry, be happy'.

Luckily for me, my main coping mechanism to cover up what's going on inside my body following dark health situations is to keep my internal flame lit. This helps to switch off the worries in my head. Light, humour and laughter are my armour to protect me from the darkness of CF. More often than not only a smile can brighten up a dark day.

Is it easy to always be happy rather than sad? Recent research has proven that people really do look on the bright side of life. Scientists have found that humans are unrealistically upbeat because the brain is programmed to remember positive signs and forget about negatives. So it would appear that a 'faulty' brain wiring makes us better at processing information supporting our outlook as opposed to facts challenging our beliefs. So my smile behind the frown is my natural default but I'm aware that this has to be sustained, which is the tricky part.

Having a sunny nature has never felt like too much of an act as it comes fairly naturally for me and I feel healthier for being happy and positive rather than being downcast and negative. After all, we use fewer muscles to smile than we do to frown.

I try very hard to have a happy disposition with everyone I meet and in everything I do to counter the seriousness of my 'bigger life picture'. That morning, being around Katie and Felix, I played down the shocking night I had just endured.

I work extremely hard at smiling, making myself and others laugh, often with cheesy jokes. Having a 'happy-go lucky' persona seems to manifest better health inside my body. At work, after a bad night or difficult morning treatment, I'll go to the extreme of trying to be the happiest person in the room or office. In turn, it means that I don't allow myself to dwell on the dark moments for too long.

I am a cheeky chap but there's method to my madness. Life has always felt too short and harsh to take it overly seriously. Dealing with CF is the serious part of my life, so the rest of it needs to be as light-hearted as possible. 'Sunshine on a rainy day', I suppose you could call it.

This approach has to come from within and I have to work hard to turn off the mental demons in my head. I start thinking happy thoughts and being happy. I'm convinced that when you possess light within, it is seen externally – people see my light and humour; they see an upbeat seemingly healthy person, not an ill or downbeat person. This has a positive effect on me and the people I come into contact with.

This doesn't just apply to work situations, but on visits to hospitals, surgeries and chemists. Especially for these mundane health related appointments, I cast aside all negativity and try to be nice, smile, crack jokes – anything that makes the experience more palatable. When I'm down, I firmly believe that laughter is the best medicine and often joke with Katie that "at least I've got my health!"

Like some form of non-stop comedian, I look for humour in everything and in anything. The power of laughter and joy helps dissolve disease in my body. It removes the physiological stress that builds up from the burden of a relentless illness.

We all walk in the dark to different degrees and have our own cross to bear; so finding ways to lighten the load is paramount. For me, humour and happiness are my guiding lights to deal with any dark moments.

I've yet to meet a person in this life who hasn't got some difficulty or inner demon to contend with. Everybody hurts to some degree. It's all relative I guess. As I'm continuously battling the proverbial CF elephant in the room, I do get less worked up about the smaller 'mice' sized issues. However, for a lot of people, I assume there's a propensity to magnify the smaller issues as being larger than they actually are. Either way, what I most definitely know and often say is that life is too short.

Even though I've had a troubled night and everything should make me miserable and morose, I see Felix and Katie clowning around and it makes me smile. The cloak of darkness has lifted and the healing light has taken over. The sky outside our holiday home is a rich blue and the sun is beginning to warm our bodies. I'm looking forward to a fun family day at a newly discovered beach – swimming in the sea, ice-creams and most importantly lots and lots of fun and laughter.

JF Kennedy once said, "It's better to light a candle than curse the darkness." I know what he meant.

17. Final Chapter

Sunday 27 June 2010

It's late evening and I'm sitting in the lounge of our mobile home stretched out relaxing with a glass of wine. I've finally got through all the English newspapers that I bought in Gatwick Airport and I've just picked up my holiday book for the first time. I love these moments on holiday – some alcohol and starting a new book.

It's called 'Invictus'. The story is based on the John Carlin book 'Playing the Enemy: Nelson Mandela and the Game That Made a Nation' about the events in South Africa before and during the 1995 Rugby World Cup, hosted in that country following the dismantling of apartheid.

Early on in the book before the opening chapter is the short 1875 Victorian poem 'Invictus' by the English poet William Ernest Henley that inspired Mandela during his long prison sentence on Robben Island. It's the poem he offered to François Pienaar, the captain of the Springboks rugby team, to help galvanize him and his team to greater deeds on the rugby pitch.

Invictus

Out of the night that covers me,
Black as the Pit from pole to pole,
I thank whatever gods may be
For my unconquerable soul.
In the fell clutch of circumstance
I have not winced nor cried aloud.
Under the bludgeonings of chance
My head is bloody, but unbowed.
Beyond this place of wrath and tears
Looms but the Horror of the shade,

And yet the menace of the years
Finds, and shall find, me unafraid.
It matters not how strait the gate,
How charged with punishments the scroll.
I am the master of my fate:
I am the captain of my soul.

The title 'Invictus' is Latin for "unconquered" or "undefeated" and is very appropriate considering the state of the author when he wrote it. I understand that due to his tuberculosis, Henley, aged 17, had one of his legs amputated in order to save his life. He was only able to keep his other leg by undergoing intensive surgery on his remaining foot. While recovering from this surgery in the infirmary, he was moved to write the words of 'Invictus'.

I was particularly drawn to the final two lines of the poem. *'I am the master of my fate; I am the captain of my soul.'* These words really resonated with me. It was the first time I've read them and I found the poem moving and very powerful.

I closed the book followed by my eyes. I was held captive in my own thoughts. It's often through extreme suffering that people can mine their souls enough for such profound words.

This got me thinking – what if a book was the narrative of your life? I know of people who like to read the end of a book before the beginning in order to discover how it all ends. What if that book centred on the outcome of their life-threatening illness? Would they still want to read ahead? Would they be keen to know how their life story ends?

In my own private version of 'Invictus', I have chosen to ignore reading ahead to my final chapter and deliberating on when and how my story might finish. Instead I think in more practical terms of the here and now; focusing on the things I can control and making the best of the health I do have rather than project too far about the poor health that could come my way.

I've always preferred not to have too deep a knowledge of all the things that could go wrong or the likely side-effects of both my CF and diabetes. I tend not to overly procrastinate about the worst-case scenarios and scaring myself unnecessarily. I strongly feel the less I think about these possible eventualities, the less they are likely to manifest in me. My preference has always been to visualise better health than I am expected to have. Instead of concentrating on having wretched lungs, I instead envision good lung function where I can run for longer without coughing and where I have surplus energy to achieve all I want in life – work, play and family.

Hypothetically, if a formal written contract accompanied CF, stating how and when my body would deteriorate, I have made the conscious decision not to read my condition's obligatory 'small print'.

In my life, on a daily basis, there are countless negative thoughts and triggers that fill my head that I need to quash. This psychological warfare or what I refer to as the 'battle royale' taking place in my body every day is a mental conflict between pessimism and optimism. I once read a newspaper article that stated that 'seeing the glass as half full rather than half empty can be a positive thing – it can lower stress and anxiety and be good for our health and wellbeing.' I have found that by continually crushing my negative thoughts, more often than not, my cup of life remains half full rather than half empty.

I've learnt through good and bad times that staying on top of terrible conditions like CF and diabetes takes a lot of physical strength and belligerence. But just as significantly, my mental approach has been just as decisive a factor in still being alive today and defying the survival odds.

The diagnosis of diabetes in 2009 was a significant turning point in my mental approach. Inheriting another significant illness on top of my CF felt like a real body blow and it would have been all too easy to have become overly cynical and grumpy. I had reached a crossroads moment in my life with one road to negativity land and the other path to positivity planes. Thanks to an intervention from a work colleague who recommended Rhonda Byrne's positive thinking book 'The Secret', I was, over a period of time, able to develop an internal strategy to manage my mental demons.

I cannot highlight enough how critical the art of positive thinking has been for me. When negative thoughts on a particular health-related matter spring up, I work hard to swat them away. I have discovered that this coping mechanism of switching my mental channels to block worry and stress helps to develop better health for me.

Rather than focus on the facets of my life that are perversely affected by CF and diabetes, I flip my thinking and compare myself to healthy people, sportsmen and businessmen in order to create a different benchmark that helps me to thrive. As my health kinesiologist, Vera Peiffer, would say: *"The quality of your thoughts determines the quality of your life."* Most of the time, my cup is topped up with positivity rather than negativity.

In my world there really is no time for moaning or whinging about treatments – what's the point in complaining about something that I do so regularly and can't change? I'd spend a large portion of my day getting all morose and that's not my desired state of mind. I have never wanted to sound like a broken record for those around me – always starting each conversation off with a negative statement on my CF existence. Believe me, this would be the easiest mode to fall into. On most days, I have to work exceptionally hard to override this emotion with an up-beat demeanour.

I try to manage the disease rather than let it manage me, making CF live with me rather than the other way around. I work very hard to compartmentalise my condition, where possible putting the illness in the corner, so that it fits in with my day and life plans rather than dictating them. All the medication is just something I need to do at certain times of the day, in order that I can get on with my life.

To assist with this approach, at the start and end of each day, in a quiet moment, I re-set my mindset through concentrated inner monologue. This is where I guide myself with the state of health that I require and what I expect to achieve that day.

Throughout the day itself, I have developed 'Jedi-like' mind tricks to deal with the variety of health situations and dilemmas that are constantly thrown at me year after year. Whether it be bouncing back from the awful effects of a cold, as I've done on this holiday or going into work and being all bright and breezy following a shocking morning coughing session.

During my intense intravenous treatments, I have learnt to read the signals in my body and how my lungs are responding to the drugs. I used to perceive extra mucous production as a showstopper and get very upset. On one memorable occasion, as a way of venting my anger, I resorted to stomping around a local wood in my steel toe-capped boots kicking trees (sorry trees!).

I had to work hard to understand what was actually taking place in my body and thus switch my mood from one of hysteria to calm reflection. Usually the reality was very different and the extra coughing was a good sign as the intense drugs were getting into parts of my lungs that hadn't been treated in a while. 'Refreshing the parts that other drugs cannot reach', to use the Heineken beer metaphor!

Another way that I have had to enforce a different mental approach was with my insomnia. In my twenties, I developed a poor attitude towards the need for sleep often telling people that *"I'll get all the sleep I need, when I'm dead"*. This stemmed from the projected life expectancy of 30 hanging over me, where sub-consciously my body told itself that those hours intended for sleep were better served living what was left of my life!

Recently, I have improved my mindset towards sleep by trying to break down this bad sub-conscious habit and alter negative thoughts for positive ones. I work hard to change my thought process to *"needing all the sleep I can get to live as long as possible"*. This has proved even more important with all the broken sleep that comes from being a parent to Felix.

I'm glad I've brought the 'Invictus' book with me on this holiday. I feel there's some serendipity about reading it and immersing myself with Henley's thought-provoking poem.

By writing this countdown health journal, my own life now feels like an open book, but it does make me question whether I'm near that final chapter – or am I still in the middle of my life story? Will I live long enough to be able to benefit from new treatments and be fully or partially cured? I do think about a possible cure that future medical interventions like gene therapy might offer, but I can't afford to dwell on it for too long or get my hopes up. Unfortunately since the CF gene was found on the chromosome back in 1989, I have been let down by far too many 'cure' sensationalist stories and false dawns.

Maybe one day I will have the need to delve into that final chapter of my life book; but until that day comes, I'll visualise good health, stay on the positivity path, ignore that small print and keep drinking from my half-full cup.

After all, I am the master of my fate; I am the captain of my soul.

18. Giant

Wednesday 7 July 2010

Today was a tough day at the office, and one that brought all my CF-related quirks and insecurities flooding out. I was in a new client's office just off Warren Street, London, trying to secure some early strategic alignment around a set of communication proposals. To add to my troubles on a hot summer's day, there was no air conditioning in our meeting room, making it incredibly warm and stuffy. The tense business conversations took place in an unfamiliar environment full of tall, middle-aged and senior looking men.

It wasn't long before my worst work nightmare kicked-off. I became overheated in that room and began to sweat profusely through my face, forcing me to remove my suit jacket, roll up my sleeves and mop my brow ad infinitum throughout the discussion. To add insult to injury, my nervousness induced a coughing attack that took what seemed like an age to suppress. To cap it all off, I struggled to establish any rapport with these strangers and they didn't seem to be taking my recommendations that seriously.

In the break, I tried to make some small talk to bring my personality to the forefront. I started with the fairly obtuse but apparently important American chap and initially got some traction via our mutual interest in the basketball team, the Boston Celtics. I mentioned that back in 1998, I was in Boston when they were demolishing the old basketball stadium and replacing it right next door with the new 'Garden' as it's famously called. I mentioned that one could look into the old stadium and see all the championship winning banners in the high ceiling. This guy took a look at me and most disdainfully said: *"1998 huh, what age were you then? 12?"*

My reply was my default one in these situations and a line that I've used on countless business and social occasions throughout my life: *"No I was 27. I'm actually older than I look!"*

Over many years of being on the receiving end of similar reactions from business people and strangers who meet me of the first time, it's hard not to get a little paranoid about this. Was the client's reaction because I look reasonably young and I'm fairly small in height at just under five feet seven inches. Quite possibly, in business circles, my appearance might give me reduced kudos and gravitas. It's not a case of me having 'small man syndrome'. Well not much it isn't...

I've noticed working in many Top FTSE companies that leadership teams and boardrooms tend to be made up of 'well-worn' and relatively tall men and powerful direct women. Also as a professional consultant in a business environment, there could be, for some clients, the concern that knowledge, experience and expertise are more easily positioned with a more senior looking person. "How can this young-looking chap be a consultant?" I have a sense that height and seniority carry more sway, especially in those early work exchanges.

These scenarios remind me of the Tom Hanks hit 1980s comedy 'Big', where a 13 year old boy, Josh Baskin, is trapped in a man's body and embarks on a day job working for a toy company. In the film a boy looks grown-up in an adult world and in my reverse situation I am a man who looks too young in a grown-up world.

I'm not the only CF sufferer who has to deal with these quandaries. There are many strange quirks that come as a result of having CF that make it a rather unique and curious condition. It may come as quite a surprise to the uninitiated but CF is not just about the lungs...

The Peter Pan Effect

I've noticed during 39 years of hospital appointments that for the majority of CF sufferers with a serious form of the condition, our more distinctive features are the small build and youthful demeanour. Most adults with CF are not that tall, are slim in build and youngish looking. I'd say that we are a reasonably non-threatening bunch. So much so that I doubt there are many nightclub bouncers with CF! Why do we struggle to thrive physically?

In people with CF, thickened secretions block the normal flow of the digestive juices from the pancreas, so digestive enzymes can't get into the intestines. Without these enzymes, the intestines cannot properly digest food and the sufferer does not get the nutrition they need to grow normally and gain weight. Most of us have to take enzyme pills to digest our food but they are not as effective as having them produced naturally.

A lot of sufferers also have significant issues with their stomach and bowels including cramps and blockages. My main problem has been when I have not taken enough enzyme tablets to cover the amount or type of food eaten or forgotten to bring the tablets out with me. This has led to loose stools, not insignificant amounts of pain and long stints in the bathroom.

As I'm approaching 40 years old, there's definitely one thing that doesn't fit with hopefully reaching this milestone – I don't look that old nor do I have any middle-aged bulk that a lot of people that age seem to have built up. As I encountered again with this client today, very few people who meet me at work or socially would ever guess my real age. I wonder if I'll have to carry my birth certificate around with me to prove that I've actually made it to 40?

Just occasionally life can imitate art, with the art in this case being the short book by F. Scott Fitzgerald: *'The Curious Case of Benjamin Button'* and the recent Brad Pitt film of the same name. I'm not looking to draw a complete parallel with the Benjamin Button film but the main premise behind both the film and the book is of a person who ages in reverse starting off as a crumbly old pensioner and aging backwards and ending up as a baby.

I'm unwilling to state that people with CF are aging in reverse BUT CF does seem to keep me and other sufferers looking eternally young, almost as if we were never meant to look older than our young life expectancy. This condition seems to lock us in and keep us small in stature and youthful.

It's as if our heavy drugs regime acts as a form of formaldehyde – somehow preserving us in a child-like state. As a parent now myself, I can understand why a lot of parents always visualise their children, no matter what age, as their young baby or child. Most parents of CFers will have to make less of an effort to see their children as eternal youngsters as we rarely look that old.

There are people all over the world desperate to discover the secret of eternal youth – well it appears that having CF is one of those options but trust me it's better to enjoy growing old gracefully than to battle with something as cruel and debilitating as this condition.

Having said all this, I do have some grey and silver hair which I embrace. For most of my life, I never thought I'd live long enough to actually have hair that greyed. As well as offering hope to the CF community that longevity can potentially be achieved I'll show off my grey hair as a badge of triumph!

Yes, Sweat

CF also affects the sweat glands, with a lot of salt being lost through sweat, which disrupts the delicate balance of minerals in my body. In essence, I sweat a lot, it's very salty and unfortunately it's mainly through my face. So you'll often spot me on busy and hot tubes, bars, meeting rooms, sport pitches wiping my brow furiously as the human version of the Niagara Falls erupts!

As I once again encountered today, this is something in business meetings that can affect my self-esteem. Sweating heavily makes me feel very self-conscious and can give off the impression that I'm stressed or not confident in a particular work or social situation. It's not terribly pleasant and at times, can be hard to control which is very frustrating and embarrassing. I find that when my core temperature is up, there is really nothing that can be done to prevent the perspiration, except for sitting in front of a fan or taking a cold shower.

Club Tropicana

One of the prevailing physical signs of CF is 'digital clubbing', where our tips of fingers or toes have an unusually large amount of excess tissue. This results in the nail bed taking on a curved appearance. Some CF patients acknowledge this trait saying their fingertips look like the character 'E.T.' or even that their fingers have a certain "gecko-like" quality. Please believe me when I say that we are not actually lizards with a human skin as in the TV series "V".

Steep Sleep

In order to prevent a coughing attack at night, I tend to prop my head up in a steep vertical angle with a couple of pillows. This helps to raise my head position and allow my body not to be flat all night, hence reducing the amount I cough. I often joke with Katie that I sleep stood up, apparently like the 'Elephant Man', John Merrick, who slept virtually upright due to his deformity. I want to be clear though that this is where our similarities end!

Pill Popper

I have so many different tablets to take throughout the day that it's inevitable that I will have the frequent predicament of needing to pop a pill or eight when in the company of strangers. At this point one can be unsubtle and take them in full view, explaining their requirement, or as I tend to do, take them surreptitiously so as not to draw attention to myself and my condition.

Also, a shocking effect of a life-time of medication is that nearly half of my drugs regime is now aimed at countering the side effects of my antibiotics and 20 years of steroids has led to the development of my recent diabetes and osteoporosis. Still it does make for a colourful cocktail of tablets – I just have to remember to take them all and remember which one should be taken with which drugs to act as the counter-balance.

I hope that it's easier to understand why I don't look and feel that impressive at times, especially in important work meetings and social occasions and why I might feel so insecure. But I do try to have a sense of humour about my little CF quirks. During difficult engagements, I have learnt to counter people's first impressions with astute and well-timed banter, sometimes being self-effacing. At work, I often use the classic consultant technique of listening intently (after all, we have two ears and one mouth), and bit by bit, establishing the respect of people by shrewd comments backed up by business acumen and successful case studies.

What I wouldn't give to tell certain work and non-work strangers my shattering truth – explain my real situation to them, perhaps to elicit some empathy and get them on my side. However, I hardly ever do as I'd rather not let my condition and health-related issues be a factor in how I'm judged. In part this is because I've realised that particular businessmen remove all emotion out of their work personas and are less sympathetic to people they don't know or have to care about. So with this in mind, I keep my powder dry, get through these stressful encounters and walk away with my dignity intact and my head held high. Walking tall in deed, if not in actual life. That's exactly what I achieved in my meeting today as I finally walked away with ringing endorsement for my communication recommendations.

Remember this if nothing else: Dealing with the constant grind and hourly frustrations of a life-threatening condition like CF– the heavy relentless drugs regime, physiotherapy, nebulisers, IV therapies, coughing attacks; and all its maddening side-effects is not for the faint-hearted and needs indescribable amounts of guts and determination. On some days to even get out of the house is a triumph of the spirit, let alone commute to work and mix it with the big boys. On some days, competing in that meeting room requires a warrior mentality that few possess and even fewer will ever have to experience.

We may predominantly be small in build, be vertically challenged, appear young and inconsequential, sweat uncontrollably, have amphibian qualities, and if you shook us

19. Made for Me

Monday 19 July 2010

Today marked Katie's and my seven-year wedding anniversary. Falling on a Monday was not the best day to celebrate as we both had to work. Tonight we paid for a baby sitter and went out for the evening, driving up to the grounds of Cannizaro Park Hotel, located to the side of Wimbledon common, for a picnic.

Not the most practical of people, I ended up scorching the turf a tiny bit with our disposable BBQ. Nonetheless, it was a warm summer's night and we had some lovely food, reminisced about our much-coveted wedding day and raised our glasses of champagne to each other.

This sort of event was of course unthinkable for most of my life. I never thought I'd live long enough to ever be married, let alone to be toasting wedding anniversaries. I've noticed over time that some CFers, mainly the girls and often in their twenties, tend to marry early; but I was on a different plane.

During my younger single days, I could spot pretty quickly whether a girl was going to be the right sort of person to deal with the issues of CF. If they were too high maintenance, it became obvious early on that they would struggle to deal with my condition. I remember some previous dates when from the outset the girls were out of their comfort zone around my condition and were uneasy with what to say and do. The odd ones were not ready at certain times to put someone else ahead of themselves. They often never got a second date.

When I lived at home, my parents and particularly my dad would look to protect me and when I wasn't in the room would mention my illness to prospective girlfriends. This more than often put the wind up them and the relationship never got off the ground. I can understand why they did this- desperate that I dated a girl who would know what she was getting herself into.

I did however have a few main relationships before Katie, each of which lasted about two years apiece. They each had the ability to mentally and physically handle my illness, rise above my inner turmoil and help me with my physiotherapy which can't have been pleasant. Luckily, I was able to enrich my life from each of these longer relationships and still maintain an overriding friendship with them.

But for most of my teens and twenties, in keeping with my mindset around living for the day as tomorrow might never come, I didn't think much about actually planning ahead and settling down. The cosy image of marriage, two kids, and a lovely house with a picket fence was one that I never envisaged. I chose not to look too far into the future and mainly adopted a similar approach to relationships.

And then something changed in me. As I reached the grand old age of twenty nine, with the unobtainable age of thirty looming on the horizon, I began to wonder if my marriage script might have a different ending after all. I had many soul-searching moments when I thought I would never meet the right kind of girl – the one that could get on with me and my CF.

In December 2000 things changed dramatically following a Christmas hockey party liaison and soon after I began dating Katie. I had already known her for over six years from the South London hockey social scene. She was part of a different club called Wayfarers while I was with London Edwardians, but on Sundays we occasionally played for a mixed hockey club called London Strollers. Katie was a pretty skilful player in her own right and was very quick, being known at university for running 'like a gazelle' down the left wing.

Katie and I had always socialised at Wayfarers and Strollers parties and I would often make a bee-line to share a drink with her. Up until 2000, the timing was never right. When I was single Katie was involved and vice versa. But as I've discovered over the years, life is all about timing.

Ironically, in October 2000, I bumped into Katie in a Battersea pub prior to a league game and asked her how the dating game was treating her. She replied that all men were lacking in moral character and she was unlikely to find the right man (she may have used slightly harsher language on the day). To which I replied, "That's because you've never dated me!" Little did we realise just how prophetic those words would turn out to be...

Katie, a senior urology nurse, understood my condition and has always taken the harsh sights and sounds of CF in her stride, never making me feel overly conscious or affected. She understood the bigger CF picture but was never really phased or unduly worried, maybe feeding off my own penchant of downplaying it. I'm sure it probably helped that she had been a nurse on a busy hospital ward with all the patient caring and hard work which that entails.

We shared similar family backgrounds, both growing up in the 1980s. We had the same hockey friends, a mutual passion for sherbet lemon sweets, and a similar sense of humour. Early on, Friday nights were spent at Katie's flat in Streatham with the TV off, where we would listen to Heart FM radio 80's night and swap stories of our youth.

Katie would helpfully laugh at all my jokes... even the ones she didn't understand. She in turn was funny without intending to be, a trait that I found and still find most endearing. We had nicknames for each other – she was called 'Borneo' as her long curly hair resembled the wild woman of Borneo one morning and she referred to me as 'Lovely One' (still not sure why I merited that moniker).

As we got to know each other during 2001, we noticed more and more of our good and bad traits. Katie is not that sentimental while I'm inclined to want to forge memories and take in my surroundings when out socially.

I'll always remember this occasion when we went for a walk in Bushy Park, near Hampton Court. Crossing this little bridge, I came across a river with rabbits on one side of the bank, and a heron stood opposite with a fish in its mouth. I was aghast and transfixed by the visual utopia in front of me. After a minute, I turned to get Katie's attention so that she could share in my moment of ecstasy, only to find her captivated by this couple on a nearby bench and the sticky buns they were devouring!

We had and still have a habit of whistling to each other in order to get the other one's attention or indicate where we were situated in a house or supermarket. We adopted a whole series of different whistles depending on what we needed to alert each other about.

As with most women, there were times when she needed to talk about her day at work and I had to be the listener. On our first valentine's night in February 2001, I had romantically placed a red rose on my bed. Unfortunately, Katie had endured an awful day on the ward and was so upset that she didn't even notice the flower and in her animated state sat directly on it – romance is never dead!

On the rare occasion that we did have a cross word, it was more likely to be me that apologised first after an argument. Katie was more likely to storm off into the kitchen and bang the pots and pans around.

In March 2001, Katie helped me to celebrate my 30th birthday. This was a major tipping point as I had made it to the average life expectancy (as it was then) and the noose around my neck suddenly didn't seem so tight. By reaching this milestone life felt different and I had an eye on a renewed future with someone special to live it with.

In June we went on our first holiday together to California in the United States of America where we stayed for some of the time in San Francisco with my old flat mate Stephen and his wife Bella. Even then, it was becoming obvious that my feelings were becoming stronger by the day and I instinctively knew I wanted to take our relationship to the next level. Previously, when married friends had said that they 'just knew' they were with the right person, it used to wind me up, as I hadn't felt that way myself. With Katie things felt different and there was an ease to our relationship.

During our first summer, my feelings towards Katie compelled me to have a serious life chat with her in a park near her parents' home town of Southend-on-Sea. I gave her the opportunity to pull out if she didn't want to take on board my long-term health concerns and the issues surrounding my known inability to naturally conceive. Marrying someone when you know that their life could well be cut short can feel extremely daunting. It's the true test of our love to have my longevity permanently hanging over us. We agreed through a smattering of tears that for better or worse we would continue; joking that our wedding vows should be changed from 'in sickness and in health' to 'in sickness and in sickness'.

We soon bought a house together in South London and on Katie's birthday, 4 November 2002, I proposed. She duly said yes and we married on 19 July 2003 in Southend-on-Sea in the same church where her granddad had been married during the 1940s. This was followed by a marquee reception, speeches, fireworks and dancing on the family lawn of her parents, Colin and Stephanie.

Neither of us felt nervous in the lead up to the big day. That all changed when we separately entered the church and saw the congregation waiting for us. Katie looked amazing – she was never lovelier than on that stiflingly hot day in July. During the wedding service, Katie's best friend, Sam, read exerts from a children's book by Sam McBratney 'Guess How Much I Love You'.

Benjamin Franklin, one of the Founding Fathers of the United States of America, once said of marriage: "Keep your eyes wide open beforehand, and half shut afterwards." Well on that day my eyes were most definitely open and I felt blessed to marry Katie with all our close family and friends at our side. For me, it was another defining moment in my life where CF was not the focus.

Before our first dance, the habitual speeches took place. In my groom's speech, I referenced that Katie liked the music of Michael Bolton, didn't watch rugby and didn't understand cricket, but I was willing to marry her. Since then, she now likes rugby and understands cricket. As far as I'm aware though, she still likes Michael Bolton. Well, two out of three is progress…

Back in Cannizaro Park, we finished our anniversary toast and shared a moreish pudding together before stretching out on the lawns. Throughout the meal I took my digestive enzyme tablets and at the end I injected myself with diabetic insulin.

As I lay there I reflected that it's bizarrely liberating that I'm able to openly pop pills and do my insulin injection in front of Katie. Such acts that I normally keep hidden away from people can be conducted with a sense of freedom around loved ones. In this sense, Katie is one of the chosen few, the 'CF circle of trust', from whom I don't have to hide away my CF treatments. Although not immune to the sights and sounds of my illness, she is someone that deals with it unflinchingly.

There are a lot of functional activities that come with living with someone with CF; from physiotherapy, constant coughing and nebuliser sessions to intravenous (IV) treatments – these are not fun, sexy or interesting times – it takes a special type of person to be around these daily treatments and keep seeing the person 'behind' the illness and not get too sad, disheartened or bored.

Katie tends to go into nurse mode with my health issues, in order to not only assist me but to protect herself from the relentless nature of handling the condition. My mum was also a nurse so I chose well!

Katie shuts out my habitual coughing and has to manage her frustrations when an episode wakes her at night. She came into her own with my diabetes diagnosis, having had first-hand knowledge of injections from all her IVF cycles, which allows her to understand and 'feel my pain'. On occasions, Katie brings her stethoscope home to listen to my chest for 'crackles' in my lungs. For most of our relationship, she has helped out with my physiotherapy when she is able and at times can take out any annoyances with her percussion on my body!

She manages the huge majority of the household chores and has taken the largest hit on the childcare of Felix, especially the years of night time wake-ups. Katie has also taken the brunt and acted almost as a single mum when I'm away having much needed IV medication. It is these interventions that have enabled me to concentrate on my vast medical regime and helped me stay reasonably well, when it could have gone the other way.

Katie tends to conceal her emotions about my illness and not really overly discuss it with me unless I bring up an issue first. She will reference it if I've just had a nasty coughing fit, hospital appointment or she can see my angst seeping out. We always discuss the outcome of each of my outpatient check-ups and she engages me as part wife part nurse.

Katie certainly doesn't obsess over it and mollycoddle me. This I believe is a good thing as it doesn't make CF bigger than our relationship, just something that needs the appropriate amount of daily respect and attention.

As I hardly ever complain about it, she is probably prone to thinking that I'm not annoyed and frustrated by my everyday struggles. When I do 'break my silence' or am upset she instinctively knows that she needs to listen and support me. On the very rare moments that I utter the words 'My CF is making me angry!' she knows that things must be serious.

Most poignantly, in February 2003 when my lungs were in a bad state with just a few months to go before our marriage, I cried in her arms just before an IV course.

On these rare occasions that I have broken down and cried in front of Katie, her resilience is affected and it sets her off as well. We can be defiant and resilient together but when the situation arises, we can also cry together and hold each other. Perhaps, that's how it should be...

As with most marriages, it's not always been a bed of roses. We both do things that can irritate the other person and we're both prone to being forgetful and lacking thought of each other's feelings.

We've been through a lot together and learned to get better at dealing with the stormy situations, usually meeting half-way on arguments, and not take for granted the times of plain sailing. A vicar's sermon at a friend's wedding enlightened me that more growth occurs in the difficult times of a marriage. I keep those priceless words close to my heart.

Katie and I have been through both thick and thin times in the last decade – we have traversed many traumatic cycles of IVF, raised a busy boy, endured countless relationship-stretching IVs and battled with her debilitating post childbirth nerve damage. By navigating through the turmoil, we certainly are better at being able to identify and appreciate the good times.

It felt good as the two of us, and it feels amazing with Felix. When we've had a happy day out or shared one of those heart-wrenching proud parental moments with Felix, life seems to stop still and we could die happy.

Katie was the maid for me before I married her. Now she's made for me.

20. The Hardest Part

Thursday 29 July 2010

Every year around July time I have the 'joy' of spending a whole day at my annual CF review in the CF unit of Frimley Park Hospital. Today was that day. This involves seeing all manner of medical practitioners from physiotherapists to dieticians to pharmacists. It's a long painstaking day but it's crucial to keep my health regulated. After all, it was during my annual review last year during a standard glucose tolerance test that my CF-related diabetes was diagnosed.

Typically there's quite a bit of hanging around on these days. Initially I sit waiting for my first appointment in the reception meeting room surrounded by paintings and murals dedicated to previous patients who had sadly lost their lives to CF. One of the murals is in memory of the son of a work colleague during my days with the energy company British Gas. Just shows what a small world we live in...

In between appointments, I was instructed that there was going to be a long wait so I moved into the television room to watch the England versus Australia Ashes cricket coverage. While enjoying the delightful sound of willow on leather, I was joined by a fellow CF adult who I vaguely knew. During our usual 'how's your health' chat he informed me about someone we both knew that had recently lost their battle with CF.

For me, hearing about the premature death of another CF sufferer has always been the hardest part of this struggle. It's another tragic facet of living with a life-threatening illness that you tend to hear of in others that have died along the way. One day someone will hear about my passing in similar circumstances.

This chap and I gave each other that knowing look which didn't need any words but articulated 'there we go by the grace of God'. We both know the harsh reality of our illness... that one can be doing pretty well but a bad infection or run of bad luck can quickly spiral and lead to one's ultimate demise.

Once he had left the room, I sat slumped and took time to remember fellow sufferers that were sadly no longer alive. I think of the lives lost to this horrid illness including my CF friends who died before reaching 30 who all deserved to live as long as I have. From an early age and throughout my life, I can recall how I received the bad news of their deaths which always left an indelible mark on my soul.

There was this young girl with doll-like blonde hair and an eye patch during one of my pre-teen in-patient stays in Southampton General Hospital. We got on well. I would offer her my sweets and I got to know her mum, exchanging home numbers. Imagine my deflation a few months later being told by her mum on the phone that she had subsequently passed away. Since then my life has been littered with similar heartbreaking news. That could be one of the reasons I have tended not to get to know too many CFers that well.

But by far the biggest and most soul-destroying were the departures of three of the 'four CF musketeers' as we called ourselves from Hampshire. Ziggy, Mark, Samantha and I were a well-known quartet, often attending appointments together from an early age. The bond was strong. Our parents knew each other and we all battled this illness collectively.

This carried on into adulthood and even though I would see them less often, I would still hear of their current state of health from my parents. In my twenties, I used to have occasional calls with Ziggy as he was a bit older than me and it was good to seek his advice on CF and more adult-related coping issues.

Similar to how people reacted on hearing the news that JFK had been shot, I remember where I was when I was told of the deaths of each of my CF friends. On each occasion, time seemed to stand still and I felt frozen to the spot. It's a most surreal experience, where life is going on around you, but you can't make any sense of it. I know of people that are almost struck down on hearing of the death of people they revered but had never met. People's reaction to the untimely death of Princess Diana springs to mind. In my experience to hear of the demise of people you actually know with the same illness as yourself is like a shot through the heart... and lungs.

Each time my parents were told of the sad news before me and I'm sure they would have looked to protect me by initially holding back what they knew would be devastating news for me to hear. They were probably searching for the right moment to break it to me as gently as possible; to be with me so that they would be on hand to talk and hug me. In my view it would have been just as sad for them as well and equally as demoralising as it would stir up their worst fears.

There was one time while I was in Southampton having an IV treatment when my dad had heard the news of Samantha's death and was acting sheepish. I picked up on this and interrogated him as to why he was acting in such a manner. It quickly dawned on me that there was some heartbreaking CF-related news that he was obviously harbouring. I shall never forget our dialogue in the hallway of their house as I implored him to tell me the secret. When he finally relented and told me who had died, I walked slowly upstairs into my bedroom and wept uncontrollably. I was caught off guard, preferring to be alone to get my head around it.

Each of their deaths drove a wedge deep into my soul and forced me to take a good look at myself. This act of soul mining allowed me to search for any possible reason or logic. Thousands of scrambled thoughts would rush around my head. The question underpinning my procrastination centred on my own longevity more than at any other time in my life. It raised the eternal questions: *Why them and not me? What did they do to deserve this fate so early in their lives? What am I doing that's different to them?*

These extremely dark times allow me to put myself into the shoes of the deceased and I consider how they might have felt when they could see that the sand in their hourglass was finally running out. I often wonder if there's a sense of relief that my friend's life-long punishing ordeal was finally over. There might even be the smallest consolation that they wouldn't have to fight for each of their breaths anymore or cough like a 60-a-day smoker. That any pain they were in could be switched off forever. That their parents, family or loved ones would not have to suffer any longer watching their health deteriorate and feel powerless to help them.

After clinging onto life for so long, I'm sure they wouldn't have wanted to depart when there was still so much to enjoy, do and achieve. They would know the stark realisation that for them there would be no more changes of season, rain, sun, sport, films, tears, laughter, smiles, frowns, sunrises, sunsets, dawn, dusk, television, radio, alcohol, holidays and hugs with their family.

No doubt they would probably have had enough of the relentless struggle with a terminator of an illness that doesn't take many prisoners. Enough would surely be enough and their ravaged bodies which had fought so courageously for all those years would have likely cried out *"NO MORE!"*

No more pill taking, nebulisers, inhalers, physiotherapy, injections, pain, weariness, intravenous medication, lung function tests, coughing fits, wheezing, hospital appointments, operations and in-patient wards. No more obdurate suffering.

I expect after fighting against CF for so many thousands of days they would have wanted some longed-for peace and tranquillity, to breathe easy for the first time and be set free.

Would their final breath in this world be accompanied by a smile or a grimace that it was finally all over? I wouldn't blame them if their final moments were laced with anger and frustration that their whole lives were affected and bullied by this genetic condition that they did not bring into themselves and most certainly didn't deserve.

It's hardly surprising that the news of CF deaths makes me dwell upon my own situation and eventual demise. This leads me to hone in on my likely thoughts during my last days, hours, moments and then more pertinently in my dying breaths. *How and when will it happen? What age will I make it to? How old will I be when I finally draw my last breath and say good riddance to mein kampf? Will I have my family around me? Will the last faces I see be those of my wife, son and immediate family?*

After a few of the deaths of my CF friends, I decided to write a letter to the parents of the deceased. It must cut to the very core for them to see their child suffer and then die before them. As a parent myself, the pain must never depart and there might be some niggling guilt that they could have prevented it. I can imagine that they may have felt emotionally torn knowing that their child had perished to the illness while I had survived. They certainly wouldn't begrudge me my continued existence but would naturally want their child to live longer.

These letters were one of the most excruciating things I've ever had to do and I can honestly say that I cried as I wrote the words. I felt compelled to share with them my thoughts and I've been indirectly told since that my letters provided much solace and aided their grieving.

In essence, I would have said that in their short life they would have had their eyes open to some harsh realities but would have experienced and appreciated more in their short amount of years on this earth than most could achieve in a lifetime. They would have lived life to the full, making sure every second counted because they knew that life was likely to be short.

They would have loved and cherished their parents, family and friends because the CF struggle creates such a strong bond. Together, the family and friends shared their journey, their infectious personality and unquenchable spirit, celebrating all the highs and witnessing the many lows. They should take amazing solace and pride in the fact that they outlived all expectations, defied so many odds and made a positive impression on so many lives. Their lives did make a real difference and left a lasting legacy which is critical when your time is up. Finally, I would have tried to put the parents at ease by saying that they had given everything to make their child's short tenure a happy one.

I also took time to reference each death with my CF consultant, Dr Ron Knight. He must have been devastated each time one of his patients lost the ultimate battle with CF but, ever the professional, he never showed it and maintained his extra positive approach and kept the façade in place. In the depths of my despair and just when I needed him the most to show me the path forward he remained steadfast, preferring to look forward than reflect.

As well as losing actual CF friends over the years, unfortunately there have been the sad departures of other CF sufferers who I was aware of through the grapevine and the occasional one in the public eye. One such loss in 2003 concerned the young English musician, Alice Martineau, who died aged just 31, whose debut album I owned and was a vital source of hope for many. Even though I never actually met Alice, her unexpected and untimely death hit me hard, seemingly bolting another nail in my own virtual coffin.

When you have lost so many of your dear CF compatriots and endured the pain when they leave you, it does become a bit of a gamble getting to know other CF sufferers. These days this quandary has been slightly negated by the all too real issue of cross-infection which limits my face-to-face interaction with other sufferers.

Under current medical guidelines CF patients have been advised to no longer spend time with each other. It's all down to the risk of making each other more ill from cross-infection. Cross-infection is an issue of considerable concern for the CF community. Those with CF attract different bacteria or 'bugs' that grow in their lungs, which may be harmful to others who have CF but who do not have the same 'bugs'.

Bugs such as B. cepacia complex and Pseudomonas aeruginosa can be transmitted from person to person by close personal contact, such as sharing rooms, sharing medical equipment, sharing cutlery or crockery, and by kissing or coughing. There is little risk of transmission of 'bugs' in an outdoor environment, but travelling with other people with CF in a car or a coach, or meeting them socially would introduce a higher level of risk.

There is a worry that CF patients are more likely to pick up strains of these bugs from each other that are more difficult to treat than strains picked up from the environment. For this reason, in the future, most CF units don't have a waiting room but use segregated treatment rooms.

And so I remember those that have gone before me. They are sadly gone but definitely not forgotten. At the going down of the sun and in the morning, I will remember them. There I go by the grace of God.

A large majority of CF sufferers endure a life of considerable suffering and it comforts me to believe that God is holding their hands as they depart this world and that they have gone to a better place, free of medication and coughing, a place where they can be spontaneous and run around like Olympic athletes.

I will endeavour to make my life count in their memory and carry their torch within me wherever I go and in everything I do. Their spirits will live on and shine brightly – a beacon of light and hope for all of a tough life well lived.

21. Praying Alive

Sunday 1 August 2010

There are often some defining moments in your life where your direction changes. I had one of these moments a decade ago and ever since I've been praying for a healthier life rather than just wishing and hoping for one.

This morning I took Felix to morning worship at Queens Road Church in Wimbledon. Felix went into the crèche area and, after assisting him for a while, I headed into the main part of the church for the sermon, which was about the power of prayer. At the end, the congregation were invited up to the front to receive healing for any health issues they had. Did I join them?

My 'faith' is a very personal and private one. I do enjoy the neutrality of fellowship, but it can feel like a lonely path at times, especially as Katie does not have such faith. I don't go every Sunday and I'm unlikely to preach to people whom I meet. In my experience, internal reflection feels more appropriate for me rather than boldly going to the front of the congregation. Having to explain all my health woes to a stranger feels awkward, even though I know they would be empathetic. It's not a quick conversation introducing my conditions and it's a noisy environment so quiet contemplation is just the ticket. I decided to stay seated, not draw attention to myself, and pray for improved health.

It's not always been thus. Praying for extra time in my life has been a fairly recent activity and my faith has not followed a straightforward path.

For nearly 30 years, there was no place in my life for God, whom I used to blame for my ailments and suffering. I felt he had personally dealt me a big enough blow and pain. I could not see how God might change anything in my life. After all, it was a done deal being born physically disabled with no cure on the horizon. I chose never to blame my parents so I suppose I had to find another culprit to reproach. My eyes were closed to see him and my ears were blocked to hear him.

In my teens and early twenties, two of my Southampton Christian friends tried to intervene and help me see a different path. They must have seen something in me that I couldn't or didn't want to see.

Paul Chrispin offered to pray for me and often didn't take no for an answer. He would stand with me, praying out loud for my lungs to be healed and for me to encounter his Lord. On a few occasions, he also suggested accompanying him to his church but I couldn't see how it could help me. I thought it would be a waste of his and my time, so I politely declined the offer.

Becky Herbert, who had met me through my brother Jez, rang me out of the blue when I was in my late teens and asked to meet on Southampton Common; where she explained that she'd had a calling from God to tell me that "God loved me." I know she felt uncomfortable when telling me this news as she knew I was unlikely to understand and my head was in a different place. I think she showed the utmost courage to say such a thing to someone who was socially off the rails and angry with life because of my health problems. We recently joked about this event and how it made both of us feel.

Paul and Becky, thank you for your persistence and kindness. I was hopefully worth your efforts.

If you have not been brought up in a Christian family and attended church regularly in your youth, you usually need a catalyst in your life which throws all your balls into the air.

Not that I realised it at the time, but my faith-changing moment arrived when I was given the desperately sad news in the late 1990s that one of my close CF friends from the Hampshire region had succumbed to the condition after many months of declining health. Ziggy Kruk was one of four CF sufferers I knew pretty well and the one I often spoke to on the phone to tap into his survival knowledge. Giving me this news was of course horrible for my parents as they understood what his death would signify for me.

This awful news coincided with having a tough time anyway. I had also felt for the preceding year that my approach to battling CF was being gradually dismantled by a dramatic reduction in my energy and positivity.

At that precise moment, with my own internal alarm bells tolling, I felt there wasn't anyone else in the world who could help me or indeed save me from the same reckoning as Ziggy. It had to come from within. I had come to the end of my physical and mental tether. I had nothing more to give and couldn't fight my CF with my current resources and strategy. I was hanging onto a precipice and my fingers were about to let go. I couldn't speak to my beloved parents about how I was feeling but instinctively felt the utmost compulsion to visit the nearest church in Southampton, St Michaels.

It was mid-afternoon when I walked into this empty but creaky church, taking a seat in a pew near the front. Perhaps I felt that by being closer to the front of the church I was sitting nearer to God and he might hear me. Then without knowing what I intended to do or what was going to happen, I started to pray. As it happened I was actually praying for my very existence. I explained about Ziggy's death and how I knew that I needed extra help if I was to survive. I asked God to provide me with solace whenever I felt powerless and the strength to carry on despite the odds being stacked against me.

Ziggy's sad death was my spur to cry out to God: "Why him? Why not me? Why have I been spared? How long have I got left?" And finally, "Am I being kept alive for a particular purpose?"

I felt an overriding sense of relief that I had offloaded and this sensation was duplicated whenever I opened up and prayed. At home, on my own, I would often pray, cry bitter stinging tears and then pray some more. The burden I had carried for so long was slowly being lifted and the internal tension and anger was dissipating. Most importantly, I put a halt to the feeling of anger and bitterness towards God. Instead I asked him for help and instantly it felt like a weight had been lifted. Unwittingly maybe I had removed the cross that I'd been stoically carrying on my shoulders for nearly 30 years.

What I encountered surprised me. Starting a conversation with God felt easy and natural, like being put on hold on a phone call and then a knowing voice starts speaking again after a long silence. This newly acquired faith seemed to be innate, lying dormant and waiting for me. This is backed up when I hear how previously non-Christian people in their hour of need cry out intuitively for divine intervention. An obvious example of this is some of the survivors of the 2005 tsunami in Indonesia who recounted calling out for God when they saw the devastation coming in their direction.

Six months after my moment of salvation I felt drawn towards an increased level of faith. After some research, I enrolled onto an Alpha Course introduction to Christianity in February 2002 at Wimbledon's Queens Road Church. As the course reached its conclusion I had to face up to some harsh questions. Was I prepared to do the hard work of facing painful situations, uncovering bitterness, and admitting to deep, resentful anger? Was I willing to give up my stubborn excuses that allowed me to stay the same, seeing my sickness as more secure than my health? Was I actually ready to step into faith and away from fear?

On the last day of the course, I decided to take a leap of faith and switch my animosity towards God for my illness into an inner peace and strength through prayer and fellowship. Trust me this was not straightforward and it took courage, energy and pain to take that first step.

My declaration was reinforced when reading through the Psalms, in particular discovering Psalm 116. The words could have been written for me in my moment of despair when hearing Ziggy's news, empowering me to focus on defying death with the help of prayer.

Psalm 116

I love the LORD, for he heard my voice;
he heard my cry for mercy
Because he turned his ear to me,
I will call on him as long as I live.
The cords of death entangled me,
the anguish of the grave came over me;
I was overcome by distress and sorrow.
Then I called on the name of the LORD:
"LORD, save me!"
The LORD is gracious and righteous;
our God is full of compassion.
The LORD protects the unwary;
when I was brought low, he saved me.
Return to your rest, my soul,
for the LORD has been good to you.
For you, LORD, have delivered me from death,
my eyes from tears,
my feet from stumbling,
that I may walk before the LORD
in the land of the living.

Slowly I was turning all the old negative thoughts and habits into positive ones. I worked hard at showing my own version of GRACE – 'Give Readily And Cherish Everything'. However, I soon found that having faith wasn't some form of magic wand for behaving perfectly. It didn't stop me from making mistakes, being inconsiderate and sometimes saying the wrong things to family, friends and work colleagues. But I was more likely to be aware of my misgivings and try to seek forgiveness when I knew I was in the wrong rather than be obstinate or ignorant. Having faith and daily prayer helped to centre me when I could have gone off the rails and done something foolish.

I soon learned that the easy bit was to take the initial leap of faith. The hardest task is to maintain your faith and values when life challenges and tragedies cross your path. Being in faith does not make you immune to bad times, but in my experience, those bad times are more palatable because I've got somewhere and someone to hand over my worries and angst to. This inner peace has carried me through our stressful IVF cycles, my battle with CF, my diabetes diagnosis, the early deaths of my beloved cats, being in between jobs and countless testing moments in my work and domestic relationships. Even though I may stumble at times, I will not fall as God is holding my hand.

What I do know is that prayer provides me with an additional strength and solace that I didn't have previously and it underpins my fortitude to keep battling CF and diabetes. It acts as another element of my physical and mental battle to stay ahead of my life expectancy.

Trust me when I say that one of the most powerful things I do on a daily basis is to be thankful in my prayers for my on-going life and the health that I do have, rather than bemoan the health I do not. I gain contentment by praying for the courage to change what I can (especially my mindset), the grace to accept what I cannot (most things are acceptable when we stop resenting them), and the wisdom to know the difference.

A lot of Christian focus is on the afterlife but an additional facet that I concentrate on is the here and now and the preservation of my health so that I can live as full and happy a life as possible.

One of the attributes of a true Christian character is a willingness to encourage and lift people. My suffering enables me to help others. It's the broken who become masters at mending. It was almost as if I had to be broken in order to be re-moulded into the person that I am now. I firmly believe that my most effective ministry and story-telling have come out of my most painful experiences. The thing that for so many years I was most reluctant to share is now the very thing I am using to help others.

I'm sure my move towards faith would bemuse and surprise a lot of people based on my earlier life and behaviour. As a former hell-raiser, this change would have been the last

22. Shaken, Not Stirred

Wednesday 11 August 2010

Following a day at work and after Felix had been put down for the night, just as the evening was drawing in, I went for a run behind our house in the local park. It had been a sunny and warm summer day and one I knew that I had to make the most of to find time for some exercise.

It always makes a refreshing change in England to go for a run in the warmer weather rather than on the roads during the cold and dark winter. After all, it's the hard yards I put in when it's warm that set me up for the harsher winter weather. If I can't make an effort and bust a gut (and a lung) on a pleasant night like tonight then it's a missed opportunity and I'd feel that CF was beating me. I'm too determined to let that happen. So I must seize the day as it were. Well, seize the *end* of the day, anyway...

After the compulsory stretches learned from years of playing hockey, I set foot out of the house and down the small passageway that leads to the entrance of Morden Park. I take in the smell of freshly cut grass and early evening birdsong as I start jogging up the track that works its way from the entrance of the park through to the fields above.

The summer time has historically been better for my general health and lung capacity and hence my ability to exercise. On the whole I try to stave off my dreaded intravenous (IV) treatments in the summer months so that I can make the most of the warmer weather. That way I'm making my CF fit in with my life rather than the other way round.

For many years on the trot, I've needed two of these IVs – before and during the winter period. This time I only needed just the one back in September 2009. This does mean that for this particular summer I'm in unchartered territory as I decided to abstain from my usual February IV treatment- feeling well enough to 'push on' and not need it.

This was a surprising but nonetheless pleasing knock-on effect from my CF-related type 1 diabetes. As I had religiously monitored my blood sugar levels and been diligent with taking my insulin, I began to have extra energy and slightly less lung infection. The jury's out for now about one IV treatment per year rather than the habitual two that has been the way for so long, but I've made the decision now so I have to live and breathe with the consequences.

However, the cracks have started to appear in my health and I've been coughing a lot more of late… my energy has been sapped. What would have been a hard but manageable jog even a month ago, is now feeling like an opening scene from a Mission Impossible film. My mission, should I choose to accept it, is to force my way around this local park in the name of exercise.

The slope up to the top of the park suddenly feels like my version of reaching the summit of Mount Everest. Getting to the top in one go without stopping makes me feel like the fictional boxer Rocky Balboa striding up those famous steps in Philadelphia. Unfortunately, I've noticed that I can run less far up this slope in one attempt with each passing year.

This is a real struggle – like running through treacle. It's not just my legs which are giving me grief. My lungs are beseeching me to stop. This brings a new meaning to 'screaming at the top of my lungs'. I will myself on, imagining my lungs can and will respond to this physical and mental barrier. My normal inner monologue cries out:

"I won't be beaten. I can do this. I will do this. JUST DO IT!"

But after a short while, it's more like the reverse of the Nike strap line: *"Can't do it!"*

I have to stop three quarters of the way up the track and have an extended breather. I then decide to do interval running where I run for a while, then stop but keep walking slowly until I get enough breath back to pick up the pace and go running again. I joke to myself that my adaptation of the instructions to rugby union front rows at scrum time would be – 'run, stop, cough, pause and engage'.

As I'm running I ended up swearing out loud – partly at myself as a form of gee-up and partly at the frustration of my harsh health situation. While I'm swearing, it amuses me to wonder whether anyone that sees me considers if I have Tourette's syndrome!

"Look at that poor chap – panting, coughing and swearing. He should be resting somewhere quiet and not out running in that state!"

When jogging is this awful, I tend to dig my nails into the palm of my hand to keep going as a jockey would use a stick to gee on their horse. I turn my iPod to the Tom Petty song 'I Won't Back Down'…

I won't back down.

After about 30 minutes of interval running I arrive back home. Panting like a dog that's too hot and needs some shade, I bypass the front door and go into our back garden, through the side gate, grab a drink and sit on the garden bench to catch my breath. I turn my iPod music from upbeat and motivational to chill out and reflective to suit the change of mood. My breathing is getting less heavy and I mop my brow with my t-shirt sleeve. I look to the sky and watch the swifts perform their hypnotic nightly ritual of manic swooping.

Bloody hell, that run was tough! I'm 39 and nearing 40 but at this precise moment in time I feel closer to 100 years old. It just doesn't get any easier this survival game.

Katie pops out into the garden and asks me how the run went. Just by looking at me, I'm sure she already knows the answer.

"Harder than ever," I reply in a deflated tone.

These moments sitting on my bench following a run allow me to take both physical and mental stock of my health, happiness and life generally. When a run goes pretty well, the feeling is bordering on euphoria; but when it's been rough, as it was just now, I have to mentally strive to pull myself together and not get too morose and down-hearted.

I watch the last rays of daylight for another day as dusk settles in. I have an out-of-body experience where I feel that I'm levitating. An experience in which I hover and look down upon myself. I frantically search for context and inspiration to spur me on. What positives can I take out of that desperate attempt at fitness?

Historically, my motivation to exercise has been both physical and mental. What's more of a benefit to me – running and a short-term discomfort or not running and letting the effects of CF build up. Exercise and sport have always been my two fingers salute to CF. That's why I put myself through this trauma time and again like some deranged masochist.

When the going gets this tough and my lungs are screaming at me to stop, the power comes from within to see my race to its end. I have to draw on my own motivation to keep running with breaks to stop and cough. There's no winning for me anymore. It's all about the actual doing as I know the importance of exercise to my on-going health and survival.

I won't back down.

My thoughts swing from positive to negative just like the pendulum on a grandfather clock. I'm definitely slowing down. My lungs are a lot more productive. To use the James Bond vernacular, I'm shaken. But do I feel stirred?

I need to address this situation and find a strategy to strike back. They say the best form of defence is attack. It's also said that when the going gets tough, the tough have to get going. Well, this is one of those times. I need to dredge my mind for the formula that keeps me buoyant when all I want to do is relax and let myself drown in self-pity. In these disturbing moments, I ask not what my body can do for me, but what I can do for my own body.

I've realised that staying healthy doesn't just rely on a compliance in taking my medication, it needs something more – an absolute commitment to keeping well. Actually 'wanting to' rather than 'having to' be healthy is very empowering. When I distil it down this is my intrinsic motivation. After a lifetime battling a relentless illness, I've learnt to fight it by being just as relentless back. I achieve this through a mixture of exercise and being diligent with my medical regimen.

Why would I want to cut corners and miss my medication? Even when I take all my medication, it just about maintains my health – it never cures. I would feel a lot worse if I missed any of my treatment regime, so what's in it for me to risk that? After all, I'm only as healthy as my last treatment. It is important to control the parts of my illness that can be controlled. Manage the manageable. In rowing terms, I control what's going on inside my own boat rather than fixate on external factors.

I have calculated that for every 24 hours in a day, at least two hours are spent doing something medical. A positive way to view this is that leaves me with 22 hours to do what I want to do each day so I take pleasure in the hours I have and not the hours I lose.

22 hours for Tim Wotton and 2 hours for CF.

My treatments are something I do to get out the door and get on with my busy life – they are my enablers – they have become a second nature activity like brushing my teeth. This is engrained in my subconscious by constant repetition so that eventually my body begins to remind me what to take and when. This can only happen by taking ownership of the condition rather than relying on others to be my conscience. For me, it's been a case of building habits and over the years I have become pretty competitive with myself to adhere to the regimen. Conversely I am prone to getting annoyed with myself when I forget any part of my treatment.

If my routine is altered which is likely when I'm travelling, on holiday or in a work conference, it does affect my medical management and I have to focus even harder not to miss any facets of my regime.

In dealing with CF I have tended to match fire with fire. I'm bullish about getting my own way from hospital visits and I'm probably a pain to medical staff at times. I read my own body signals and thus don't always wait for the doctor to tell me about changing my antibiotics when I already know what drug to take and when to take them. I try to keep on top of the condition and look for new ways to 'boss' my illness with changes of drug, alternative therapy or new ways of positive thinking.

I won't back down.

I one hundred per cent respect my illness, know my many limitations and look to avoid the 'CF banana skin' of trying to dismiss it and not take it seriously enough.

A lot of willpower is required to win this ongoing battle. When you get to a certain age you tend to balk at doing things that you just don't want to do and believe me doing my treatment is the last thing in the world I want to do. I have to knuckle down every day of my life and continually do these unpleasant acts of medication. I only get out of my body what I am prepared to put into it.

I do at times have to bite my tongue when people I encounter complain about their short-term health issue but do nothing about it. Or those that make a big fuss at the dinner table about taking just one tablet. I've also witnessed guys who milk their condition or injury for all it's worth and feed off of the novelty factor. These are often the same people who don't take any medication to get it fixed but prolong their own agony and that of those around them. I prefer to say nothing and let my actions do the talking. But I've had nearly 40 years to get used to my afflictions – I've never known anything different.

I have to respect this illness 365 days a year and especially at times when I would rather kick-back and have some time off: Christmas day, birthdays, my wedding day and honeymoon, holidays, travel, before and after work – I don't get a day off with this condition. The symptoms of CF and diabetes don't take a day off and neither can I. I can take a holiday but CF doesn't take a holiday from me. I've calculated that if I had just two weeks off from taking all my various medications, I would be seriously ill in hospital.

If I fail to prepare for daily eventualities, I am preparing to be caught out and potentially be affected. Following a 'just in case' mantra, I always plan for the next day, work, social commitments and the weather. My work bag is always stocked with my daily pills, insulin and dextrose energy sweets. I bet

I'm one of the few men who would go out on a stag do armed with an umbrella so that I don't get wet and damp! As soon as I've played sport or if I get caught in the rain, I'll take a shower to avoid catching a chill. It's being spectacularly practical rather than spontaneous. Spontaneity is something that happens to other people who live in a parallel universe to me.

I get angry on a daily basis about my drug regime, but I have learned to channel that anger and frustration. I focus my thoughts on what activity – tube to work, playing sport, game with my son, meal with my wife, night out with friends – I will do once that piece of medication has been completed, rather than on the actual treatment itself. I very rarely vent my anger and frustration with those around me and I'm learning to be more open as I write this diary.

I re-join my body back on the bench. I'm now calm and at peace as I sit in the delightfully calm twilight moment that only really pervades on a still summer's evening. I think of friends who can just exist without having to put themselves through this form of exercise torture and I envy them. My God, I envy them. Sometimes I feel that ignorance would be bliss.

However tough it is for me to bear, exercise is my version of treading water in the ocean. Once I stop, I'll drown and that will be it. I've literally got no other choice but to keep on going with it. By forcing myself to breathe hard while exercising, I in turn breathe life into my lungs. While there's still breath left in me, I will continue to run for my very life.

Everyday I'm shaken by my disease but I try not to be too stirred and respond by shaking it back. After all, I'm still here. I'm still running. I won't back down.

23. White Flag

Tuesday 7 September 2010

D-Day for most people with CF has commenced for me. The deterioration of my health has dictated that I need one of my much dreaded but much needed intravenous (IV) treatments and it's booked for today at Frimley Park Hospital in Surrey.

There are different layers of suffering and corresponding medication with CF. For most of the year I undergo the daily regimen slog of 40 pills, nebulisers, injections and physiotherapy. However, when my lungs are ravished enough I need to take my treatment to an extra dimension... and that means having two-plus weeks of high dose IV antibiotics. I refer to this as l having an 'MOT'. These are the times when I need to wave the white flag and strategically surrender to CF for a while in order to re-group and come back fighting.

In the lead up to initiating this course of treatment, I always feel like the Duracell bunny, but minus a battery or two. I can get on with my usual daily activities but everything is at a reduced pace, in mind as well as in body. Tiredness eats at me and my body feels as if it's in freefall. Imagine the way one feels when leading up to a break from work but times it by a thousand.

In my experience, IV antibiotics make such a difference because they help to clear my chest of the built-up infection. The liquid drug goes directly into my blood stream through an IV catheter and is then dispersed quickly around the body. This in turn churns up the mucous in my lungs so that it can be coughed up more easily. An IV may require a hospital stay, but can also be done at home, which is the route I prefer – splitting the time up between home in London and my parents in Southampton.

As I left my house, leaving Katie and Felix behind in London this morning to drive down to the hospital felt like the axis of my world had turned in a different direction. Only three days ago, I was out enjoying myself having one last hurrah weekend of fun. I call it my health rattle. I feel it's important to do something fun and normal just before entering the twilight zone of IV medication.

It also allowed me to celebrate a pleasant summer, although the last month has been somewhat of a struggle health-wise as I only had one IV treatment in the last year rather than the usual two. Being a sentimental beast, it offers me one final memory of summer 2010 that isn't distorted by CF and all the grimness that my illness brings. It provides another deposit in my happy bank that is invaluable when times are tough.

In keeping with my socialising philosophy of 'Windows 7', I had a Saturday afternoon sporting activity followed by a friend's evening garden party. During the afternoon my ex work colleague Stephen and I had tickets for a double header rugby union event at Twickenham, where they start the season with two concurrent games featuring London-based teams. One of the winning teams was my club Harlequins who I've been supporting for over 20 years since my university days, so it was a splendid event.

The sport of rugby is quite a passion in my life. Even though I was never the right size for it, I played at school and enjoyed getting stuck in. However, at just under five foot seven inches and with a slight build, rugby was never going to be the sport for me but I do thoroughly enjoy watching it.

I like the ethos behind rugby – take and dish out punishment during the game, shake hands at the final whistle, smile and then have a drink together and compare tall stories. Like battling CF, you can't take to the rugby pitch anything less than one hundred per cent prepared, where the gloves are quite literally off and you have to front up to survive and give your best. The determination and resilience needed by the players, especially the forwards, really resonates with me – to keep on getting up time and time again – to give as good as you get and still be ready for more punishment.

After some celebratory drinks post match in Richmond, I joined Katie and Felix for the evening bash, which was an outdoor house warming party just outside Richmond Park for one of Katie's best friends. A good time was had by all.

That seems in stark contrast with where I am now. I've just suffered an awful two-hour ordeal as a doctor tried unsuccessfully to insert a PICC line into the vein in my arm and along to the right area, near the heart. After three attempts, three holes in my right arm which involved a lot of pain and quite a bit of blood, the doctor suggested that I should come back tomorrow and try again. At which point I candidly retorted:

"Somebody in this bloody hospital will get this line into my body so that I can start my treatment. It has to happen today. I'm on a tight schedule and won't be coming back tomorrow."

Back in the reception room while waiting for a more experienced doctor to have a go at inserting the line, I sat disconsolate trying to fight back the tears. It's a two-hour wait for my knight in shining armour to arrive and try again, so I put my iPod on, relaxed and ruminated about the whole debacle...

Reflecting on IVs over the years, I calculated that this is roughly my 60th IV session – that's a lot of holes and scars on the inside of my arms! I've had so many of these that my veins have almost had enough and it takes a lot of effort, blood and swearing to get the lines in these days, and that's even before I start any medication.

I do count myself lucky as my veins have been kinder than most and I have staved off needing a 'portacath'. This small medical appliance installed beneath the skin would feel like a permanent reminder of my CF and I've tried to avoid having one at all costs. That does however mean that I have to put up with these line insertions and the trauma that comes with them.

For most of my youth, when I socially lived for the moment with great gusto, I did get very run-down and my lungs were often in a horrible state of infection prior to needing IV treatments. My mucous production and subsequent cough would get so bad that I became part-human, part-cement mixer. Nowadays I try not to let myself get quite as run down and scar my lungs. I also try to time them with the end of work assignments and either side of the winter. For me and the majority of CF sufferers, they are a necessary evil.

I have a ritual on the day my IV commences as I'm driving to the hospital. I think of the Steve McQueen film 'Papillon' and the iconic scene when Papillon is put in solitary confinement for trying to escape. When at low ebb when starving, he would look to the heavens via a small window in his cell and shout, *"I'm still here!"*

At these precise moments when I drive away from my normal life into the abyss of IV medication, that is exactly how I feel, though I'd be shouting those words out of my car window instead of through prison bars. Maybe IVs are my version of a prison sentence?

Each and every one of those 60 IV sessions has entailed some form of drama, pain and exasperation. In my teens and twenties there was a lot of heartache for my parents and me. This was caused by blocked, leaking catheters and physically drawing up the drugs using water for injection and the powdered antibiotic.

A number of my IV drugs have caused some horrific side-effects over the years. A sample of these reactions includes fevers, hallucinations, stomach upsets and severe body rashes. I once fainted and had to be fetched out of the bathtub by my Aunty Mary who was looking after me at the time. There was also one session around my seventeenth birthday where we didn't realise that the IV drug was causing an allergic reaction and so we kept injecting it for a few more days which in turn made the side-effects intensify. I was finally put out of my misery by a visiting doctor who urged me to stop taking the IV drug.

I've been on an IV and conducted my treatments in all manner of places in my lifetime from my different homes, to University halls of residence, to nightclubs, hockey pitches, weddings and holidays. I even took my treatments to parties while at college.

Although there are more horrid medications for CF sufferers, with organ transplants being the most traumatic, I always explain to the non-CF community that these IVs are my version of chemotherapy. They stretch me both physically and mentally – it's extremely gruelling and feels like trench warfare.

Physically, the power of the drugs wears me down. I feel lethargic and sapped of energy and spirit. During an IV drug treatment I painstakingly inject the liquid drug into the catheter in my arm from either a syringe or via a drip bag. One session can last well over two hours and I often need them three times a day. This is all done on top of my usual medication regime, which makes for a long day where I seemingly go from one treatment to the next in a vicious circle. If anyone can manufacture a pill that has the same effect as IV drugs, they would be bought dinner for the rest of their lives by appreciative CF sufferers!

Mentally, it's a rollercoaster trying to remain as positive as possible even when things don't seem to be going well or when my body sends me mixed messages on the effectiveness of the medication. It's definitely when I feel at my lowest and least capable of coping.

Psychologically, IVs are a harsh reminder that CF is very much still calling the shots and affecting my health and fragility. It takes away any spontaneity and makes me feel like the 'sick boy' all over again. I find IVs rein me back in, exclaiming: *"Don't get too comfortable, feel normal or get too ahead of yourself and feel like all those healthy people!"*

Generally, patience is a huge virtue when handling CF and my recently diagnosed diabetes but it's required in bucket loads during these sessions. I need it on days like today when I'm struggling to even get the PICC line into my body let alone start the actual medication. Also, there's often a lot of waiting around in hospitals for doctor appointments, plus patience is needed during the frustrating down time of the treatments themselves. I try to get myself into a 'Zen-like' state of calm to manage this whole process. But most importantly, I need to hold my nerve and stay the course of the medication so that my lungs can reap the full benefit from the drugs.

Historically, I'm not always a nice person to be around during IVs – I'm prone to being grumpy, incoherent and forgetful of the simplest words. Katie and I joke that I once couldn't remember the term 'seat belt' referring to it as a 'driving strap'. I forget the names of friends or the simplest details when I'm on IVs, which can be most embarrassing.

I would certainly have struggled dealing with these IV sessions if it were not for the amazing and consistent support from my parents, brothers, Katie and friends who share the burden with me. My mum has particularly gone the extra mile and been involved with each and every IV course. She has been through thick and thin, blood and gore, tantrums and agony, but also through humour and laughter which is our overriding medicine. Most boys have a special connection with their mums but I'm sure that ours has been intensified through this on-going strife. What my mum and I have dealt with together, in particular these horrendous IVs, has created a bond of resilience and love that would be hard to match.

There's a tough side-affect for my relationship with Katie. Every IV treatment causes extra stress for us as a couple and as parents to Felix. When I'm away at my parents' home, it leaves Katie to be a one-parent family. And when I'm back at home, it's immensely frustrating for both of us that I'm off work and around the house but incapable of doing the usual tasks to help support as husband and father. I am able to spend time with Felix but I'm not able to be my normal exuberant self with him.

On a positive spin, these sessions have given me time with my family which my normal busy life in London wouldn't offer me. Once you leave home, these 'quality' times are few and far between. Despite the fact that I'm often higher than a kite, I do remember these times with some fondness.

I can't deny that it's an almighty faff taking time out from work, sport, family life and not being able to be there for Katie and Felix. The older I've got it seems apparent that these IVs clash heavily with normality. They are always inconvenient and conflict with work and social commitments. Luckily, I have the support of an understanding employer who grants me this time off with open compassion.

As with most things in life, as you get older you tend to become wiser. With these IV treatments, I have found a way that works for me – a more measured and realistic approach where I listen to how my body feels before, during and after the IV course and try to act accordingly. I have to quite literally stay the course and make the whole medical process work for me.

Finally, after a 90-minute wait, the line was successfully put in by a doctor who I knew from the past who had supported me a few times before. The sense of relief I felt once the IV catheter was correctly in position was palpable. The battle within the battle had been won and the tension lifted as I made my way to the CF unit for a test dose of my IV antibiotics. In my experience, most IV courses have a series of these dramas that keep me on my toes and force me not to get too complacent that everything will just work automatically.

By this time it was early afternoon and I had to spend well over an hour wired up to drips in order to have my test dose of the IV drugs. While waiting in the day room to check that I didn't have any adverse reaction to the medication, I had some late lunch. Feeling tired from the day's exertions and mental trauma, but desperate to check out of the hospital, I drove the 40 minute journey to Southampton for the commencement of my week of TLC with my parents.

Initiating this latest IV session, I have kick-started a mental and physical rollercoaster journey. However tough it gets, I always try so very hard to keep my eye on the end goal and project in my mind how I will be post treatment – back with my family in London, working hard, playing hockey, exercising, enjoying a night out with my chums, taking Katie for dinner and playing rough-and-tumble with Felix.

It's half time in my hypothetical game of rugby. I'm losing, bruised, bloodied and battered but there's still a lot to play for. The game can still be won.

By realising when the time is right to change my treatment and seek help, I temporarily wave the white flag so that I can get better and live to fight another day. As I see it, I may have lost the battle but I've not lost the war.

24. Journey's End

Tuesday 14 September 2010

I'm back in London and having a very annoying day enduring my IVs. The medication has been doing what it's supposed to and is churning up the mucous in my lungs, but I just couldn't stop coughing. This is quite typical of the early stages of an IV session when the medication impacts areas of my lungs that have gone untreated in a while but this time it has felt worse than usual.

This was greatly magnified by the wet and damp weather today. My lungs just wouldn't let up and the non-stop coughing made my throat sore, my voice hoarse and at times drove me to despair. There seemed to be wave after wave of phlegm that needed clearing. The waves in time became tidal and eventually resulted in a coughing tsunami. Even after such a long time of coping with CF, there are some days where my illness feels more incessant and unforgiving than ever. Today has been such a day...

I wasn't feeling too bad yesterday so today has been rather a curve ball. Confused by this change of direction, I pathetically ask my lungs, *"Where has all this extra coughing come from?*

Come on. Give me a break!" my inner monologue screamed, looking for a resolution.

"No chance," was the defiant and spiteful retort from my lungs.

Like the cumulative effect of water torture, the relentless hacking caused my mind to launch into a stratosphere of doom and gloom. What Holly Golightly from the film 'Breakfast at Tiffany's' would refer to as her "mean reds".

On most days there are many small frustrating CF-related triggers that I can overcome. It's very rare that I let them elicit a seismic reaction inside me and plummet to these depths of darkness. Luckily, I can normally stave it off with positive thinking and the standard distractions of everyday life. However, while I'm trapped inside the CF bubble of an IV course. I'm at a heightened sense of awareness and I find that it doesn't take much to set me off. If my life was a cartoon, I'd be the roadrunner and my condition would be the pursuing coyote. In the cartoon the coyote always gets defeated, but with CF it catches up with me from time to time. This is especially true during IV time when CF's existence is magnified.

In this higher state of consciousness, I think I have control of the situation and I've pulled myself together and then out of the blue, my house comes crumbling down – often by something innocuous or unexpected. The catalyst for my downfall usually consists of a TV programme, innocent remark or a song heard on the radio.

Tonight Katie and I watched an episode of the American medical drama 'House' which had an ending that totally floored me and dredged up all the anxiety of the day's suffering. The programme concluded with a young adult man, who had been ill all his life, and his gut-wrenching decision to quite pragmatically take the opportunity to finally put an end to his discomfort and die. For him, after a lifetime of pain and hardship, it was the right time to go. He did this alongside his dog, whom he cuddled tightly as he passed away.

That feeling of slipping away really resonated with me. In fact it cut to my very core. I could completely understand and appreciate how that young man would have felt in making that decision – I know more than most how it feels to constantly fight a relentless illness and that there's only so much fight in anyone's body.

After watching the programme, we went to bed but I just couldn't talk to Katie about how I was feeling and the well of emotion that was building up inside me. It usually takes quite a lot for me to break down and cry but I knew that tears were close on this occasion. One word to Katie and the floodgates would open and my dam of emotional defiance would be breached.

I didn't even know where to begin. I felt a swathe of sadness envelop me. Like being hit by a big wave and being dragged under with the strong currents. A plunging underworld of sinking, you might say.

The power of the IV drugs and the all-day coughing fit had been escalated by the mind scramble of the TV drama, and it was looking to pull me into a vortex of sadness.

Everyone with a long-term illness will have considered the following questions. *How will it feel when I know it's my time to depart? How will I react? What will it feel like? Will it be a relaxed feeling of peace at last? Or will it feel like welcome release from all the suffering and heartache? Will I be angry that my condition has finally beaten me?*

As I lay on my bed, in the depths of my despair, I could almost feel the blood coursing in my veins. I could hear the heavy rhythmic beat of my thumping heart and my mind was frenzied by fear. Different memories and songs flittered around my mind. All I could think of were lyrics that referenced people making the decision to die or bring an end to their suffering.

I decided to turn to my iPod in order to calm my manic state. It unfortunately offered me little redemption.

I couldn't seem to escape from this web of morbidity. Was this my journey's end?

The futility of war has always held a great fascination with me. Anyone on the frontline of a war zone will surely have questioned their mortality. When your days are likely to be numbered – due to an incurable illness or as a soldier – there's something quite empowering in acting as if you're dead already. In my experience it can break the chains that could tie you down. Both CF sufferers and war combatants have poignant moments when the whistle blows and they have to confront their inner demons in order to proceed and go over the top.

Whereas the WW1 poet Siegfried Sassoon commented on the battlefields of Belgium, "I died in hell, they call it Passchendaele," my version would be, "I lived with hell. They call it CF."

As I entered more deeply into my temple of doom, I reminisced about some of my harsher moments and unpleasant experiences battling CF over the last 39 years.

This may shock my friends, but I have wanted to kill myself on a few occasions. In particular, in my late teens when in our family kitchen with my twin brother Jez after a night out when I picked up a knife with the intention of cutting my wrists in desperation of my plight. Jez came to my rescue that night by talking sense into me and allowing me to cry my frustration away.

Other lowlights include:

The countless IV treatments which have stretched me both physically and emotionally.

Making myself sick in order to clear my lungs before playing sport in the late 1980s and 1990s.

My first year at university and the rollercoaster of my health and lung deterioration.

Writing a damning two-page list of my ailments and CF-related side effects in 1989 when at a peak of annoyance.

The grim aftermath of a shockingly bad cold in the mid-1990s and seeking reassurance from my good friend Paul that I would eventually overcome it.

Being forced awake in the middle of certain nights; choking and desperately trying to catch my breath.

The embarrassment of a bag of my IV syringes and needles falling down from a train's overhead compartment onto startled commuters – *"It's not what you think!"* was all I could muster.

I drift back to listening to my music. A little while later, the song 'Novio' by Moby came on and quite literally pinned me to the bed.

This is my chosen song – the song I wish to be played at my funeral, in the church as my coffin is brought in. Up till now, I've never disclosed this song choice to anyone, even my wife – let's call it my morbid secret.

I doubt Moby would have intended for this song to end up signifying the demise of someone, but to me, it's always been so haunting and atmospheric that I feel it's entirely fitting.

The only problem is that the song is not that long, so it would need to be played on a loop.

But this song has been chosen for other deeper reasons than its acoustic wonderment. This song makes me feel childlike. CF has always kept me looking youthful and boyish.

This boy has lived long enough to become a man, though I feel I'm always cocooned by my condition. However, I can never really escape from what I used to be – a sick boy. Could CF be the Alcatraz of illnesses?

My final thoughts on this most sombre of nights centred on the perception of others about my CF. I honestly believe that it would be a profound surprise and a shock for a lot of people to realise how serious my condition actually is. As it's not well known or understood, the majority of people have not the faintest idea how cruel and life-threatening the disability is. CF does kill and it finishes off sufferers early in their lives. It brings to mind comedian Spike Milligan's request for his tombstone: *'I told you I was ill'*.

There might be an even bigger surprise for those that know me that I even contemplate such depressive and morbid thoughts, let alone that I have already chosen my funeral song. To them I normally seem pretty positive and stoic. The bottom line is that I would defy even the most spirited and upbeat person not to occasionally succumb to and be beaten down by such a relentless illness as CF.

For now as tiredness takes me to a more relaxed state, this CF soldier is ready for sleep. Today's journey has come to an end. It's all quiet on the Wotton front...

25. Something Changed

Thursday 16 September 2010

Something changed today. I had an awakening. I have decided to share and open up to the outside world about my struggle with CF. This epiphany came to light during a discussion with Ailsa Herd, a friend of a friend who had previously supported the UK CF Trust with its public relations.

We met in a coffee shop near London's Tottenham Court Road to discuss my CF life and story. Predictably, as soon as I began to talk about my health experiences with a total stranger, the underlying emotion came to the fore. When I breached the subject of the CF friends who had died I was unable to suppress the tears and eventual sobbing.

For most of my life, this is how it's been for me. It was never that easy to talk openly about my life-threatening illness as it's such a personal and sensitive subject. That's why I've tended to opt for silence on the matter. It's telling that I've waited nearly 40 years before I felt I was in the right place emotionally and physically to find my voice and share my story and insights.

I've always been too emotional and it felt quite a struggle to even mention it to my nearest and dearest, let alone spread the word to a wider public. Inside and outside of work, I've tended to reveal my secret on a 'need to know only' basis. I had little outlet for this emotion and decided to bottle it all up for all these years. That's a long time to leave it all pent up. But that's how I chose to handle my health time bomb.

Over the years, I chose to suppress all my emotions about CF and be very guarded about disclosing it to strangers or raising it too often with family and friends. I never wanted to be viewed as the 'ill person' and be defined by my CF and I certainly never wanted anyone to feel sorry for me or to be pitied.

I feel that a lot of my silence stems from the fact that my condition is unfortunately not that well known or understood and it cannot be easily seen or ever properly imagined by most people. This harsh reality most definitely added to my strong desire to keep my condition tucked away as much as possible. Indeed, it became my inconvenient truth.

From my perspective, because I knew that my illness was not going to magically disappear, there seemed little point in 'going on' about it to others. I never wanted to sound like a broken record by mentioning it or complaining too much or too often to those around me. I also felt that by minimising the time I spoke about 'mein kampf', I would reduce its importance in my life which would in turn make me feel less affected by it. I'm sure these verbal barriers were a subconscious form of self-protection.

On the surface I have always looked fairly well and I'm good at covering things up. I'm sure at times that a lot of my friends would be inclined to almost forget I had an illness. As I didn't raise the subject most people probably felt I didn't want to talk; which led to a stand-off that was mutually beneficial for both parties. It truly became the illness that dare not speak its name.

People are not mind readers and over the years they would not have been able to predict how I would respond to being probed about the state of my illness. I can only imagine that this must have left them with a conundrum: *"Do I mention it to Tim or not? Do I ask him how his health is or do I wait for him to bring it up? Surely, he'll let me know when he wants to talk about it. I don't want to upset him. He doesn't like to talk about it so I'll do the same."*

At one end of the spectrum, I've noticed that there are some people I've encountered in life who really don't want to feel uncomfortable, even for a short while, by asking about someone's ill health or difficult times. These 'human ostriches' – with their heads in the sand – ignore the situation and hope it goes away. At the other end, quite a lot of my friends have always made the point of asking me how I'm fairing every time they see me.

Similarly, in my sporting life, it was preferable to keep my illness under wraps as it always felt at odds with my healthy pursuit of exercise. I never wanted to seek sympathy, but in particular, I never wanted it while playing sport and trying to keep up with my healthy peers.

But after so many years of secrecy and protection with my inner turmoil, bitterness and frustration locked away, there was a huge amount of unresolved sadness, resentment and emotion under the surface.

When I did attempt to speak in public about my CF at charity fundraisers and at formal events, like the time I was invited to engage a big audience at a sports related event in the Houses of Parliament in 2006, the emotion would seep through the cracks. Usually tears would be right around the corner.

Over the last few years, there's been a groundswell of change rumbling in me and I felt the desire to be more open with people about my condition and what it has taken for me to still be here when so many with CF have sadly passed away. I now really want friends to ask me how my health is going.

I'm sure that the birth of my son Felix, the enormity of being a father and the repercussions for my longevity acted as a catalyst. It helped to open the emotional floodgates. I sought out my first ever course of counselling from a local church. I might have taken this up before then but it had never really been available or on offer to me by the UK National Health Service.

I didn't feel as if I was losing the plot as such, I just felt that the time was right to talk and unburden myself of some of my inner demons – unpick a few of my layers of distress – in order to ease the tension of my built-up well of emotion. At that point, it had to be someone completely neutral to listen and navigate me through the choppy waters from silence to sound.

Only this summer, following a difficult situation at work, I had the revelation that surviving CF had been the biggest achievement in my life but it was hidden away and I wasn't talking about it or using it for my own or others' benefit.

During my chat with Ailsa today, sitting outside that coffee shop on a pleasantly warm September afternoon, I decided to take the lid off my 'CF Pandora's Box' and reflect on my life – past, present and future – my trials and tribulations, happy times and my survival strategies. I felt inspired to identify what it was that had made the difference in keeping me alive and defying the odds.

With my conscience stirred, I stepped out on a journey of self-discovery that began to shake up my mind and awaken my soul to the overriding desire to share my hard-fought but enriching life-lessons in order to help myself and others. At the same time, I felt the need to increase the understanding of CF and inspire people that there is usually a way to overcome difficulties.

While Ailsa went inside to buy us coffee refills, I was left to ponder how I was going to make my story feel compelling. It was obvious that I would need to look deep within myself for the answers.

I instinctively knew that I'd have to consider my past – what had my illness taught me about life and what wisdom had it bestowed upon me? What could my past tell me about my future?

I had to look around me for support in my quest to be more open and visible. Who could help me to fulfil my burning desire to share my narrative? Who would be the right people, familiar or strangers, who could assist me on my journey of discovery?

I also needed to gaze ahead to my hopeful and desired future and how that might shape my messaging. As Helen Keller said, "The only thing that's worse than being blind is having sight but no vision."

I started to contemplate what resources were available to spread my news? What books, technology, mentors, contacts and networks could I tap into? I definitely understood that the magnitude of what I wanted to share would require help and resources.

Finally, I felt the need to look above me and pray that I was doing the right thing and the right people and resources would come into my life.

As Ailsa and I sipped our next round of drinks we made the decision to start a blog based on my diary extracts during 2010 and my life experiences and insights. It would build on the journal I had already been writing and push extracts of my CF insights to the general public, CF community, family and friends. We would launch it at the start of 2011 via social media and see how it progressed using a viral approach.

There's a hypothetical law of the universe indicating that what you give out or transmit is reflected back at you. In my case, as soon as I had decided to open up, people would be drawn towards me.

Well this law began right then and there outside that coffee shop. Something amazing happened when a complete stranger, who just happened to be sitting next to Ailsa, reached out and handed me a freshly written note containing his name, phone number and some academic text. Before leaving, he mentioned that he had overheard some of our conversation about my health and felt compelled to share the helpful quotes. On the back of the paper were his contact details and a quote by the Swiss psychotherapist and psychiatrist Carl Yung:

"He who looks outside dreams;
He who looks inside awakes."

To say that we were dumbfounded would be an understatement.

A little while later Ailsa and I hugged and parted company. As I strolled back to the tube, it gave me time to consider what had just happened.

This newly decreed declaration to share my inner feelings and CF journey to friends and strangers alike induced a mix of emotions in me. In part it would be liberating to break the silence and cathartic to share my inner feelings but it would equally be laced with some level of dread that I was planning to be so bold and open after so many years.

I hoped it would offer me the much needed opportunity to reduce the underlying sadness and tension that had built up for nearly 40 years. Overall, my gut instinct told me it was the right thing to do and over the next few weeks, I decided to share my idea with some close friends to get their feedback and hopeful endorsement.

This afternoon I felt some of my hefty burden was lifted. It was a new beginning. Something had changed.

26. As Good as It Gets

Friday 1 October 2010

Today's the day. I go back to see my doctor at Frimley Park Hospital to establish whether all these rotten weeks of intensive IV treatment have made a substantial difference to my lungs and general health. It's the day I hope beyond all hope that my IV treatment will be finished and I can get my life back.

I had what I hoped to be my last dose of IV drugs this morning in order to reap their benefit on my lungs as much as possible while the IV line was still inserted. After all, I feel that while I've got the damn line in my body, I might as well use it!

After driving to the hospital, I endured the habitual wait in the CF unit reception area for my appointment with Doctor Knight. This allowed me to reflect on the last few weeks of IV hell – all the usual trials and tribulations that punctuate these treatments. That awful ordeal trying to get the PICC line into my arm seems a lifetime ago. Since then I've had over three weeks of IV drugs and countless difficult and frustrating moments. The last week in particular has dragged on horribly and felt most onerous.

It made me smile when I remembered a recent visit to a work colleague's house for morning tea and the shock for those who saw me looking drowsy from my drugs. I'd come straight from my elongated morning IV session and was feeling at a naturally low ebb. One of the other colleagues initially thought I was a bit aloof, even withdrawn and uncommunicative, which is not my usual persona in the office. I later explained to them that they had met the other Tim Wotton, the drug induced one!

Finally I got called into see my doctor. I had butterflies in my stomach. I was just so desperate to impress on him how much my lungs had improved and how ready I was to stop the IV and get on with my life.

Adding to my anxiety, it was raining that autumn morning which always makes my lungs more productive and could mask how well my lungs actually were. Would my doctor rate my health well enough for the IV course to finish and hence deem it necessary to remove this awful long line in my arm?

It's not always been a foregone conclusion and it hasn't always gone my way. One time an IV session during my university days was extended by my doctor for a week longer than I'd expected. Even my procrastinations didn't make any difference. I had to suck it up for another whole week in order to really clean up my health. I distinctly remember being so annoyed and frustrated, that I marched to the local town centre, where I entered the nearest bar to down a pint and a cocktail shooter!

After a bit of a chat it was time for the dreaded breathing tests into the standard spirometer machines. I've performed these peak flow tests well over a thousand times in my lifetime and on each occasion I'm willing for my results to be improved from the previous appointment. How I hate blowing into these devices. Each time I blow into one, I feel like the sick patient and child all over again. It's as if the mouthpiece is some form of time machine transporting me back to my first paediatric appointment.

My breathing and blowing go well and luckily my tests are good enough for the IV treatment to come to an end. I finally hear the words I've been waiting for all morning: *"Tim, I think we can complete this course and take that IV line out!"*

A nurse takes the long tube out of my arm and clears up all the dried blood and dead skin that have built up over the last three weeks under the dressing. With my arm feeling surprisingly lighter and all bandaged up, I go to the pharmacy to pick up some oral medication prescribed by the doctor to help transition me back to post-IV life.

It's an odd feeling as my body is still heavily fatigued from the heavy IV drugs, not least the session I had first thing this morning. However, once an IV course is completed, it feels quite euphoric despite the tiredness. In fact, I will remain wiped out for a couple of weeks as a result of the debilitating drugs. Only those people who have had to suffer such medication and time away from their normal lives will fully appreciate how it feels to get your life back on track – it's probably one of the purest highs I ever feel!

At the same time, it's one of the rare moments when I feel normal and bursting with hope. I waved the white flag to begin the IVs over three weeks ago when it felt as if everything I did was like walking through treacle. I am now finishing them, weary but jubilant, walking on air!

The sense of freedom and release is so intense that it almost feels as if I'm being let out of prison after a short sentence. As I walk out the exit, my natural reaction is to think to myself "What now?" I look around, watching medics and patients busily getting on with their day, and I try to figure out what to do next. I quite literally stagger out of my medical-induced hibernation to face the real world again.

To make all this more palatable I have tended to follow a stick and carrot, pain and reward approach to medical appointments and especially IV treatments. After a bit of suffering I feel the need to treat myself. Historically, when my hospital was the Royal Brompton in London, I would indulge myself in some retail therapy by going shopping on King's Road after appointments. Since I've been going to Frimley Park Hospital, my ritual has changed to frequenting the nearby McDonalds for some fast food on the way home.

Things have changed in the way I conduct myself following an IV course over the last 39 years. I have matured my approach and learned the best ways to reintegrate myself back into society in a more measured and sensible manner.

For most of my late teens and twenties, when my social life was all important, I felt that the IVs held me back and I hated to miss out on socials and league hockey games. So as soon as the course was completed, I used to get straight back onto the hockey field or bar – usually on the same day! I would often then go hell for leather for the next few weeks and burn myself out far too quickly. This stupidity would invariably hasten a cold and affect my lung function. Back then it became a vicious circle but I was loath to change my post-IVs madness.

Nowadays, I try to lead a monk-like existence during the IVs so that the drugs can work as well as possible and I gradually ease myself back into normal life once the course is completed. That way the IV treatments are an enabler for me and act as a springboard to more seamlessly get back on with my family, sporting, work and social life once again.

I feel delighted that this eventful IV course has now come to an end. Ahead of me lies a weekend of relaxation before I have to climb back on the proverbial bicycle of life and begin to pedal again. The realistic truth is that I'm going to feel as good over these next few days as I'm ever likely to feel at any stage this year.

It will be a special weekend of feeling reasonably healthy. The magic of these post-IV days is tough to put into words. I can do my forced expressed air technique – a huff to us CFers – and it doesn't produce a full-on coughing fit. I can laugh again without triggering a spasm. I've got my arm back – where the IV line was – in use and can play rough and tumble with Felix. I'm once more a helpful dad to Felix and husband to Katie. I can do some athletic warm-up stretches and go for a jog in the local park. I can do my weights and press-ups again to boost my physique after nearly a month of inactivity. It will be the reverse of healthy people who complain of just one weekend per year when they feel unwell.

I can return to my 'usual CF regime' minus the additional IV drugs. Amazingly, getting back to just my normal drug regime feels oddly bearable after three weeks of IV hell. Imagine a life where reverting back to a regimen of only 40 pills a day, nebulisers, inhalers, injections and physiotherapy feels like a welcome break?

Tomorrow, I'll get up early in the morning when Felix calls out. I'll enjoy spending some quality time with him and at the same time give Katie a well-deserved lie-in. It's only fair as she's given so much of her time to Felix and his early starts. She's also been protecting me while my IVs progressed and shielded me from the extra tiredness of being a full-time parent.

Weather permitting, I'll also go for my first light jog tomorrow afternoon. As much as my body will feel alien to me, my ankles will hurt, my lungs will burn and I'll have little energy, I know it will be a worthwhile effort to push my body through. Like an antique car that hasn't been started in a while, I need to turn my engine over to breathe life back into my body.

Even though I'm keen to be more open about my CF struggle, I still want and need to give off the persona of being fit and able – this includes the ongoing perception of me as a healthy and fit business consultant and sportsman.

Quite a lot of my time living with CF feels like a giant act covering up how I'm feeling physically and mentally. My coping mechanism at these times is to have a positive rather than negative front for everyone I encounter.

When I see people at work on my first day back this coming Monday, I expect someone will greet me with the often said remark: *"I haven't seen you for a while. Have you been away on holiday?"*

"Yes, I had a great time, thanks," I'll say, tongue in cheek. Little do they know and how much it would surprise them if I replied instead, *"No. I've been having an intensive course of intravenous drugs to treat my incurable illness cystic fibrosis, which you've never heard of!"*

This special time doesn't last for long though. I'll enjoy the rest of today, the weekend and most of next week feeling relatively well with little or no coughing. What is most people's normality is only fleeting for me. It's maybe how a dragonfly would feel during its short couple of days of life. For me, it's as good as it gets.

27. The Phoenix

They say a week is a long time in politics, but it's also a long time for a CF sufferer following an intravenous (IV) course. This week has been all about resetting my mindset and positivity following the hard-hitting course of treatment. I have learned the hard way over the past 39 years that it's best to ease myself back into all my usual life activities.

In Greek mythology, a phoenix is a bird which is cyclically regenerated or reborn, obtaining new life by arising from the ashes of its predecessor. After coming back from around 60 of these traumatic IV sessions, it definitely feels as if I'm rising like a phoenix from the ashes. Following each IV a tangible feeling of starting all over again pervades- of being born again and getting another chance at living my life. Indeed, I often joke that I've made more comebacks than Frank Sinatra!

The IV drugs have helped my lungs by reducing the infection in my chest and I know that I'm healthier than before it all began. Trust me I wouldn't sign up for the whole rigmarole of IVs if they didn't produce some improvement in my lung function. I know that I'm feeling better; I just don't have much energy and exuberance straight away. My body whispers and the respiratory tests at the CF clinic last week have indicated an improvement. Yet there's still a 'but'...

Similar to the after-effects of chemotherapy medication on cancer patients, it's not an instantaneous return to energy for the initial two weeks after my IVs have finished. I'm utterly jaded, sluggish and out of kilter – imagine having severe jet-lag for a week and that will offer an insight into how I feel post-IVs.

For me the rehabilitation lasts for exactly a fortnight before I can definitely feel a sense of vitality again. Insult is added to injury during my first week back as insomnia kicks in and I tend to need herbal sleeping tablets to get any sleep at night. This is mainly due to the dramatic change in my body from being zonked out from the IV drugs and then reverting back to normal medications which don't have the same sedative effect. It's a huge frustration that I'm desperate to get on with my life again but all the while, I'm feeling sluggish because of the effects of the nightly sleeping pills.

Despite these extra limitations, getting back into physical activity is an important part of my 'Road to Wellville'. As stated before, exercise has always been so integral to my battle with CF, acting as a barometer of exactly how my health is. It also serves to bolster my self-esteem that I'm not being beaten by the illness and I can keep up with my healthy peers.

During the preceding week, I initiated this latest fitness riposte with a couple of light jogs around our local park. After leaving the house looking and feeling fairly good I returned after about 20 minutes of interval running looking as if I've been dragged through a hedge backwards and panting like my brother's dog.

These first couple of runs post IVs are extremely tough. My whole body seems to creak these days, not just my lungs. But I'm drawn towards pushing myself on. Once I have this new lease of life, I know I've got to get back out there to make the most of the health I could have and want to have rather than drift back into mediocre health.

Following the warm-up jogs in that initial week, I still have a deep burning desire to once again play field hockey for my club London Edwardians. The jogs serve as a loosener. An actual league game of hockey against a healthy bunch of men is the real test for my fitness regime.

What's more, this is my twenty fifth consecutive league hockey season and it's a run I don't want to end while I am still able to get on that pitch and make a contribution while at the same time 'tuning up' my lungs. My benchmark is my own dad who played hockey non-stop for well over 55 years so I've got a long way to go to beat his record.

Few 39 year olds I know are still partaking in competitive sport and they all have their reasons not to. I'm sure most find it's easier not to be active once they've got a busy work and family life. Some people need a goal to get running again – something to aim for, like a 10K run, marathon or triathlon. For me I have my hockey.

To keep going with my favourite sport provides me with the ultimate motivation. This exercise has an obvious correlation with being as healthy and active as I can be and in turn hopefully being able to live as long as possible to be around for Katie, Felix, family and friends.

This has all led to my return to hockey action today for the first time since May. I have been selected to play for London Edwardians men's third team in a league game in Epsom, Surrey. In keeping with my 'Windows 7' weekend activity plan, I've been invited this evening to join some old university friends for Steve Kerin's fortieth birthday party in a bar around Clapham, London. To use Star Wars parlance, it's time for my empire to strike back.

As I drive mid-morning to Reigate to play the local team, I'm finding that the health-kick I felt last weekend is rapidly dissipating. A few light jogs are useful but they in no way prepare me for running full-pelt around an AstroTurf pitch. For some reason, my lungs seem to pick up on the tension filling my body and I nervously start to cough more heavily than I had done for a while. What great timing I thought to myself – this is the time for my lungs to behave themselves, not to play me up!

This then kick-starts all the doubts and insecurities that fill my head prior to playing a league hockey game these days. For a lot of the previous 25 hockey seasons, I would just turn up and play and not have any real self-doubt about how my lungs would hold up. Nowadays, my mind is awash with worry and I flit in between feeling capable and incapable of playing, often changing my mindset a few times during the course of an hour.

But I've been picked to play and play I will. Having said that, I actually started the game as a substitute. This was no bad thing as it allowed me to view the opposition, where I would be playing on the pitch and who I would most likely be man-marking. After about fifteen minutes when my team was already two goals down, I get the call from the captain to get warmed up and ready to come on to play.

As I did my stretches on the side of the pitch, I recalled the battle cry from William Shakespeare's historic play Henry V: "Once more unto the breach, dear friends, once more…"

As I step across the white line and slap hands with the team-mate that I'm replacing, I amend the Henry V call to arms, defiantly shouting to myself, "Once more unto the pitch, dear friend, once more…"

However, there was no dream ending to the game as we were quite easily beaten 7-1 by a more youthful opposition. I played for 15 minutes either side of half time which was more than enough as this stage in my rehabilitation. I couldn't have tried any harder but boy IT WAS HARD WORK…

After the match, I went for a warm down run around the pitch in order to prevent my muscles from stiffening too much. This got me reflecting that in my playing prime, I had to think hard after a game to remember any mistakes. Now it's quite a mixed bag. I'm not able to fully make a difference to the outcome of the game anymore as I could in my younger playing days. Plus, my coughing at times can be pretty shocking for those on the pitch and is difficult for me to control.

But while there's breath in this body of mine, I'll keep playing on. The sense of achievement is magnified each time I play competitive sport and that is a worthwhile feeling. It's also a sensation that I cling onto when the going gets tough battling CF.

Tomorrow after such an onslaught on my body, I know I will suffer and my limbs will be stiff. There's little doubt that I'll be doing an impression of the Tin Man from Wizard of Oz. It's all worth it though. After all, there's no gain without some pain.

As I head out this evening to join my college friends for a night of revelry I felt proud of my earlier sporting accomplishment. I had this well-earned tiredness coursing through my body but at the same time I felt extremely alive and vibrant. After having done the hard graft, I could now go out to have some fun.

Tonight's party begins the year of fortieth birthdays for a lot of my peers and my own landmark is fast approaching. Five more months to go until 17 March, 2011 – wow, I believe I'm really going to make it!

As I triumphantly enter the bar tonight and see my dear friends, I will change the words of that Henry V rallying cry to, 'Once more unto the bar, dear friends, once more...'

Over the next few months, I will strive to improve my fitness and build my immune system by sticking to my daily drugs regime, managing my diabetes, taking pretty good care of myself and having my flu jab.

I'll keep my feet on the ground after this half game of hockey today and won't get too ahead of myself. I'll keep playing and gradually build up my health but the amount of exercise I can achieve is all relative to my level of fitness. I certainly won't be taking part in an Iron Man competition any time soon.

My sport and socialising help to keep me going, feeling as if I'm conducting a normal life, and helping me to defy the ravages of my illness. I emphatically know it makes a difference to the outcome of my health and my longevity on this planet.

The phoenix has flown from the ashes once more...

28. Regeneration

Saturday 23 October 2010

Today I returned to the Old Cranleighans Hockey Club in Thames Ditton, Surrey for a league game for my club team against London Academicals. As well as another step in my way back to fitness, it's also the 10-year anniversary of a life-changing moment that took place at this same venue.

People often refer to an 'event' or 'moment' that changes their lives forever. Mine came after a frightful experience here. In theological terms, I had a spiritual awakening. Biologically, I endured a restoration of my body and lungs. As I drove into the car park of the ground and saw the AstroTurf pitch vivid memories started to flood back...

A decade ago on Saturday 25 November 2000, I was due to play an early afternoon league game of hockey for the men's first team of London Edwardians. I was approaching 30 which was the average life expectancy age of CF sufferers as it was then. This significant milestone for a CF sufferer had been hanging over me my entire life. In reality, this life expectancy was like a version of kryptonite hanging around my neck, weighing me down.

For the majority of this time, I had physically battled the condition by my sheer determination and will to survive. Mentally, I didn't really have an identified approach to dealing with the condition. Spiritually, I had no real faith, tending instead to be angry at God for my suffering.

Back then, I chose to keep CF hidden away from all except close friends and family. I was especially selective with which work and sport colleagues I confided my 'secret' with as I didn't want to be stigmatised as sick and be treated any differently.

I recall that by the age of 29 my relentless desire not to be beaten had taken its toll. I was flagging severely, physically worn out from using up any remaining inner strength needed to carry on the fight. I had sadly seen the majority of my fellow CF friends pass away before the elusive 30 milestone which made me question how long I could survive myself.

Ten years ago, I was attempting a double comeback. I was resuming my hockey career after the habitual three weeks off for intravenous treatment and had managed to force my way back into a competitive and thriving first team squad.

This meant a lot to me. Hockey was my *raison d'être*. It mattered more than anything in my life back then. Using the ability I've been given and winning with my friends was what Saturdays were all about. I knew that the majority of CFers would be closer to death at the age of 30 so getting ready to play competitive sport always felt liberating and powerful.

However, what I hadn't taken into account was that my mind was a time bomb waiting to explode. Looking back, I'm convinced I was subconsciously affected and troubled by the sad news received the previous week that one of my closest friends with CF had died. Their lungs became so infected that they coughed up a lot of blood and this culminated in their premature death.

Over time, CF can cause thinning of the airway walls. As a result, teenagers and adults with the condition may cough up blood – *hemoptysis*, as it's known medically. Coughing up blood is usually caused by a ruptured small blood vessel and this is a common complication in people with CF.

This spitting up of blood or bloody mucus comes up from the lungs and throat and often looks bubbly and is usually bright red, because it is mixed with air and mucus. I had coughed up blood before and it always felt scary, especially the first time when I was unaware what was happening. It normally constitutes a couple of tablespoons worth of actual blood and then the blood tapers off after a half an hour.

There's this gurgling sound in my chest which is the warning that this particular cough is different. Instantly I know I'll be coughing up some blood instead of mucous. One can taste the blood on the way up and it's very warm.

Up to this point I had never had a severe haemoptysis which is when more than half a pint of blood is discharged. But I was aware that this acute level of bleeding could be life threatening.

Back on that fateful day in November 2000, as is typical of any pre-match routine, the team went on a warm up run around the near-by field. Out of the blue, I coughed so hard that I must have ruptured one of my small lung blood vessels. Straight away I heard the ominous gurgle followed by the metallic taste in my mouth. I immediately knew what this signified and what was coming next. My lungs didn't disappoint me. Next I had a mouth full of blood which I had to surreptitiously spit out. I broke away from the team and hid behind a bush, where I began to ceaselessly spew thick red blood.

I expect the rest of the players must have thought I was taking a comfort break. How wrong they would have been. The last thing I was taking from the amount of blood produced was comfort.

Still in the nearby field, we got in a huddle for the team talk and I was asked to start the game as a defender. Suddenly everything was in slow motion – similar to the madness of a car crash. Was this blood a pre-cursor to my own death? Did it feel like this for my CF friend before her demise? Was my body finally ready to cave in and was this game my last bow?

It was very surreal but at the same time calm and delightfully peaceful. I felt completely at ease with the world. I remember looking skywards as our team captain delivered the match tactics. It was a beautiful sunny autumn day with blue skies – almost heavenly – as if I was ready to be received above. I felt the urge to reach up in order to be grabbed by the hand as if God was welcoming me to join him.

It seemed fitting that if today was the day that I departed this world, then so be it and playing the sport I loved was the ultimate way for me to go rather than malingering in a hospital bed.

"Come on Wotton; for one last time take it all in – birdsong, warmth of the sun on my face, the hockey stick in my

hand, smiles of my sporting friends and their laughter... life is beautiful!"

I even had a vision of one of my brothers delivering my eulogy in a packed church, explaining that I was playing hockey in my last hours and saying the immortal words, *'It's what Tim would have wanted.'*

I kept this dramatic secret from the rest of the team except for my good friend Julian Hale, who knew about my health. I alerted him to the situation and asked him to look out for me on the pitch.

I was still generating blood from my lungs. As I walked onto the pitch with tears in my eyes I never considered backing down and not starting that game. I suppose I felt that this was my fate and a relief at last from a 30-year battle with a relentless and unforgiving disease.

I had a flashback to Mohammed Ali's 'Rumble in the Jungle' fight. After feeling the superhuman power of George Foreman's punches in the first round, Ali stood in his corner waiting for the bell to start round two. He had a look in his eyes where he knew that this was his moment of destiny: he'd need to reach down into his very soul to find out whether he could defy the odds and win the fight of his life.

In the seconds before the whistle commenced the game, I made the decision that if this was my time to die, then I was going to go out on my shield.

"Enough is enough. You can't fight this illness anymore. It's your time now. You've done more than anyone expected. No-one will ever forget what you achieved in your life!"

Something happened on the way to heaven.

That day I did survive the game and I stopped coughing up blood after 15 minutes of the match starting. It clearly wasn't a major haemorrhage. On reflection I suspect that the death of my CF friend played with my mind. The blood I was coughing up wasn't that awful in the scheme of things but at that very moment in time I was scared and had convinced myself that it could be fatal.

At half-time, Mark Twain's quote, after hearing that his obituary had been published in the New York Journal, sprung to mind: *"The reports of my death are greatly exaggerated."*

Little did I know in the clubhouse after the game that rather than being my demise that this event was actually the first day of the rest of my life. Heaven could wait for now. The heaven I thought that I was going to that day was actually here on earth and I instinctively knew that the time had come to find new ways of battling this condition. Through this drama I realised that my physical approach on its own was never going to be enough. Perhaps God was looking to introduce himself to me that day rather than actually take me away from Earth?

I felt the need to share this story with my close friends as a way of coming to terms with how it made me feel and what it meant to me. It goes without saying that it was and still is a very emotive anecdote for me to convey. As a direct result of that game, I have become more open about my CF with the sporting world and the majority of my fellow players would know about my health dynamic.

Significantly, the poignant nature of this life-affirming occurrence had such an effect on me that ever since, it has dictated how I approach living with CF.

My fresh beginning took the direction of my life down a different path. A month after that ominous game, I began dating Katie, which in turn led to marriage and the later birth of our cherished son Felix. Six months after the incident, I felt drawn towards exploring some level of faith. During the Alpha introduction to Christianity course in Wimbledon, while reading the Bible, I discovered a passage from Hebrews 2:15 which liberated me: *'free those who all their lives were held in slavery by their fear of death.'*

I now felt released from the shackles of impending doom that had imprisoned me all my life and instead of blaming God for my illness, I asked him to help me conquer it! As a positive consequence of this newly discovered inner peace, I realised the potential of and developed my mental approach to battling CF to complement my on-going physical intensity.

29. Far from the Madding Crowd

Wednesday 3 November 2010

We went on a trip to the sea-side town of Brighton the day before Katie's landmark 40th birthday. For us, it's a convenient place to visit, being only an hour's drive from where we live in South London. But it's more than that. It's been our bolt-hole over the last ten years to hide away together for a mixture of happy and sad reasons.

We stayed in Brighton during our early courting days. It's where we've escaped to for days and nights out, including our third year wedding anniversary over a few extremely warm days in 2006.

This morning we both enjoyed the relaxation of a spa treatment at Champneys. This was followed by a lovely lunch at a seafood restaurant I'd found online called 'Due South' which is located on the beachfront near the old pier.

We experienced some particularly heavy winds that day which was of course magnified by being on the coast. As we strode purposely to the restaurant over the heavy shingle we were practically swept off our feet. On taking our seats at a sea-view table, it was virtually blowing a gale outside with all the advertising boards being heavily buffeted. The irony was not lost on us that even though there was a storm taking place outside, we were trying to escape from our own personal hurricane.

The timing of her milestone birthday was not very kind on either of us, but particularly for Katie. Only a short while before, we had attempted IVF again with frozen embryos that were left over from the fresh IVF cycle that had given us Felix.

To have just one child when battling with the uncertainties of IVF felt unachievable so we hadn't previously planned or dared to dream of having a large family. During the IVF rollercoaster where the odds are less than 25 per cent success, we hoped for the best but feared the worst. IVF is such a strange dynamic because although a single child would feel amazing, we had to be prepared for the double whammy of twins. So when you do IVF, you've got to plan for more than one child when realistically getting lucky with one is highly improbable.

A few weeks ago, despite having never had any previous success with frozen embryos, amazingly Katie became pregnant... with twins. Our dream didn't last long. Unfortunately, both embryos didn't hold for long and Katie suffered another miscarriage before the 12-week mark.

It was against this torturous backdrop that we escaped for the day to Brighton. We probably needed to get away from everything that reminded us of our loss. It was particularly tough on Katie for such a tragedy to precede her 40th. Today was designed to blow away the cobwebs of despair and the heavy wind outside the restaurant was doing its best to achieve that.

I believe that the majority of our friends and family would have been shocked by our latest IVF attempt, especially after all we'd been through with our previous struggle to have a child. Additionally, there were the difficulties we'd negotiated since the birth of Felix and I'm sure it would have been the last thing they would have expected. We decided therefore to keep it to ourselves and not let anyone know what we were doing – not even our closest family.

In so many ways my relationship with Katie had at times been to hell and back during the preceding years. To begin with, the six cycles of IVF were a significant hardship for us to endure. A long and painful forty-eight-hour birth felt cruel for Katie as she had to suffer again following all those years of IVF. The subsequent nerve damage that Katie suffered while giving birth to Felix left her needing to sit on a cushion for the last three years. To add insult to injury, Katie's body and mental state were seriously affected by the nerve pain she was constantly enduring.

If asked during those initial dark years if having a child was 'worth it', I know that she would not immediately have been able to answer in the affirmative. It's a brutal but true fact that our beautiful son came at quite an initial cost to my relationship with Katie.

It took years for us to become accustomed to all the little ways we could fall out with each other over big and small parenting scenarios. We never used to really argue before we became parents so the adjustment was considerable. We'd even managed to successfully navigate the stressful IVF cycles which can test a couple's fortitude and in some cases be the cause of separation.

After three emotionally draining years of IVF we didn't plan our collective strategy of how we'd actually cope as parents when our child was finally with us. This included not having an agreed approach to child discipline. After going through so much, including a horrendous miscarriage with our first IVF attempt, we probably didn't want to jinx our luck by planning too much before we had that baby safely in our arms.

In short, Katie and I really struggled as a couple over the initial couple of years as parents. I know that's not uncommon for first-time parents but add in Katie's nerve pain, my ongoing CF regime and health protection and it was almost too much for us to bear.

There were many harsh moments when it would have been easier for me to quit and leave the relationship. Indeed, in the depths of our despair we actually discussed whether we'd bitten off more than we could chew and perhaps it would be best for us to separate.

However, these dramatic discussions were often 'in the heat of the moment' and splitting up was never seriously on the cards. From my own perspective, I was damned if I was going to go through six IVF cycles with Katie in order to have our much longed-for son, only for that prize to be the prime reason for us to finish. That very thought drove me on; guiding me to hang in there, learn the parenting game, pray hard and keep refining how Katie and I managed our relationship as a married couple and as parents.

The cumulative effect of parenting on our marriage and the enormity of being a father whilst shielding myself from worsening health acted as a catalyst which opened my emotional floodgates. I needed to do something different. Katie and I needed to talk through our issues but at that time, I really don't think we could have gone to a counsellor together – it would have been too raw for both of us.

As part of her pain management, Katie had the chance to discuss her struggle with her pain consultants. But what was there for me? This form of psychological help had never before been available to me by the National Health Service. After some local research, I sought out my first ever course of counselling from a local church. I didn't feel as if I was losing the plot as such. I wasn't in a state of disarray, but I knew that I had to chat to someone neutral.

Initially, it felt very odd to talk to someone I didn't know about such intimate issues. Surely enough, as I began to unpick my layers of tension and worry, tears followed. It was like unravelling the layers of an onion and dealing with the usual crying that would accompany such an act.

It soon became apparent that I could only take eight sessions with my counsellor. A lot of ground – and tears – had been covered and I couldn't see the value in exposing myself to digging even deeper into my psyche. I discharged myself as I felt it had done its job and helped me talk about some of my underlying stress – the cause and effect of our marital discord. It also empowered me to go home and engage Katie on the topics covered in order that we could examine the 'elephant in our room'.

One huge issue that affected me and in turn frustrated Katie was my interpretation of our situation, believing that we were a pair of 'lame ducks' during Felix's early years. I felt that we were victims – Katie's nerve pain and my CF– and that we couldn't manage anything normally. In the midst of our chats, often on the bench in our back garden, we learnt what was required to fix our problems. As with most discourse in a relationship, it wasn't just one of us that needed to change. We both had to meet half way and amend our ways and mindset... and keep sharing how we were feeling and acknowledge the good moments.

To further contextualise this for me and understand that we had hope in our marriage, we attended a good friend's wedding at this time and I latched onto the vicar's sermon where she conveyed that there was often more growth in a relationship in the attritional trough periods rather than in the peak happy times.

Punctuated throughout our early parenting years were the times Katie and I went away together for trips without Felix. We had nights and weekends away around the UK whilst our boy stayed with his grandparents. These moments of escapism proved invaluable to us on so many levels. Most significantly it showed us that we automatically reverted back to our pre-parenting calm and convivial dynamic. There were no arguments – we just got on well again!

These reviving times away from the daily grind reminded us why we were a couple in the first place and why we had made the commitment of marriage to each other. For me, this always felt gratifying and allayed my anxiety concerning the 'real' state of our relationship.

I instinctively knew that if we could resume being a married and loving couple again when it was just the two of us, that we were going to be OK in the long run. It felt positive that we could traverse through any number of storms in our lives and reach the rainbow on the other side together.

Once we got through the early couple of years and began to re-discover ourselves, we started to have the natural feeling of wanting to give Felix a playmate. We began to really notice the standard question from other parents when out with Felix: *"Is he your only one?"*

Having more children was something Katie would have wanted years ago but I was concerned that we needed to get back on track in our relationship before we attempted IVF again. I think Katie was seeing it through an emotional lens whilst I through a more practical one.

This dilemma coincided with another course of counselling I undertook; this time with Michelle Conn at Frimley Park hospital, which I was now eligible for. The hot topic was this – 'do we or don't we' go for another baby?

Michelle was very helpful in assisting me in writing a pros and cons list on a flip chart for attempting IVF again. Then in a coming together that closely resembled a business meeting rather than a romantic liaison, Katie and I had an extremely functional meeting where we both shared our pros and cons lists. It really was a stark contrast to the usual way a second child is planned by the majority of couples we know.

Interestingly, our pros lists were longer but the cons were bigger issues. After much soul-searching and deliberation, we decided to use our remaining frozen embryos in another IVF attempt. And that led us to today and our escapism to Brighton.

After lunch we went for a stroll, holding hands, on the seafront. From time to time, we would stop, look out to sea and hug. He had held each other in a similar way after each of the initial five IVF's that hadn't worked on the long and winding road to bring Felix into this world. We were both sad that we had lost the twins; Katie was understandably inconsolable. Sometimes in a relationship there are no words that can do justice to certain situations.

When dazed by all the horrible events that can rock a couple, we are always able to console each other with a timeless embrace.

I used the 'moment' to reflect on what it had taken to keep us together. I felt like it was a triumph of the spirit that we even attempted to go for another child, whatever the outcome.

We were lost on the way to Brighton but found each other again on that seafront.

30. Less Is More

Thursday 18 November 2010

For most of today I was in quite a depressed state about my life and lack of normal health. It definitely started off as one of my dark melancholic days. Then my eyes were opened again and I saw the light. It seems that whenever I'm in dire need of some context, I often discover it right there in front of me. These awakenings are integral to keep me humble and appreciative of the life I can lead as opposed to the life I can't...

My day started poorly after an awful morning getting ready to leave the house and get to work. There was an extended bout of coughing, followed by being sick on myself. As I was trying to rush through breakfast, I ended up bleeding onto my work shirt after the injection of insulin.

I expect it's the same for anyone with a long-term health condition that some days are worse than others. On certain days whatever could go wrong goes wrong. These mornings are just wretched and test my nerves to breaking point. I think my strong reserves of patience broke at about 8am this morning. The banks holding my river of perseverance were most definitely breached.

I got myself into a real strop about my health and life. I felt sorry for myself. I just didn't feel terribly alive and the morning mishaps added fuel to my fire. This carried on when I was in the office and built up throughout the morning. I had a face like thunder and was not my usual self at all. My normal sunny facade had been removed and I was replaced by a mean-spirited person.

As much as I tried to break out of my self-induced sulk, nothing seemed to be working. All my thoughts oscillated in a vicious circle of frustration and anger. Feeling generally fed up with my lot in life, the words "Everything is wrong!" continuously cropped up in my mind.

All this amalgamated into what I refer to as one of my "Why Me?" moods... "Why am I suffering when so many people go around without a care in the world?" "No one understands my daily struggle! People would be shocked if they knew what I have to go through every day!"

All that morning, I was consumed with self-pity. All my usual methods of breaking a negative mindset were not working. I went from meeting to meeting in a state of discord. This continued to my lunch break where I was going to a local restaurant to meet an old school friend for a catch up.

And then the phenomenon struck. As it always does when I'm desperately in need of a dose of reality; I saw something that changed my outlook instantly and brought my sorrow to an abrupt end.

As we sat down with our drinks and studied the food menu, I saw someone who put all my needless worries into perspective. At the next table, sitting in a wheelchair, and being assisted by a young female carer, was a twenty something man with what I believe was cerebral palsy.

He was so profoundly disabled that he needed his head strapped to a head rest and the carer needed to show him a board of letters so that he could point out what he was going to eat. All the time he was bobbing about in his chair, dribbling from his mouth and making high-pitched noises. I was spellbound by his desperate predicament and the diligent patience of his carer.

Throughout my life, when having a very dark CF moment, I will more often than not see someone out and about who is more disadvantaged or disabled than me. I can recollect when and where I witness these unfortunate and helpless people and the deep emotion they stir inside me.

These moments stop me in my tracks and practically freeze me to the spot. I feel immensely humbled by their situation and it completely brings me back down to earth with a bump. I realise immediately that my own circumstances are really quite bearable in comparison. "What have I got to worry about?" is my overriding sensation.

This in turn keeps my feet on the ground, helping me to rationalise my plight and see how my worries fit in with the bigger scheme of life. I automatically cogitate on all the normal things I am able to do and the sensations I can feel every day that are not possible for these poor people. I hone in on all the little things I can do for myself that are unimaginable for them – my ability to speak, touch, hear, walk, run, laugh, wash, drink, eat. The list is endless and very gratifying. These are the lowest common denominators in life that can be easily taken for granted and underplayed.

It's a cliché but it's true that whatever I battle with CF is insignificant alongside some people. There's always someone worse off than me. When I'm struggling with my own woes, this plain fact is all I need to remember is to rise above my angst and be thankful and happy again.

I believe that my pain and daily struggle have enhanced my own humility and allow me to see and appreciate others who also suffer mentally and physically. Time and again I'm more likely than my friends to spot other sufferers when out socially. Am I more pre-disposed to see them?

As much as I despise my daily battle with CF and diabetes, it has given me a perspective on life that many people will perhaps never attain or will only encounter later in life. I'm convinced that this rich appreciation of what life has to offer has made me the person I am today.

The perpetual likelihood of less time on this planet has given me a unique opportunity to appreciate the simple things more. In many ways, I believe that if a person was informed that their time on earth was severely limited from day one that they would have more appreciation of every living moment. In this scenario, less could well be more.

It's marvellous what you can see when you really open your eyes. Nearly 40 years of relentless suffering have taught me that life is far too precious to miss anything. Life really can be beautiful. One just has to stop and take it in from time to time. I expect that I value my continued existence more than healthier people that should appreciate it more.

Rather than counting each day, I think it's important to make each day count. I look to seize each and every day as much as possible. As I can't be sure how long I've got to leave my lasting legacy, I try to live for each moment, wanting to make my life matter in so many ways and with so many people.

I definitely see life as a privilege rather than a right. For me, every day feels special. Every extra day I'm alive feels like a bonus. Without wishing to sound fatalistic or too dramatic, I look at each day as potentially my last day on Earth. I feel the urge to dress accordingly – as if it's the last outfit I'll ever wear. Rather than waiting for that 'perfect day' to wear my favourite or newest clothes, I'll go ahead and put them on.

Each difficult moment surviving this unforgiving illness – and there have been many tough times like this morning and far worse – has opened my eyes and opened my heart. This 'awakening of my soul' has made me more sentimental as I want as much of my life as possible to be punctuated by worthwhile memories rather than mundane events.

My quality time playing rough and tumble with Felix matters. Each game of hockey I play has significant meaning. Every day of married life counts. Indeed, being the nostalgic one, I'll be the one that mentions our wedding anniversary date every month to Katie. Each new dawn and sunset I experience gives me hope. Every time I leave the house is another opportunity to make a difference to my own life and the life of others.

Living with this chronic condition has opened my eyes to the things in life that are really important and my level of appreciation for the simpler moments has been enriched. Life is too short to worry for long about minor issues. It's not always easy but I work hard to identify my blessings in life and be thankful for them. It's a short and merry life. I focus on what I can do rather on what CF stops me from doing and on what I do have rather than what I don't.

Because of these hard times any small pleasures and feel-good occasions really stand out and make an impact on me.

Through my exploits, I've been able to master one of the hardest and most sought-after tricks in life – knowing and appreciating when and why I'm feeling happy and content.

In a life of upheaval, where I face the eye of the illness storm every day, to counter it I instinctively look for tranquillity and peace around me. I'm able to find serenity and can calm my troubled soul by seeing beautiful surroundings, people and images where ever I am.

I find amazing inner peace in the beauty of nature – rainbows, blood-red sunsets, mysterious cloud formations, birds flocking, rays of light breaking through clouds, waves crashing against the shore, the roughness of the sea on a winter's day – these spectacular moments frame my life, allowing me to reflect and stand rapt in awe. I don't take for granted all the little things that I see around me that I want to remember for the time I have left.

Every day at work, home or socially, I need to experience a little human kindness or a natural miracle that serves as a reminder that I'm still alive to witness it.

As grim as my illness has been, I do feel blessed and while I'm still on this earth, there's so much to see and feel that there's no time to have my blinkers on and block things out. People can go a whole lifetime and not know what I know, see what I see and feel what I feel.

Every step of a CF life is a challenge and there seems to be hardly any low hanging fruit or easy pickings to get what you want. Nothing is taken for granted, particularly my health, which in turn has given me a richer perception on what is significant in life. This is even more vital on days, like today, when I've been struggling at a low ebb.

Even on such a day of hardship, there's usually a way for me to see the wider picture, smash the negativity and start appreciating what I do have rather than getting fixated on what I don't have; appreciating what matters and doesn't matter in life. Some days the sun doesn't shine, but with my eyes wide open, I can still find warmth in my heart and soul. Today was such a day.

31. Get Up and Go Again

Sunday 28 November 2010

I had a monumental dilemma on my mind today – a life-changing decision had to be made – one that could change the direction of my life and possibly the outcome of my longevity. I was forced to seriously consider whether it was the right time for me to retire from playing field hockey, my beloved and life-affirming sport...

This all came to the fore after an innocuous but extremely poignant incident yesterday during an away league game in Surrey for my London Edwardians team versus an experienced Epsom side.

I'm definitely at a stage of my hockey career where my mind plays tricks on me in the lead up to any game. Outside of the state of my fluctuating lung function, rain is and has always been a large factor for me in the lead up to a match. Even more of a quandary is rain that wasn't forecast and appears after I've already committed to play. That was the situation I faced yesterday on the way to the game due to commence at midday.

Throughout the forty minute drive to the Epsom pitch, I went through scattered rain showers which intensified my concerns about playing. It's not just the effect of the damp conditions on my lungs, making me prone to cough more; it's the real possibility of getting a chill on my chest that could cause long-term damage. The anxiety of this unexpected rain cranked up my inner fretful monologue...

"Should I play? This rain is making my lungs more congested. It's crazy to play. Will the rain ease off as it will be tough for me to play in this wet? Perhaps I should pull out?"

As is typical in the lead up to a game affected by rain, every five minutes my mind changed on whether I felt capable enough to play. The barrage of questions continued...

"Have they got enough players? Can they manage without me?"

"Maybe I'll play the first half and then stop?"

"I'm almost at the ground. I can't duck out now. I'm ready to play so come hell or high water, I might as well play whatever the conditions!"

It was raining very heavily on my arrival. I sat in the car questioning why I put myself through this ordeal... *"What should I do now? This is worse than I imagined."*

And then one of my team mates walked past my car, spotted me, cheerfully waved and pointed me towards the rest of the squad who were getting ready for the pre-match stretch and chat. It was only at that moment that I knew that I had no other choice – I decided to play.

I started the game as a substitute; a situation that I didn't mind as it was still raining. My team went two goals down in the first five minutes from two well-taken goals before we woke up and found some rhythm. After 15 minutes I joined the fray and played for three quarters of the game as a defender.

Due to the intermittent rain during the game and the persistent damp conditions, I did need to cough harder at certain times to help clear my lungs to enable me to keep up and do my bit on the pitch. This included some pretty heavy coughing fits where I had to stop and physically retch. This cannot have been pleasant for people to hear, especially for those playing who didn't know about my health problems.

We battled on and went close to scoring on a few occasions, including missing a penalty flick, but the game ended in us losing 2-0. The final whistle blew to signal the end of the game. As is customary we shook hands with the opposition players and both umpires. And then my world was turned upside down... the Epsom umpire said to me upon shaking my hand, *"My God you sounded awful! Are you sure you should be playing with a cough like that?"*

Over the years, many players, both team mates and the opposition, had made comments to me during and after a match about my coughing. I've often wondered what the opposition think when they see me in action, coughing and wheezing like an old man? Some light-heartedly ask if I have been smoking too many cigarettes, had a night on the town or am suffering with a bad cold. Most references kindly check on my well-being. This time it was different, very different.

This was the first time in over 30 years of playing the sport that an official had said such a comment to me... and it really hit home. It was only a throw-away remark and more than likely a polite gesture with good intent; but the way it came across completely deflated me.

I felt as if I'd been struck my lightening. I just stood there and didn't move for what seemed like an eternity, but was probably only a few minutes. I was upset and crestfallen. The words of that umpire came as a bolt out of the blue, triggering a chain reaction of doubt and confusion.

Ironically, during the warm-down run the rain finally halted. After a quick shower we went to Epsom's clubhouse. Normally I pride myself on being the life and soul of the party. Not this time... I was quiet and deep in thought.

That afternoon back at home I spent some quality time with Katie and Felix which was a useful distraction. I did briefly mention the incident to Katie but down-played the whole thing. But by the evening, the comment from the umpire would not leave my conscience and kept spinning around my head. I played back the events of the game again and again, always finishing with the harsh comment...

"My God you sounded awful! Are you sure you should be playing with a cough like that?"

I ruminated on what the man had said. A hundred different scenarios came to me, followed by a string of questions that I had no answer for.

Was this an opportune time for me to pack up playing hockey? Should I retire from the sport forthwith? Was this perhaps some form of divine intervention? Maybe the comment was exactly what I needed to hear and my on-going hockey playing was foolhardy and not doing me any good anymore? How would my retirement be interpreted by my close family, friends and fellow hockey players?

Should I stop at 39 years old before I make it to 40? But I so wanted to still be playing at this milestone age.

Does this mean that I won't make it to 40? Does this signify that by giving up on my hockey, I've given up on life itself?

As one should always do with such a dilemma to figure out, I decided to sleep on it and see if my thinking was any clearer the next morning. However, as soon as I woke up this Sunday morning, the first words that sprung to mind were...

"My God you sounded awful! Are you sure you should be playing with a cough like that?"

I began to wallow in my predicament. Every half hour I would internally decide to either play on or give up hockey completely... and then immediately change my mind again.

After much deliberation, I realised that I would benefit from a consultation with someone close to me who could help me with this colossal predicament. They had to know my hockey career and health dynamic inside out in order to offer me the appropriate counsel. Within minutes it became obvious to me who the right person was – I needed to speak with my dad. I had to ascertain his thoughts on whether I should retire from playing!

After all, it was my dad who introduced me to this wonderful sport and it was through his dedication and support that I have been able to play for over 30 years. He knew better than most that my hockey has been the key differentiator in my life – keeping the ravages of CF at bay.

But equally I'm painfully aware that the idea of me stopping my and his beloved sport would cripple him. It's our mutual barometer for how my health is. In both our minds if I can still play my hockey I can still beat off my illness. If I stop playing then CF is winning. If there was one person in this world to have this conversation with it would have to be my dad.

That early evening, it was my usual Sunday call home to catch up with my parents in Southampton, so it was the perfect timing to have this discussion. Upon dialling their phone number, it was one of those rare occasions when my dad answered the phone instead of my mum.

As is typical of a lot of fathers who believe that their children have rung up to primarily chat to the mum, he quickly said, "I'll just pass you onto your mum."

"Actually dad, it's you that I really want to speak to."

My dad, ever the hockey enthusiast, always began our conversations with his hockey-skill related question, "How's your wobble son?"

"Actually, it's not so good at the moment. That's what I need to chat with you about."

I relayed all the details about yesterday's game – the weather, my coughing and of course ended my diatribe by quoting the thought-provoking comment from the umpire. *"My God you sounded awful! Are you sure you should be playing with a cough like that?"*

I then launched into a barrage of questions to help me off-load my angst and indecision about my hockey-playing future...

"If I sound that terrible on the pitch with all my coughing, why am I bothering to play anymore? However, no other sport makes me feel as alive and gives me a clear indication of how well my lungs are doing. I still need to play, no matter how my lungs sound at times.

"I desperately wanted to keep playing till the age of 40 and beyond but now I'm not so sure. Perhaps it's the right time to retire from hockey and swap over to tennis instead?"

Phone conversations with my dad were historically not all that animated with me doing the majority of the talking. Tonight's chat was in no way different. I spoke and he listened. After going through the full gamut of my emotions, I asked him directly whether I should retire or not. Even though I may have been breaking his heart with all my talk of retiring, he was thoughtful and kind. "Timbo, I'll support you whatever you do."

I told him I would think more about it and let him know the outcome. We said good night and he concluded the chat as he always did with me, "Bless you my son."

I was still in a quandary but chatting to dad had at least given me some solace that I would arrive at the correct judgment in due course. Later that night, as I was preparing to get into bed, I felt the inclination to pick up the Bible from my bedside table. Miraculously, upon flicking through the pages, I stumbled across a passage in Kings that I was unfamiliar with. The text I blindly discovered shouted so loud at me that I almost dropped the book. There in 1 Kings 18:43, I came across the line, *'Get up and go again'*.

I felt a surge of relief. I had my answer right there on that page in Kings. Those words gave me the strength to carry on... I knew in that instant that I shouldn't retire from hockey. Not only should I not pack it in, but I should push on till I reached 40 and beyond. I had to get past the 40 landmark and like father like son, look ahead to coaching my son Felix how to play. While there's breath left in my lungs, I have to keep playing.

Get up and go again – play hockey, go to work, be a husband and a father – I felt vindicated about my decision. This would be my mantra whenever I hit a life obstacle or health slump.

The first person I'll tell of my decision to carry on playing will be my dad. He deserves to know that I've decided to get up and go again...

32. Winter's Tale

Saturday 18 December 2010

Today really did kick-start the winter of my discontent. It was still pitch black outside when I was awoken early by Felix, and I immediately started to feel groggy with some of the usual cold-like symptoms – sore throat, headache, tiredness. It had been a hard couple of weeks at work and I was feeling rather weak and at risk of succumbing to an infection.

Everywhere I go at this time of year I am engaged in the dual conflict against the wintry elements and the preponderance of colds and flu in the office, on the London underground or generally around and about.

As with the majority of people, it's quite natural to feel at a lower ebb, which in turn makes me even more susceptible to coming down with a cold. It was almost inevitable that I'd catch something at some point during this fateful time.

Getting a cold is harsh for everyone but it's the way that it affects the chest of a CF sufferer for a long time afterwards that sets us apart from fellow, healthier humans. The actual cold symptoms are not dissimilar but it's the pronounced ramifications for our lungs once the cold has depleted that we find crippling.

Most people without CF who wouldn't have the habitual need to cough in order to clear their lungs will likely undergo a week or so of intensive exacerbations. For CF sufferers the infection in our lungs post cold is often ten times as bad.

If my concerns this morning are proved correct and I am acceding to an annoying cold, then my lungs can go from being relatively clear – well, clear for a CF sufferer anyway – to sounding like the rumblings of a cement mixer, almost overnight.

Coming back to better health after the ravages of a cold is a long, frustrating, debilitating and all-encompassing journey.

More often than not, a dreaded course of intravenous antibiotics and increased medication are the only ways to properly negate the build-up of infection caused by a cold.

This morning we went to visit Katie's uncle, aunt and cousins in Putney, South London for pre-Christmas drinks and bites. The forecast had been predicting heavy snow but the intensity of what came to pass could not have been expected.

As we sat in their lounge enjoying mince pies and watching Felix play with their terrier dog, it started to snow. It wasn't a small flurry but a full-on, fat-flake snow storm which settled on the streets and roads instantaneously. As this weather looked so threatening, we all realised that it might be a good idea to take our leave and head for home – a half-hour drive.

The windscreen wipers were working overtime to clear the snow as we headed towards Putney Hill. It was like a scene from the disaster movie 'The Day After Tomorrow' with cars wheel-spinning everywhere and people slipping about on the pavements.

While waiting to actually turn onto Putney Hill, the DJ on the car radio must have been in a mischievous mood as he played Dean Martin's winter hit 'Let It Snow.' In the end it took us over 20 minutes to turn right from one junction onto this main road, so bad was the mobility of cars affected by the heavy snow fall.

As we finally arrived home, driving extremely carefully, we heard on the radio that all of London had ground to a halt by this blizzard that seemingly caught the city unprepared. Even the main Heathrow Airport was snowed in with no flights taking off or landing.

Some harsh winter realities were beginning to sink in. A chilly climate that produces such a colossal dump of snow has severe repercussions for my health. This is one of my worst nightmares and really stokes my winter blues – all intensified by my worrying cold symptoms that were not abating in any way. In fact they were getting more pronounced by the hour. My throat was burning and four-hourly pain killing tablets were barely taking the edge off my washed-out sensation. As a diabetic, I couldn't even enjoy the small consolation of tasty cough sweets to soothe my sore throat. Instead I sucked non-stop on sugar-free Strepsils.

During the exceptional harsh days of a winter, anyone battling with a chronic lung condition like CF will struggle more than ever. From my own perspective the cold and damp days are without exception my worst health days. My chest feels tight and restricted and I never really get a break from coughing.

My lung capacity in the cold, damp and wet weather is always reduced. Add to that the fact that there's less light and with that a decrease in everyone's energy levels. However, most CF sufferers already have less energy to play with so we really notice how winter diminishes our energy stocks. All in all, everything feels restricted and I have little vibrancy. Like the Overlook Hotel in the Jack Nicholson film 'The Shining', my body seems to close down during the winter months.

So far this UK winter has been very cold, particularly since we entered December. I find that my lungs are like a barometer. In the mornings on waking up, I can detect what the weather's like before I even open the curtains, based on how my lungs are feeling. If I wake up coughing more than normal, it's never a surprise that it's damp or cold outside.

In some ways CF is similar to Seasonal Affective Disorder, as it's not just a disorder for one season but a condition for every season with seasonal symptom variations depending on the climate and conditions. These require the appropriate seasonal adjustments to effectively manage the variations and stabilize my health.

Exercise is never straightforward in the colder months. Running is not simple for me when I'm feeling relatively well but at this time of year it is doubly hard. This reduced lung capacity can feel very dispiriting. When I feel capable of exercise during winter, I tend to favour runs on the local pavements rather than in the park behind our house.

Indeed, trying to find an appropriate window of opportunity to get outside to exercise can be a challenge; in between the rain and the bitter cold. All this snow today will have far-reaching ramifications for my capacity to get any exercise as it will be far too dangerous to run on the pavements. This snowfall has also coincided with the Christmas break from league hockey, so I won't have the opportunity to play my beloved hockey on Astroturf till early January at least.

Historically, I've never been one for gyms and have never had a membership. This is partly due to the feeling that I would be in 'competition' with healthier people therein; but predominantly because if I needed to cough hard or clear my lungs, a gym is not terribly conducive or discreet.

In my experience, there's a tough balance to be found between letting the weather curtail all exercise and being bold and going out for a run when it could do more harm than good. In the past I have been too bullish for my own good and a jog at this time of year has led to a chill, followed by a cold and long-term infection. Without access to a gym, I will struggle to get any form of exercise for two to three weeks which is worrying for my lungs. This is the paradox that I now face.

A lot of people I know get their exercise in the winter from skiing or snowboarding. In my 39 years, I've never gone skiing. Outside of my general distress from being in a cold climate, for me there's a substantial risk of developing a serious chill. I would likely get hot while skiing on the slopes and then my body would cool too much before I could take a shower. For someone with CF, this could cause untold damage to my lungs and even pneumonia which would be catastrophic. I know of an older CF adult who went skiing and as a direct result had problems with his chest from which he never fully recovered. This in the end led to the drastic measure of him requiring a lung transplant to save his life.

As well as the potential concerns with the cold, I have never gone on a skiing holiday because I was desperate not to injure myself in any way that would prevent me from playing hockey or any other form of exercise. I've always felt that it was never worth the risk and I suppose what you never try you tend not to miss.

This afternoon we are due to visit some friends and their children in near-by Southfields. We'd got to know them in the lead up to Felix's arrival as part of the National Childbirth Trust. The heavy snowfall had let up enough so that the roads miraculously allowed us to drive there for this Christmas party.

As we got Felix ready to go out the door I thought about making my excuses and asking to stay behind as I wasn't feeling that well with the cold symptoms. However, with colds, I try not to make a fuss to people around me, not least because having a condition like CF tends to dwarf minor ailments like a cold. I also try not to let the magnitude of the cold take over my body and especially my mind.

I fervently believe that the least amount of fuss I make about a possible cold gives the infection less of a foothold inside me. In effect, I don't want to make myself more ill by acting ill and playing on it. By doing this, I don't project the effects of a potential cold to my lungs and enable it to manifest into something really debilitating.

Sometimes this approach works and I'm sure I have averted a sniffle from turning into a full-blown cold. Other times, there's nothing to stop the path of destruction that is going to come my way whatever I do mentally and physically to dodge it. Which way is this potentially looming cold going to go I wonder?

Eventually I decide to accompany Katie and Felix to the children's party. Keep calm and carry on, as they say...

Especially throughout the winter months I am largely proactive with tactics to counter the likely threat of infection. I have the flu jab which prevents me from getting the flu which would be disastrous for my lungs. I also take St. John's Wort, extra Vitamin C and other over-the-counter immune boosting supplements. Additionally I use a lot of sanitizing hand gel where ever I go to avoid picking up any stray germs on surfaces. This seasonal strategy is designed to build up my defences and fortify the ramparts of my health sandcastle.

With some of these preventative measures comes a further annoyance. The extra immune system vitamins and supplements all take that extra bit of time to swallow, along with my usual cocktail of medication. This delays me even more when rushing to get to work in the mornings.

For practical reasons, the winter months are more frustrating when dealing with my CF and diabetes medication. I am usually wearing more clothing layers so to get to my skin for insulin injections is sometimes a real feat of engineering. I often have to add in another nebulised drug in the evenings which again takes time, planning and effort.

Added to this, my physiotherapy usually takes longer in the winter months as there's more phlegm to get up. Due to the increased amounts of mucous I occasionally give myself extra 'dream sessions' of physiotherapy just before bedtime. This takes place when I'm almost too tired to do the chest percussion but I know that I'll get a better night of sleep if I knuckle down and do it. This often means going downstairs from where Katie and Felix are asleep and hoping that my coughing does not wake them.

We returned home at 5.30pm in total darkness from the Southfields gathering. Back in the house, while running the night-time bath for Felix, I cast my mind back over the events of the day and my dilemma about whether I've got a cold brewing.

My winter's tale is not unique but nevertheless it's one I have to endure as best I can. In a life perpetually battling CF, it's the wintertime, encompassing the months from November through to the end of February, that's the toughest to combat and stay healthy.

We all tend to smile behind a frown at this time of year, but for people struggling with a chronic lung condition like CF this frown is harder to remove. Despite all that winter throws at me, I certainly have to be unyielding to stay upbeat, jolly and optimistic.

Will these cold-like symptoms I've been feeling all day result in anything serious and perhaps be the start of my downfall? I'll find out tomorrow but for now, I've chosen to ignore it, carry on and keep calm...

33. Wonderful World

Saturday 25 December 2010

Most people I know really enjoy the long build-up to Christmas Day; the never-ending festive songs on the radio, Christmas carols and of course the day itself with all the presents and food. For me, Christmas Day is at its most memorable in the late evening when all has been said and done.

I find these moments when another Christmas Day is drawing to an end to be the most poignant and I often use this time to contemplate how it measures up with all my previous 'special' days. I ponder on the Christmas Days I have already had, where they took place and the various festive antics. I remember stand-out times on this day and who I shared them with. I think it's important for me to contextualise another year having survived CF.

I also scrutinise how many more I'm likely to enjoy in the future…

In many respects today was a traditional British Christmas Day. We spent the first part of the day at home in Morden before driving down to see my parents and close family in Southampton.

Since we were married in 2003, Katie and I tend to alternate between our sets of parents on Christmas Day. This year we were with my folks, where my brothers and sisters-in-law also joined us.

Felix was a picture of complete and utter joy this morning. Parenting can be challenging but you live for magical and innocent moments such as these – watching his delight as he found his presents under the Christmas tree next to Santa's half eaten mince pie. Such was his unbridled excitement that he performed a happy dance.

After a pretty uneventful drive to Southampton our Christmas Day really got going. On arrival, we had some champagne and opened the presents that were under my parents Christmas tree.

Felix, being the only grandchild, was the centre of attention. Acting as a postman he helped to distribute the presents from under the tree to the adults in attendance. When given half a chance he took extra joy in opening the delivered gifts himself with rapid gusto.

After a while I noticed that Felix started to get a bit demonic with all the presents around him. The actual ripping open of the wrapping paper was becoming his raison d'être rather than actually appreciating the gift inside.

A fabulous sit-down lunch then ensued with all the usual Christmas Day turkey and trimmings. Felix's attention span waned after 20 minutes so I took him into the lounge where he was happy to watch one of his TV programmes until his pudding of ice-cream was ready.

Following the Queen's Speech we all went for the habitual afternoon walk around nearby Southampton Common, which is always needed to blow away the cobwebs of over indulgence.

At five in the afternoon all the adults had tea and cake while Felix had his evening meal followed by his bath and bed. As we viewed some TV we had a light supper and then it was time for Katie and I to withdraw to bed as we expected Felix would wake early the next day.

It was at this time that I picked up one of the presents I'd received for some bedtime reading. It's one of those Christmas rituals that you tend to read any book on the day it's received. It was titled 'The Perfect Distance' and it told the story of the British middle-distance running rivalry between Sebastian Coe and Steve Ovett that reached a crescendo at the Olympic Games in Moscow and Los Angeles in the early 1980s.

What gripped me in the pages I initially read was the Christmas anecdote, where Coe decided not to take it easy but went for a long run on Christmas Day as he instinctively knew that his rival Ovett would not be letting up even on a day of rest. Those athletes knew that they had to knuckle under even when everyone else might be relaxing, drinking and eating too much.

This level of dedication and motivation struck a chord with me and got me thinking about my own plight. Whereas these athletes were not allowing themselves to have a day off from their training regime, I'm not able to have a single day off from my medical regimen.

I can't take time off just because it's Christmas Day as appealing as it always is to tell myself differently, *"On this special day I can relent from my routine and have the day off. What's one day in the scheme of things?"*

Every Christmas Day I contemplate such an eventuality. However, it never happens as I know that I still need to pop my pills and do my physiotherapy, nebulisers and injections.

Laughably, I take more tablets on Christmas Day than I receive actual presents. Indeed, I probably take more pills just on Christmas Day than most people need to take during a whole year.

The hardest physiotherapy session of the year is the one in the early evening on Christmas Day. This is my Coe Ovett moment. When every sinew in my body bellows at me not to bother and stay put downstairs, watch TV or have a drink, I have to literally tear myself away to do my important physiotherapy.

The most memorable of these Christmas Day showdowns was a few years back in Southampton when Katie and I were newly married. I had moved myself into the kitchen to watch one of my favourite films – the Christmas Day staple 'It's a Wonderful World' starring James Stewart.

I was so ensconced watching it – it was the first film Katie and I had watched together as a courting couple back in December 2000 – I was not exactly receptive when Katie politely reminded me that it was time to do my physiotherapy ahead of the evening meal. We will always remember how reluctant I was for many minutes to drag myself away to do "my bloody physiotherapy!"

She kept coming back to remind me and I was not budging even after many attempts to persuade me differently. In the end she was able to prise me away but I was not happy. It's this event I recall on these Christmas Day early evenings when I force myself to yield for the greater good.

The book offered me further perspective on my CF battle. Unlike these Olympians, my struggle is not a sprint or middle-distance race. Every day is a form of endurance event like a steeple chase or marathon.

Also I'm not in direct competition with anyone to beat them in a race in six months. No, the competition for which I'm engaged is pitted solely against me. It's Tim Wotton versus Tim Wotton. My mission is not to be fit and healthy for a pre-determined event; it's to be ready for everyday life. In the pursuit of this goal, I'm not able to let up and take my foot off the pedal even for a day and that includes Christmas Day.

It's against this backdrop that I consider my feelings about the 25th December. At this time of year, it's normal to be asked what you want from Santa Claus. The majority of people ask for their latest want big and small. My request, after nearly 40 years of living with CF is a basic need not a want – it's a present called 'good health'.

I don't wish to come across as too melodramatic or bah, humbug! I certainly don't want to quash the spirit of Christmas. I did, of course, enjoy the presents I received and I'm enthralled by the book in my hands. I got an especially huge buzz from being around Felix today and his innocent intoxication with the whole festive experience.

But I doubt there's a person who suffers with either CF or any other life-threatening illness that wouldn't secretly want to swap all those lovely gift-wrapped presents for the most precious gift of all – better health! It's all I want and have ever really wanted for Christmas.

Even for one day it would be the most magical present I could ever imagine receiving. The gift of health exceeds all other gifts. Unopened gifts contain hope and he who has health, has hope. And he who has hope, has everything.

I hope and pray for the gift of a cure and for improved health. I dream of the Christmas Day in the future when I won't have to do any treatment, especially my physiotherapy when there's a good film to be watched instead – what a wonderful world that would be.

34. Opening Up

Tuesday 4 January 2011

That's one small step for a man, one giant leap for CF awareness. Well that's how it felt when I launched my first ever blog today...

After soliciting incredibly positive feedback from certain family and friends about my epiphany to open up about my 39 years of CF survival, some of my spare time in the last few months has been spent planning the next steps.

Following that meet with Ailsa, my PR friend, last September I've been focusing on writing a blog that unpicks my journey and my techniques for handling all the adversity that comes with CF. In many ways, it's a golden opportunity to match my flair for writing with a subject matter that is so close to me. At work as a communications consultant, I normally write articles for websites and magazines about business news but have to do so within a fairly rigid framework. This was different and I could write freely and honestly which immediately felt liberating and empowering.

I wrestled for a few months with how best to frame my experiences and messages before deciding that my 40th birthday should be the anchor point. For most people I knew reaching 40 came as a bit of a shock to them. I knew this significant milestone would have a different resonance with me as historically so few CFers make it to this age. I felt compelled to harness one of the most important dates in my life to share my story.

I wanted the blog to be a weekly countdown to my 40th on the 17th March sharing my battle to stay alive and my perspectives on life. That would mean publishing different posts every week for three months and building the tension and expectation leading up to my prized day of celebration.

I then brainstormed the list of topics that I wished to cover in those countdown posts. After an exhaustive exercise, the topic list included my endless medical regime, playing sport, keeping positive, the use of complementary treatments, marriage, the IVF rollercoaster, being a dad, fitting in my CF-related diabetes and lastly my hopes for the future once I'd made it to 40.

At the same time as landing all the separate blog subjects, I needed to research the most appropriate, user-friendly and free blogging platform. I finally chose to use WordPress and worked closely with one of my graphic designer colleagues to put my homepage together. This included a photograph of my family and selecting all the required functionality for the blogging platform.

I then wrote the initial blog text and used Ailsa as my editor and sense-checker. In fact she kindly proofed quite a few of my countdown posts to ensure I was keeping on-message and coherent.

On reading my draft of the first 'Countdown to 40!' post, she challenged me to bring it to life and introduce an early hook for readers to help draw them in. As I'm quite a visual person, I pondered on what metaphor or well-known object I could use that would easily resonate with people the world over. First impressions of my message and written style would be crucial as it could mean the difference between recipients reading on or giving up.

Inspiration often comes to me when I'm listening to my iPod on the London underground journey to work. In mid-December last year, I had the 'eureka!' moment I was searching for while listening to the Echo & the Bunnymen song 'Evergreen'. It was a sentence in that song relating to time in one's hour glass that led to my use of the hourglass metaphor in my first blog.

I decided to wait until the New Year 2011 to post my inaugural blog rather than having my launch buried and lost in the busy family time between the Christmas and New Year festivities. The plan was for the blog to hopefully go viral. I would email it to close family and friends in early January with the added request to subscribe to receive future posts and also for them to cascade it to their friends should they wish to. I would also use Facebook and Twitter to promote the launch blog and each subsequent post.

This whole process led me to finally craft the 'Countdown to 40!' blog text which began with...

"Consider your life expectancy being held in an hourglass? Now imagine that the grains of sand in your glass appear to be running out very quickly... how would you feel? What would you do differently or prioritise before your sand runs out?

'As you can imagine, when your longevity in this world is perpetually in doubt, it has a dramatic effect on what you do, how you think and your priorities in life. I often felt that my hourglass was running out on me."

And concluded with...

"As I look ahead to my 40th birthday, it feels natural to also look back and reflect on the journey I've been on – my trials and tribulations, happy times and what it has taken for me to come this far. There's a saying that 'what can't be cured, needs to be endured' and by enduring all my life, I believe I have some extraordinary stories to share and some unique life insights. I want to share the approach I have honed over the years that keeps me alive and kicking, where CF does not define me but is just something I have to 'get on with' to lead my life.

Over the next few months leading up to my 40th birthday, I am looking to share some of these experiences and enlightening life lessons. I also want to increase the general awareness and profile around CF, raising the public conscience in order to create a tidal wave of interest around the condition. Hopefully I will inspire everyone (healthy or those dealing with any long-term illness) that even when you are at your lowest ebb with the odds stacked against you, that there is usually a way to overcome."

I took today as annual leave with the distinct intention of launching the blog and sharing it with family and friends via email and social media. I certainly had a mix of emotions as I got ready to hit the publish button of not only my first blog, but my first online CF exposure.

I hadn't been this public about my CF in a long time, let alone been so free with my inner feelings. Back in the 1980s a local news production company had shot and aired a short TV documentary about me when I made the England junior hockey team. Today I would be bold and go public with my CF struggle for the first time as an adult.

As my finger hovered delicately over the WordPress publish button a catalogue of questions fizzed around my head...

Would I get past the 'so what?' test with those that read my blog? Would anyone really care about my experiences? Would my style of writing be appreciated? Would people feel inspired or compelled to comment back? How would this blog and being more open about my CF affect my life? How will I know if it's been worth the effort? What would success look like?

With all these questions as yet unanswered, I didn't want to put any pressure on myself concerning how many people would read it and feel inspired to share with others, make a comment or subscribe to receive future posts.

For a lot of friends, this would be my first real frankness about my health and sharing of my inner emotions. It might even make for uncomfortable reading for some who didn't know much about the condition or may have just assumed that it can't have been that bad as I look fairly well.

It crossed my mind that my blog might possibly offend some people or come across as too preachy. There's not much I could do about that. I felt compelled to speak my mind and be honest.

I hoped it would serve to educate the non-CF community and friends while offering hope and practical help to CF sufferers and their families. Too often we underestimate the power of how words can have the potential to turn a life around.

If just one CF sufferer or parent of a CF patient received some help and even hope from my story and survival tips, it would be worth the effort of writing the blogs and sharing my journey. That was the bottom line for me.

After pushing the publish button on my first ever blog, I drove to Kingston-upon-Thames to go shopping. I felt I wanted to take my mind off any likely response to my blog launch and whether anyone was actually interested by it.

The functionality of the blogging platform meant that if someone commented, I would be sent an email to moderate and accept the comment before it was published back onto my blog homepage. As it was, I didn't have to wait too long to see that it had struck a chord with people. I received a string of comments to review while out on my shopping trip which immediately put my mind at rest and vindicated my decision to pursue this countdown blog.

Later that evening my blog site had received several hundred visits, 15 replies from family, friends and strangers; and multiple subscriptions for the next instalment. It already felt quite addictive checking how many hits my blog had received and also viewing the comments from readers. Some of the comments included:

"I hope you get much positive response and that your words spread far and wide. I'm sure with such a determined spirit, there is much more to follow. All the best for 2011 and your Countdown to 40."

    - Gus (the kind chap who left me and Ailsa that note of Carl Jung quotes outside the coffee shop last September)

"Wow mate, for as long as I have known you, you have been an inspiration to me. You have achieved so much and lived with so many challenges in your life beyond what I could imagine, but have always made everyone smile."

    - Stewart (Primary and Secondary school friend)

"Bloody hell Timmy – that was one powerful read..."
- Katy (hockey friend)

"Hi Tim its lovely to hear how well you are doing, keep up the good work. I am a carrier and my 18yr old nephew Luke with CF died 2 days ago, we had hoped he would live to 30 but it was not meant to be. Hopefully a cure is around the corner."
- Linda (CF Community)

I had lit the touch paper and there was no way of going back. The gate had been opened and my CF horse had bolted... that gate would never be closed again in my lifetime. At last I had opened up – to myself, to the CF community and to the rest of the world.

In cricket parlance, I feel as if I've been hidden away in the practice nets for the last 20 years and now I'm about to face the opening ball of a test match in front of a packed and expectant house at Lord's cricket ground.

Today, 4th January 2011 was definitely the start of something new and the end of the beginning...

35. Come Undone

Sunday 6 February 2011

It's extremely rare that I enter our family house, walk up to Katie and start crying but the events of today caused me a fair amount of inner turmoil and angst. What I experienced while out with Felix is not something I wish to repeat in a hurry…

This morning I took Felix to Wimbledon. We went to the Queens Road Church service where we sat through the initial worship before dropping him off at the children's play area so that I could concentrate on the main sermon.

By the time we finished there it was lunch time so after a quick chat with Felix, we decided on eating nearby rather than driving straight home. This led to my first 'father and son' trip to Pizza Express on Wimbledon's high street.

We both ordered pizza but his meal took a while to appear, during which Felix got over -hungry and rather agitated. It was a bit stressful dealing with him as he had played hard in the playgroup, had gone beyond his energy levels and needed to eat but was too tired to eat… an age old dilemma for parents and sometimes hard to mitigate against.

It took a lot of effort to cajole him along and convince him to finally pick up a piece of pizza and start eating. Of course, once he had navigated the first few mouthfuls, his spark returned and it was just what he needed.

My problems didn't end there. I didn't have my diabetes blood testing kit with me so had to guess how I was feeling and also surmise how much insulin I needed with my pizza meal. I had only been a diabetic for about eighteen months so I was still adjusting to all the nuances of the condition. On occasion, it's quite a science to get it just right and with all the hassle dealing with Felix I had probably got quite low in my glucose levels and may have had too much insulin rather than too little.

After we'd eaten and left the restaurant, we agreed to pop into the Tesco mini-store for a few provisions on the way back to the car. Unbeknownst to me, all the events in the last hour were triggering a diabetic meltdown inside my body. It wasn't long before everything in my world came crashing down.

While shopping in the store, seemingly out of the blue, I suddenly felt all the familiar signs of a severe hypoglycaemia coming on very quickly. This hypo as we diabetics prefer to call it would have been caused by a reduced amount of glucose or low sugar levels in my blood. It can produce a variety of symptoms and effects but the principal problems arise from an inadequate supply of glucose to the brain, resulting in impairment of function.

I felt hot, giddy, drowsy, drunk. Worryingly, I quickly lost the ability for rational thought as my brain began to be impacted by this shortfall of glucose. It's a strange sensation – like your life force is ebbing from you. I often say it's like someone has pulled your plug out and all your water is seeping out.

One feels incapable of coherent physical and mental actions. As the mind begins to slow the body movement down, speech is also impaired. To the outside world, one could be confused for looking like a drunk who's teetering around after too much alcohol.

Some people become obsessive and are 'control freaks' who need to plan and organise all those around them. As well as feeling in control of oneself, one of the more natural feelings is to have a strong level of influence over your own children, especially when they are young and vulnerable. As a parent myself, I fully understand that you systematically and voluntarily take on the care of your son or daughter, putting their needs ahead of your own.

In this instance while supposedly looking after Felix in a busy supermarket, I certainly felt out of control and it was a horrible sensation. I was rapidly turning into an 'out of control freak', to twist the phrase.

At that precise moment while I was hovering in the pasta aisle with the realisation of what was happening to me, I lamented on the many other public challenging times I have to endure due to my illnesses – other out-of-the-blue examples like coughing fits in public places, having to excuse myself from work meetings to clear my lungs, surreptitiously popping pills during lunch with strangers and injecting my body with insulin in public venues.

Some of the more frustrating moments in my life battling CF and diabetes have centred on my inability to look after my son Felix and supply the control that he needed and to play my part as a parent and support my wife Katie.

Since Felix was born in May 2007, I have needed six separate intensive intravenous therapies where for at least one week I would be away from home. Not being there for him and Katie cuts to my very core.

Keeping up with Felix, who is a very busy boy, has brought on hypos previously where the stress or exercise causes my sugar levels to drop to low levels. This is not the first time this has happened but it's the first time it's been this intense without Katie being on hand to help out.

I can hold it together when experiencing a hypo when it's just me on my own, but this felt different. Felix is prone to running off, and there I was listing to port and I felt extremely vulnerable, worried and incapable of keeping it together as a dad for him. Even though I was with Felix in this store, it was more in body and less in mind.

I asked Felix to stay close and not run away and he instinctively realised by my tone that he needed to cooperate. I've noticed that children seem to have an innate ability to know when there's a crisis taking place. They understand when they need to comply with their parent's instruction in the case of an emergency. Felix is pretty intuitive about my CF and has seen me do my nebuliser at home. He's aware that at times I'm not very well and is very compassionate.

In order to solve my hypo, I knew that I needed to restore my sugar levels quickly to normal which involves having a quick hit of anything sweet followed by something more long-lasting such as a carbohydrate food.

I had to fight back and take the initiative away from the hypo which was now enveloping my body at a rapid rate. Luckily being in a supermarket I was surrounded by the right food products to start ingesting glucose. So, I took some wine gums chewy sweets off the shelf and started to eat them which Felix thought was great as he could have some as well. He seemed to like this game of eating food straight from the shelves! But for me, this wasn't a game or fun – this was real life and I felt terrified…

Rational thoughts were hard to produce when I'm in such a state. Without my diabetes blood testing kit, I couldn't check how low my sugar levels were and hence know how much was needed to rectify matters. The only thing I knew was that when I'm sweating profusely and feeling this disorientated, it was likely to be a seismic hypo.

How long would it take to get back the control of my senses? How much longer would Felix stick by my side and not get bored and run off?

We went to one of the self-help check out tills – where there needs to be assistance on hand as everyone makes mistakes. Even when you are mentally functioning, these tills are hard work and by this point I was really struggling. I couldn't join up my thinking at all to begin the process of working these tills.

Seeking out one of the attentive assistants, I explained my diabetes situation to her and she replied nonchalantly: "We get this all time, no worries" and calmly scanned my items and helped me to pay with my card. I asked if there was somewhere I could sit down for a while as my legs were close to buckling. She ushered me to an adjacent row of chairs that would normally be reserved for grannies, where Felix and I promptly sat down. The relief of letting this chair take my weight was palpable.

This same lady found out what I needed to reverse the effects of my hypo and then kindly offered to get me a coke and a bar of chocolate. After requesting some money from me she promptly returned with the products and my change!

I sat there enjoying the can of coke and sharing the chocolate with Felix. Since my diabetes diagnosis in 2009, it's such a rare treat to now drink any non-diet fizzy drink that I savour every mouthful. It's not until something you enjoyed and took for granted is removed from your diet or is restricted, do you fully appreciate it. With me, the drink I miss the most is the high sugar hit of a normal can of coke.

I find these moments a perverse treat in so many ways. I probably have only two or three cans of normal coke per year and each one I'll remember where I was when I had it- such is the taste sensation. While the coke was being drunk, I could slowly feel my body re-charging itself with glucose. In my human bath, the plug had been slotted back in the hole and the water was filling up to restore my equilibrium.

As we sat there letting the sugar work its magic, I reflected that it's a luxury that I can mention my diabetes to anyone when in an emergency out and about and the vast majority of people have not only heard of it, but have an understanding of the condition and what's needed to rectify a dangerous situation. I can't say the same about my CF.

I would probably have to explain my CF to a stranger before receiving any form of medical assistance relating to a coughing attack out in a public place. Realistically, there's nothing that can be done to help my CF but anyone can assist me with a low blood glucose level and help to restore my sugar levels by giving me a fizzy drink or piece of chocolate.

After a fifteen minute duration where Felix and I polished off all our sugar products, I felt better and more balanced. I sought out the helpful assistant to acknowledge her kindness and we left the store and walked back to my car.

After such a traumatic couple of hours, it was no surprise that I was so emotional on seeing Katie back at home. I was desperate to explain what had happened and how it had made me feel. Tears are an unusual commodity in my world, but here they flooded out.

Out of bad often comes good. It was a hard lesson to learn but I will be better prepared in the future to mitigate the effects of my diabetes in order to reduce the chances of this loss of control happening again. Especially when I'm looking after Felix on my own. This will help me to stay in control of my life, manage my own destiny and that of my family.

I now believe my own hypo...

36. How Have I Cheated Death?

Tuesday 15 February 2011

The boomerang effect has been happening since I launched my blog last month. What I am sending out is coming back to me. The hypothetical law of the universe indicating that what you give out or transmit is reflected back at you is occurring to me.

By opening up through my blog, I have definitely noticed that the new transparency about my CF struggle has been reciprocated by many people.

My survival story and anecdotes on defying a life-threatening illness really seem to be making a difference to the lives of those that are reading it, whether they received it directly from me, have been sent it via friends, have seen it online or stumbled across it by accident.

I fervently believe that people will remember how you made them feel rather than your actual words and deeds.

This feeling was never more real and endorsed in late January when I read on my blog page the following comment from a mum with a CF child:

"Reading your comments gives me hope for a future for my CF son, when sometimes there seems no hope at all."

- Karen

On receipt of those words, with tears in my eyes, I had to get up and walk outside my consultancy office in order to compose myself. I was stunned that my words could touch someone in such a profound way and provoke such emotion in a person that I had never met. It was even more mind-blowing that I could offer them one of the most important things in life – hope.

Judging by other responses received from the CF community, I am helping CF parents to believe that their sick child doesn't have to just exist with CF but can live a relatively full life.

"I too am 40 this year but I am mum to 3 year old Eva who has CF. I would be very interested to learn about how you motivated yourself to keep fit both when you were younger and now long term. I would like to be able to pass your experiences, feelings and motivations to Eva as she grows up. I hope this is a wonderful year for you and long may it continue!"

- Penny

"I'm a mum to 5-month old George with CF. He has already endured so much. I want him to grow up as a normal little boy who just happens to have CF. Reading your blog has given me faith and the realisation that it can happen. Thank you."

- Nicola

"Thank you for sharing your story. I am a mum of a little boy who just turned a year old who has CF. We want to raise him as a "normal" kid who just happens to have CF, just like you said. Thanks for giving us hope."

- Kristy

"I have a son just about to turn 4 in January with CF and I just wanted you to know that since he was born I thought that I would like to have an approach and mind set for his condition which would be a constructive approach to living life with CF – a mind set for him and for his mother and me. I think that your story is a lesson to all people living with the condition and those supporting them. Truly inspirational."

- Jon

"My son, Jack, is 3 years old with CF. Hope he grows up with the same guts & determination that you have showed. Hope you smash the big 40 and live a longer life for you and your family… Inspirational."

- Steve

"I just read your blog and was amazed. We have been fostering a 2 yr old with CF for a year now. Prior to this we had no idea what CF really entailed. We had heard of it and knew it was a serious illness but that's all. I shall keep reading your blog, it gives me inspiration .Thanks"

- Anne

"What an inspiration! I lost my best friend at the age of 21 to CF; that was 20 years ago now... she was a beautiful soul. Happy 40!"

- Kylie

Similar to my own long stretch of silence, it seems clear that a lot of other CF adults have kept their emotions hidden away for most of their lives. Through reading my testimony, it appears that CF sufferers and healthy people with their own life issues have felt empowered to reflect themselves and consider how they would benefit from opening up more to their nearest and dearest.

"I suffer from CF and CF-related diabetes and will be hitting 30 this year. The vast majority of your post is like someone has just read my mind, when I read it I was amazed that I hadn't written it myself!"

- Al

"I turned 40 last year. Reading your first post was like reading something I had written... I even use the hourglass analogy. On a good day there's still tonnes of sand in it. On a bad day (recent swine flu and horrid chest infection) it has about a handful of grains left!"

- Audrey

Other blog feedback has revealed that the non-CF community now have a deeper understanding about the illness and are appreciative to be offered such reflection and insight.

Additionally, distant friends, all my family and parents of school pals have been in contact after reading my blog.

"I would never have guessed that you have such a major illness and be the person that you are on the outside, this happy chappy who just gets on with enjoying life the best you can without the illness being the main focus of your life. When I see you at the bus stop I have no idea that you have just downed the best part of 40 pills and injections that in itself is a feat doing it day in day out."

- Simon

"Your story puts all my so called 'worries' into perspective."

- Steve

"You've really touched a nerve here, thank you for sharing this it will help and inspire many people."

- Susan

"What a fantastic blog post, I am sure it will have a huge impact and give inspiration to everyone who has someone with CF. This is the most positive way anyone I know has approached 40. Thanks Tim I'm really proud of you for not just thinking about doing this but getting on and doing it."

- Joan

All those years of built-up emotion under the surface is beginning to be reduced as a result of my being more open with myself and others. Indeed, I am beginning to talk in public places about my CF and my voice holds itself together a lot better.

Putting my feelings down on paper has been challenging but at the same time, it has been quite cathartic and a form of healing process in its own way. Having to be completely honest with my narrative has been a good exercise. By being true to myself I instantly feel humble. This honesty has increased the flow of positivity as I've had to accept my health, warts and all.

I would say that there's a balance to be found between talking more and shouting from the rooftops – after all, it's still a very private subject. It's not easy to speak up and I'm still pretty reserved about my illness with strangers but I feel deeply touched that my words have helped others.

I have opened the window into my CF world and the silence has been broken. I can't close the window now and don't really want to as this new approach feels entirely appropriate. However, it's taken me nearly 40 years to get to this point and I wonder whether I should have started to be this open before now.

Sometimes in life, it's OK to hide your life issue away but it's important to be careful not to bury away the associated emotion for too long as cracks will appear down the line. Based on the take-up and comments to my blog, I've been pleasantly surprised when I've opened up with the response I've received.

And now the publicity for my story has increased immeasurably. I wrote an article on my countdown to 40 that was published today in the health section of the UK national newspaper, The Guardian. This stemmed from one of Katie's family forwarding my blog to the health editor of the Guardian who in turn approached me to write for them.

They were very taken with my blog and were keen for me to replicate that style in an article for them. They asked me to frame why this birthday is so important, how I have dealt with my illness over the years, how I feel to be one of the oldest people in the country with CF and why I've decided to start addressing this publicly now. This was all underpinned by how turning 40 would be more of a revelation than a shock for me.

This was a fantastic opportunity to spread my word both in the UK and globally as The Guardian has a good global online readership as well being a popular UK broadsheet. The article would also promote my blog homepage and hopefully increase my readership.

It did feel amazing this morning on the way to the office, buying my own copy of a national newspaper, knowing that I would see my picture and story inside. The title of the article 'How have I cheated death?' was a poignant reference about how I felt for so many years watching my fellow CF sufferers sadly pass away.

It also allowed me to unpick some of the main reasons why I had been able to dodge death and stay alive instead. Snatching life from the jaws of certain death one could say…

As the day draws to a close, I study the blog output and comments with renewed vigour and passion for the journey I've begun. The effect of the extra exposure from an article in a national newspaper has meant that I had the most ever visits on a single day to my blog since its launch in early January.

Today, 1751 hits on my countdown blog have been registered which takes my overall visits for the site to over 5000. As well as that, 13 different people made a comment today and I've been busy replying to them as they came in. Some highlights included:

"I just read your article in the Guardian so obviously one of your desires (of raising more awareness about CF) is already bearing fruit. I knew a little bit about this disease but not a great deal and it is great to learn more about it and to hear a bit about your story. Thank you for your bravery in 'coming out' and becoming a voice for others with this illness."

- Holly

"Just wanted to say congratulations, far too often I worry about whether or not my 5 year old who has CF will reach such a wonderful age and have a family etc. So to have someone like you to aspire to is wonderful. Thank you for your words of encouragement because if you have realised it or not you have touched lives and given inspiration and encouragement."

- Kirsty

"My 16 year old with CF was admitted into hospital again yesterday… one of those things that you all manage to deal with so well. Reading stories like yours gives us all encouragement and hope… thank you for sharing your story."

- Lyn

"It is important that 'everyone' knows what CF is about and that we are all more educated, whether for a supporting role or any other. I loved your words of 'owning' what you have and I think many people could do with reading your story just to remind themselves how fortunate they are being that there are far too many 'self-indulgent' people in the world."

- Rachel

"Thanks again for the encouragement and belief that your article (and more importantly your life) has given me... and our families."

- Nigel

'How have I cheated death?' Could this be one of the most crucial questions I've ever asked myself? Who knows who may approach me next to share my story?

Silence helped me when I was angry about my condition. Speaking up has healed some of those emotional wounds and allowed me not to look back in anger but to look forward with positivity.

37. Gloves Are Off

Thursday 24 February 2011

Tonight I met up with Anthony Earley, my long-term friend from my hometown of Southampton. We went to watch a film called 'The Fighter'. I was consulting in Sunbury during the day, so we agreed to meet outside the cinema in Richmond-upon-Thames, where we would buy the film tickets and then fit in a pre-film drink and dinner.

We did what we always do when we meet for food – an elaborate sweep around all the local restaurants in the vicinity, knowing full well where we would end up dining – the Indian restaurant right next door to the cinema.

We, like most men, are creatures of habit and this extends not just to the type of restaurant we dine in but also to the actual Indian food we eat every time. It's become our rite of passage as friends since we were in our teens. Extra hot chicken jalfrezi accompanied by naan breads to mop it all up and of course a pint of the ubiquitous Kingfisher lager.

We had exactly 40 minutes – more than enough to gorge ourselves – while conducting a quick-fire catch up on each other's lives: family, work, sport and films. We also discussed in detail the sporting biographical movie that we were planning to watch that night, 'The Fighter', starring Mark Wahlberg, Christian Bale and Amy Adams based on the early boxing career of the American Micky Ward.

Anthony and I have always liked boxing and we have followed the big title fights since we met as teenagers. We share fond memories of the fight game from listening on the radio to the Tyson versus Bruno fight in the early hours in February 1989 to watching the televised reigns of Nigel Benn, Chris Eubank and Lennox Lewis.

In fact, it was because a lot of the key moments in our friendship have been inexorably linked to boxing fights, that we were drawn to meet up to see this film while it was still showing on the big screen.

The film itself was gritty, real and offered an engaging insight into the world of boxing, showing Micky Ward's fall into obscurity and rise to prominence; fighting both his opponents in the ring and the inner turmoil of his family and dominating mum. All in all we left the cinema in high spirits and were collectively glad we had made the effort to watch it together.

On my drive home tonight the film got me thinking that battling the horrid effects of CF every day of my life is in many ways like being embroiled in a non-stop prize fight. Everyone with CF is in his or her own way 'The Fighter'.

In basic terms, I fight CF and recently diagnosed type 1 diabetes every day and I take steady punishment in the form of jabs, hooks and uppercuts that quite literally take my breath and energy away. This is relentless stuff and my conditions keep coming for me as soon as I wake in the morning to when I fall asleep in the evening. And sometimes they take me on through the night. I'm in a non-stop fight for life.

I do suffer many heavy blows in the form of coughing fits, wheezing, chronic infections, tiredness, stomach irritation and diabetic hypos. These turn eventually into physical knockdowns when my lungs are so infected and I'm so worn out that I need debilitating intravenous (IV) treatments. I take the count, dust myself down, grit my teeth and get back up for more!

Sometimes it feels like a David versus Goliath mismatch as CF makes me feel small, weak and insignificant. It's as if I'm facing some big slayer that has finished off so many fellow CF sufferers before me. As there is no cure for this illness, CF is unbeaten and at the moment I'm there for the taking.

My condition is a formidable and obdurate opponent – it has the height of Lennox Lewis, the power of Mike Tyson, the agility of Floyd Patterson and the determination of Rocky Marciano.

As a student of the history of boxing, I remember that George Foreman, the heavyweight boxer who fought

Mohammed Ali in the 'Rumble in the Jungle' in Zaire in 1974, felt that the punches he landed during that fight de-humanised Ali but he seemed to 'come back to life' time and time again.

And so it is with me. Some of the coughing fits induced by CF are so fierce that they are de-humanised and so debilitating that my soul feels as if it leaves my body, only to return to the corpse that carries me around this world, once the coughing subsides.

However, this is not a standard 12 rounds contest that I'm facing. This has been a near-on 40-year fight for my every breath; and the opponent facing me is like an unforgiving terminator who will keep on attacking me until I give up for good and am knocked down and out for the longest sleep of my life.

I've got to know my foe very well over this length of time and I get better at knowing and sensing where the next intense attack will come from and how best to defend myself against it. It's not always been easy and I've learned some valuable lessons from the multitude of beatings I've suffered.

All my medication, IV drugs, physiotherapy, nebulisers, injections, positive mindset, sport, alternative therapy, prayers and support from family and friends are my defence and resistance – they are all needed and enable me to fight back.

With each year that goes by I'm slowing down, with energy waning and lung capacity reduced. I know more than ever that my savage opponent is catching up with me. I do have some incredibly pitiful days when my lungs give me no quarter or recovery period. Unlike the real boxing game, there's no downtime in between fights. For me, it's relentless and keeps coming in waves.

On these dark days, I'm practically up against the ropes taking punch after sickening punch from CF with only the odd jab back as a reminder to my illness that I'm still there. On these occasions I'm barely able to defend myself. I feel backed up in a corner, in damage limitation mode, taking blows. To use the scoring system in boxing, these merciless days would definitely be marked as a 10/8 round to CF.

Indeed, it feels like the gloves are off and my condition is taking me onto 'the cobbles' to the pre-Queensbury Rules era of bare knuckle, anything goes fighting. There are no rules and a referee to defend me if things get out of control. I'm taking too much punishment – it's an uncompromising fight to the end. Although I'm not physically marked on the outside of my body, all the damage is on the inside. What lies beneath one might say...

On brighter days, when I'm feeling upbeat and reasonably fit, I can't wait for the contest to start so that I can show CF who the boss is. I manage this through playing hockey, tennis or going for a dynamic run. To use the boxing vernacular, I might even do some show-boating, do the Ali shuffle and throw the odd bolo punch!

I keep these rare moral victories to myself. I'm all too aware that pride comes before a fall and I must respect at all times this deadliest of opponents. Fighters are prone to trash talking their opponent in the lead up to a bout in order to steal the psychological upper hand. Well there's no point in belittling my CF as it won't be long before I'll be reminded of my frailties.

Most of the time, I'd say it's honours even and CF and I neutralise each other out- neither having the upper hand (or punch). On most days we give as good as we get, spar with each other and the judges would score us an even 10/10 round.

At the end of tonight's film, the fighter Micky Ward battles through a gruelling contest and eventually wins and claims a world title. That was a defining moment in his career and his destiny to be a world champion.

The gloves are off in my duel with destiny. However, in my contest, there's no boxing ring, bright lights, flashing cameras, cheering crowd, ring announcers, hoopla or a referee. It's just me versus this unforgiving illness inside my body trying its hardest to finish me off.

Currently in this fight for my life, I'm still standing, completely motivated to carry on battling with my conditions. I'll still get up when knocked down and I will still be there when the bell rings for the start of the next day's confrontation.

In my case, real-life is again imitating art and I am a prize fighter... and the prize is not for money, a championship belt, kudos and hero status. The winner in my daily brawl takes the biggest spoils you can imagine. Something more important than money can buy... life itself!

38. The One and Only

Tuesday 8 March 2011

Today we found out the outcome of our latest attempt to have another baby via our final ever cycle of IVF.

Following the incredibly sad loss of twins last November prior to Katie's 40th birthday, we wanted to go one last time with the embryos we had frozen at Hammersmith Hospital.

The last few months we've been back on the IVF rollercoaster. Not a ride for the faint-hearted in any shape or form. Particularly for Katie who takes the brunt of the process, physically as well as mentally.

We still felt the natural desire to give Felix a playmate. We would regularly be asked the following questions by parents in public play areas, "Is he your only one?" and "Are you only having one child?"

We had these last few embryos left and they were hanging over us. Katie had amazingly kept it together after the loss of the twins last year, in part because she knew there was one last chance at having another baby and that hope kept her going.

If we didn't use these embryos we would always have been niggled by the 'what if' scenario that they existed and we hadn't gone for it and tried to use them. It was a tempting dilemma that they were waiting to be unfrozen and used – like an important package waiting for you at the post office collection that you know is there and the intrigue to go and pick it up.

This was Katie's eighth IVF cycle spanning over seven years. This included the two miscarriages and the successful cycle that brought Felix into our world. The effect of the IVF process and the body-altering drugs really take their toll. The preceding weeks of daily injections to get her body ready caused horrific tiredness, akin to inducing an early menopause.

It's not just physically that she was changed. The drugs at times had a negative effect on her general nature and demeanour. Unfortunately the medication can make the woman tempestuous and short-tempered – not an easy situation for both of us. Unknowingly, Katie would not be the full ticket which was tough on her and difficult for me being around her when she was in a compromised mood. These mood swings were in addition to the emotional rollercoaster that accompanies every IVF cycle, such is the limited chance of success.

Financially and emotionally we knew we couldn't keep doing this. We made a verbal pact before this latest attempt that it would be our final IVF cycle – one last hurrah, if you will.

Katie had been through all the horrible injections and countless trips to the hospital leading up to having the de-frosted embryos placed inside her womb a few weeks back. Since then she has been trying to take it as easy as a mum can with a lively three-year old snapping at her heels. The doctors will all tell you that in theory you can do what you want to do and if the embryo is going to stick that it will do. But that advice falls on deaf ears to a would-be mum desperate to give her embryo every possible chance of holding on.

Since we had Felix, the process for finding out whether an IVF cycle had been a success has changed. Previously the lady would have her blood taken in the early morning and then wait a few excruciating hours to find out the good or awful news via a phone call from the hospital. This led to a nerve-wracking two-hour slot where either Katie or I would answer the phone and be told the outcome. In my experience, this wait is as nervous as I've ever been in my life and makes waiting for exam results and job interviews pale into insignificance.

Nowadays and more humanely, after the embryo transfer, the woman is given a few pregnancy testing kits and told when to start using them. This allows the hopeful mum to have her expectations matched to some degree prior to going in for the blood test. Finally, instead of that horrendous wait for a phone call, you are given a number and time to call them to get your blood test results.

Very early this morning, Katie drove to Hammersmith Hospital to have her bloods done. She must have known that the portents were unfavourable because her testing kit had proved negative the previous evening. But there's always hope and the blood test would be conclusive either way.

While Katie went off to the hospital for potentially the last time, I dropped Felix off at his child-minder and then worked from home so that I could be around for the outcome news.

Naturally, Katie was nervous and distracted until it was time to ring the hospital in the early afternoon time slot that she had been given. It was our time to find out whether our future included another child or not...

Sadly it was not meant to be. Katie came off the call in tears and we hugged in mutual grief, fully cognisant of the realisation of our situation.

The whole IVF process followed by the eventual sad conclusion cut to Katie's very core. She had gone through a physical and emotional hell, in the end for nothing. I imagine she will always hold a torch for another child. That inner angst will never completely disappear and there will always be a part of her that grieves for the loss of the twins last November and the harsh realisation that she will never have another baby.

For my part, I was hugely proud of the immense determination Katie showed during these last two IVF cycles. The utter finality of knowing that we were not going to have another child and give Felix a brother or sister feels crushing. However, it's important to know when enough is enough and when you cannot continue for an elusive gift.

Every step of a CF life is a challenge and there seems to be hardly any low-hanging fruit or easy pickings to get what you want – nothing is taken for granted which in turn gives me a richer perspective on what is valuable in life.

As an adult, becoming a parent has felt like some form of re-birth for me. I had to re-set myself and begin a completely new challenge – one where there are often no easy answers, no user manual to instruct me on what to do and where my intuition and gut instinct become my guiding light.

Parenting has not always been plain sailing. To be honest in the early years it was a mixed bag – a true blessing of our miracle boy Felix which came at quite an initial cost with Katie's nerve damage pain and our ensuing relationship struggle.

My health adds another significant factor to the equation. Before I became a dad, for 36 years I fought tooth and nail to protect myself and put boundaries in place to preserve my health. I have had to come to terms with the juxtaposition of being a dad which has meant that some of those barriers are put at risk.

In some ways, I am still getting used to the fact that I am the father to a healthy child. Quite often I think of Felix through my own lens as if he has to be as careful as me with all the same health deficiencies as I have to contend with. Katie will pick me up on this by reminding me that he's not like me and doesn't have CF.

In my defence, sometimes it's hard for me to think any other way – seeing life through healthy eyes – because it's been so engrained in me for so long. It's not like I had perfect health for a while before being struck down by an illness in order to have a comparison to draw on. CF is all I've ever known – it's my normality. It's actually quite difficult for me to think like a healthy person.

From my own experience, one aspect of being a parent that I didn't expect was the positive affect Felix has had on others – both family and friends. In particular he brings delight to my parents and parents-in-law, as his grandparents. It's wonderful how he makes them glow with pride and adoration. It's most definitely their reward for having been parents themselves and grafting to raise their own children. But a child also immeasurably changes the lives of his or her own parents.

I do believe in life you are often given what you can deal with and perhaps with my on-going health issues, we have, with just the one busy boy, more than enough for us. It's all relative to each family's dynamic, their health and wealth situation. Felix is not the first 'only' child in this world and he won't be the last.

It's at times like this, as hard as today's sad news has been for us to digest, that we have to appreciate what we do have – a healthy, exuberant and entertaining son – rather than what we don't have or now will never have.

There's only one letter more between the words 'none' and 'one'; but for anyone that has really struggled to conceive will know, there's a whole world of difference when it comes to having one child as opposed to having none. We are truly lucky that we have our darling boy.

Felix is everything you would expect in a boy. Like father like son, he's called 'handsome' a lot. I cherish my time with him and already have so many happy memories stored up. I adored going crabbing with him in Brittany when on holiday which evoked childhood holidays with my own dad. I love our Saturday trips out to Wimbledon Common and into the Village for lunch. Best of all is our shared catchphrase, "I love you to the moon… and back."

Felix and I share many common bonds. We are both high on life and looking to extract as much from our lives as possible. I keep defying the CF survival odds to stay alive in this world and he defied the IVF odds arriving in the world. With the IVF titanic struggle as a backdrop, it seemed appropriate to hold a 'Welcome to the World' party on Morden Park common, rather than have a first birthday party for Felix.

Felix is a timely extra motivation for me to keep battling on against the CF tide and stay around to be there for him and Katie. Any time I play sport or need to take my medication, one of the things that helps me to play that hockey game or pop a tablet is the thought of my son. That gives me the extra oomph to play that hockey game or pop that tablet.

When I was single in my late twenties before Katie came into my life, I felt I would 'die happy' for a hug with a long-term partner. Now a hug with Felix takes this feeling to a different level; where I feel I could 'live for eternity' for a hug with him. Recently, we have started three, way family hugs which mean the most of all.

Felix is my living and breathing legacy in this world – something of me that will continue to exist even when I'm not around anymore.

I'm sure there will be times ahead when we'll hanker for another child, but it's just not meant to be. We've got Felix – our 'one and only' and we feel blessed to have him.

In the future, if other parents casually ask me in playgrounds, "Is he your only one?" I'll happily reply, "Yes, he's our one and only Felix!"

39. This is the Day

Thursday 17 March 2011

I never thought it possible for most of my life. Slowly over the last year I dared to dream that it could happen – that I'd achieve this stupendous birthday goal. Through this journal I started to verbalise it as a possibility. From there, I actually broke my self-imposed silence and started to tell family, friends and even strangers about my desire to seek the Holy Grail for a CF sufferer…

I've finally made it. As of today, I can now shout it out loud – "I've made it to 40 years old!"

To use cricketing terminology, I'm 40 not out and going pretty well despite some heart-in-mouth moments along the way. The ball has been dropped on numerous occasions and I've not always been in flowing form but I've stood my ground and doggedly carved out a courageous and diligent life innings.

I had booked the day off work, which I don't always do on my birthdays but I knew this day needed to be kept sacrosanct. Who wants to be at work when they have reached such an elusive milestone in their life?

After taking advantage of a lie-in, I went downstairs to see Felix and Katie for a long hug and an unbridled birthday celebration. After making my habitual cup of green tea, I opened the cards and presents that I had already received. The feeling of euphoria continued as I quickly contacted my twin brother, Jez, and my other close friends who share the same birthday.

Katie had also taken the day off work so we went for lunch in a country pub called the Cricketer's Arms in Cobham, Surrey – this was definitely the right place to be when celebrating being 40 not out!

After a lovely meal, we went for a walk together down some country lanes to work off the food and just take the day in. It was a nice moment to just be us, walking hand-in-hand and snooping around unchartered countryside.

We got back home mid-afternoon in time to pick up Felix from his nursery, which is a rarity for me on a normal work day. Within fifteen minutes of being at home, a photographer from the national newspaper The Daily Mirror arrived for a pre-organised photo shoot. This was another press follow-up to the popularity of my 'Countdown to 40' blog. They intended to publish a feature on me having reached my actual birthday. As the weather was reasonable and Felix wasn't interested in joining us for an indoor family photo, we ended up outside in our back garden. After many distracting tricks by the photographer, we finally achieved the shot that he wanted of all three of us.

Over some lovely birthday cake that Katie had made and a cup of tea I opened the cards and presents that had arrived during the day. As is the modern way of celebrating a birthday, I received a torrent of birthday best wishes from family and friends via email, Facebook and mobile texts. This was broken up by the occasional phone call from my nearest and dearest and an extremely thoughtful voicemail message from my previous work client, Sam, all the way from Texas!

To be honest, I felt in a bit of dream-like state as you would when there's so much attention on you. However, one thing that did feel real was my adherence to my normal daily medical regime. I still took all my usual drugs today not wanting to miss a trick. There's no time off from my drugs not even on a special day such as this. The infection in my lungs wouldn't be celebrating my birthday so it was important to keep my relentless approach going.

Even though today landed on St. Patrick's Day, which is synonymous with partying, I decided to keep my powder dry ahead of the big birthday event planned on Saturday night in Wimbledon. Instead of a boozy night, I opted to go for a jog around the local streets. It seemed the right thing to do and gave me an opportunity for some time on my own. It felt appropriate to keep my mind, body and spirit on the front foot.

At 6.20pm, just before stepping out for the run and while Felix was in the bath, I posted my birthday blog – 'This life begins at 40' – which I'd finished writing only this morning. Hitting the publish button felt emotional and completed the countdown of eleven blog posts in the lead up to this historic day. All had touched upon different elements of my journey battling CF and were well received. I was hoping that this final one would continue in that vein…

Outside in the cold night air, I went for a standard winter-time run on the local pavements. When I'd got to the top of the nearby hill, I decided to go 'off-piste' and walk along the alley way to the entrance to Morden Park. It allowed me a chance to get my breath back following the exertion of getting up that hill!

Even though it was pretty dark already, the evenings were getting lighter which always feels uplifting having gone through a tough winter. I stood there listening to the delightful twilight birdsong and reflected on my day.

It honestly felt as if I'd reached the top of the world. My normal grimace while running was replaced with a half-smile of joy laced with pride based on my achievement.

Turning my iPod back on, I chose this moment to listen to a song that I'd been waiting to play during this birthday countdown. It was a song by the eighties band The The called 'This is the Day'.

For me it was a moment to ruminate on all that had happened on my survival journey, every minute, hour and day of my life, while looking boldly ahead to what the rest of my life had to offer.

Making it to 40 as a life-long CF sufferer was a hugely significant milestone and one that I wasn't taking lightly. It came with a mix of emotions – joy, relief and happiness, but also some guilt for those not as fortunate as me in being able to defy the effects of this condition.

I shed a tear for the lives lost to this horrid illness including my CF friends who died before reaching 30. They all deserved to live as long as I have. I remembered the blog posts since January and the response from parents who had lost young CF children and adolescents. I can only think that they might find it difficult to comprehend how I have lived my life while their child hasn't had that level of fortune.

This was definitely a bitter sweet moment. I'm perpetually humbled by the sadness of their deaths. It keeps my feet on the ground and helps to reduce any delusions of grandeur that I might be harbouring over my enforced longevity.

The inconvenient truth is that CF doesn't favour anyone it touches and there are no winners – it's harsh, relentless and doesn't take any prisoners – it's simply a horrid illness. There's a phrase I often use to describe my luck to still be here when others have sadly perished: 'there I go before the grace of God. It could have been me...'

As always when I delve into this thought pattern, it does again beg the immortal questions for me – how have I survived? How have I cheated death?

As I recommenced my jog, the flow of my running allowed me to concentrate on what my birthday might mean to others that knew me and who had helped me to reach this summit. This day is most definitely one to acknowledge my mum: today's a stark contrast to how she spent her own 40th birthday when I was still young. Her big day coincided with my first appointment with Doctor Knight, who left them in no doubt that my health was not all it should be... that must have been such a deflating way to 'celebrate' her 40th and I am very lucky that I could reach the same milestone in such a normal and fun manner.

I also see it as a time of celebration for my dad, brothers, Katie, close family, friends, medical staff and complementary therapists who have supported me and have been such a valuable part of this journey.

Not only did I make it to 40 for myself but for others whose hope I carry with me. Finally, it's for my fellow CFers who have sadly departed the world. Their spirit is still burning deep in my soul.

As I completed my jog and before I entered the house, I sat outside on our brick wall and reflected again about the magnitude of this day. Typically, my sense of elation had the lifespan of a mayfly. I soon began to consider what tomorrow and the future had in store for me...

What next? Maybe today only represents climbing to the base camp and the summit is even further for me? I'd got to a significant milestone and already I was starting to think about what my next goal would be – what's the next realistic age I could attain – 45, 50, 60? Maybe my life is just beginning at 40?

Later in the evening, I took time to read my birthday blog output, desperate to soak up each and every minute of this landmark day. I was deeply touched by the eleven comments received, which included:

"Roll on 50! Happy birthday Timmy! So proud of all you have done and so happy for you and your family!"
                                    - Stewart (Primary and Secondary school friend)

"Keep pushing on Timmy, keep pushing on. Keep writing this blog too; it is awesome."
                                    - Juliet (University friend)

"Congratulations!!! I hope many more years will follow, I also hope you will continue with your blog as life starts at 40!
                                    - Irene (Work colleague)

"Congratulations and thanks for your inspirational blog – I hope my boy with CF is as determined as you."
                                    - Cheryl (Mum with a CF child)

"It has been an amazing experience to read your blog. CF is indeed a terrible illness and one has nothing but admiration for the way you deal with it every day."
                                    - Luke (Hockey team mate)

Replying to these kind comments made me feel proud and relieved that I'd actually started my countdown blog and increased the openness about my health.

I see reaching 40 as a celebration of my life to date and what it has taken for me to survive; but I also view it as a launch pad for the rest of my life – with my hourglass half full rather than half empty. Like a cricketer, I need to build on my 40 and push on for at least another 40!

To still be here is the most precious gift I have on my 40th birthday which is not something that many 40-year-olds would think to acknowledge. Not only am I still alive, but I have a lovely wife and son to share my future life with.

This is the day when things fell into place. This is the day when my life finally changed. This is the day...

40. Live to Tell

Tuesday 22 March 2011

A few days after my 40th, I played for my London Edwardians hockey team on a crisp sunny Saturday morning and we had a hugely convincing and satisfying 3-1 win. I felt reasonably fit and contributed during the three quarters of the game that I was on the pitch. As we left the ground, no one on our team was happier than me – to still be playing, competing and winning aged 40.

As an extra reason to be proud, this was the eighth league game I'd played without losing since almost retiring last November. Back then, after a consultation with my dad, I made the bold decision not to give up but to 'get up and go again'. That decision has most definitely been vindicated by the outcome of this match.

A few hours later on the Saturday evening saw the occasion of my big 40th celebration in a venue in Wimbledon town where Katie and I were joined by my brothers, their partners and many other close friends. It was a hugely joyous event and one which I wanted to chat to everyone and be the last man standing. This was a goal that I thought I'd achieved at 2.30am when surveying the scene in the nightclub. Then out of the ether of the dancing throng stepped two of my Irish hockey friends, both called Jonny, looking as if they were just getting started for the night... I've said it before and I'll repeat it here – it's tough to out-drink the Irish, especially around St. Patrick's night!

Today, Tuesday 22 March, I have a feature in another national UK newspaper, The Daily Express, focusing on my milestone and what I did upon reaching 40. Entitled 'I have defied the odds by reaching 40', the article contained the following quote which sums up my whole approach:

"Cystic fibrosis no longer defines me. I try to manage the disease rather than let it manage me. I focus on what I can do rather than on what it stops me from doing."

Since the start of my blog a few months ago my CF story has been displayed in three national UK newspapers, I have conducted two radio interviews and shared a Boston-based news article with the CF son of a famous American football player, Boomer Esiason. I have also been asked to write an article for the Mirror Weekend newspaper in early May. With this media attention I am making waves and raising the public consciousness concerning the illness.

It appears my news has travelled well. When I walked into my local barber shop for a haircut in late February, I was greeted with 'We saw your article in the newspaper – we never knew – good on you for sharing!'

Since I started the blog in January, I have definitely noticed the new candour about my struggle with CF has been reflected back by everyone. Actually touching people with my prose feels both affirming and empowering. It seems that I'm starting to open more eyes, minds and hearts to the condition and helping to de-mystify it for people who had either vaguely heard of it or who had no idea of its existence. The vast majority in the latter camps have no appreciation that CF is such a harsh illness and kills sufferers early in their lives.

I'm increasing the awareness around CF and hopefully inspiring people (either healthy or those dealing with any long-term illness) that even when the odds are stacked against them, there is usually a way to overcome.

Judging by the responses to my blog from the CF community and friends, my story is already helping others and in some cases, offering a rare ray of hope that life expectancy with CF is what you want it to be. By enduring something so unpleasant I feel better qualified to assist others. It's funny that the thing I was most reluctant to share for so many years turned out to be the very thing that can make a substantial difference. I'm absolutely delighted that I'm having such an effect.

This countdown blog has been good for me in so many ways, not least as a means to share my experiences and coping strategies. It's actually been quite a cathartic experience; digging deep within my soul to find the right words and then sharing them via this journal, my blog, websites, newspapers, magazines and on the radio. It's a good job that I have the right face for radio!

With this in mind, I've decided to keep the blog going but to post less regularly when I've got something new or life-affirming to share. I plan to change the name of my blog from 'Countdown to 40' to 'Postcards from Earth'.

Interestingly, my narrative is having other knock-on effects. A number of family and friends have approached me about fundraising for CF via different activities. Indeed, my good friend, Julian Archer, was inspired enough by my blog, that he's doing a sponsored CF cycle ride from France to England culminating in joining me, my brother Chris and my Phantoms touring team for a hockey game in Southampton in mid-May. This will allow me for the first time ever to take part in a sponsored hockey game to raise money for CF. This is something I've always dreamt of doing – playing my beloved sport and raising funds at the same time – but hitherto had been reticent to organise. This was linked to my strong desire not to showcase my illness while exercising. Up to now these two have been kept far apart, but not anymore.

I am abundantly moved when anyone wants to challenge themselves in the pursuit of making money to help cure CF. I offer those who physically torture themselves for my condition the solace that as hard as it gets during their chosen activity, that they should think of me and remember that their lungs do work and that they should feel blessed.

I inform any fundraisers of the harsh reality that many CF sufferers cannot walk till the end of their road or will struggle to walk up a flight of stairs. With this in mind, I encourage them to cherish their own health as it's the greatest gift anyone can have and they should be proud to make the most of it for a good cause. By breathing extra hard themselves, they quite literally breathe life into the lungs of CF sufferers.

I may inadvertently inspire people to 'bust a gut' to raise critical funds for CF, but I find it works both ways. It's their altruistic efforts that in turn inspire me to keep going and defy the medical odds.

And yet... as I read my article in the newspaper today I know that my life is a double-edged sword.

My health didn't join in with the birthday festivities and magically improve. It didn't take a day off just because I happened to turn 40. All this wonderful media propaganda is taking place against the usual backdrop of my relentless daily CF and diabetes medical regime. CF doesn't go away. It's always there to remind me of my heightened mortality.

Like the majority of CF sufferers, I am often lacking in energy due to the extreme effort required to adhere to the punishing schedule. During some recent exercise, I coughed so hard that I produced some blood, which is always disconcerting no matter what spin you put on it. Yesterday, after the birthday weekend, Felix heard my early morning coughing session and proclaimed to Katie, *"Poor daddy!"*

In early March after Felix had attended a party, I brought him downstairs for his breakfast and he pointed out that one of his party balloons had withered. *"My balloon is worn out!"* he disappointedly exclaimed.

On some days, that balloon is me.

There are times, when battling my health conditions that I feel more like 400 years old rather than 40. But it makes the days that I feel upbeat, strong and energetic even sweeter and fulfilling.

Anyone struggling with a long-term chronic health condition like CF will have uttered the immortal questions, 'Why me? What did I do to deserve this rotten illness?'

I still ask myself 'Why me?' but it has a different connotation now. How have I cheated death? Why am I still here? What's the bigger plan for me? What can I do to make sure I keep alive for as long as possible?

It's one of the truest facts in life that 'time' and 'health' are the two of the most precious assets. Often these are not realised and appreciated by people until they are diminished.

For me both of these have been in short supply from the start of my life. This rare perspective fuels the intensity of what I want to achieve with my time alive.

My increased longevity has to be about making my life count – every hour is important. I'm here today, but I could be gone tomorrow. Whilst I still have breath in me I must define and create my everlasting legacy. Before the whistle blows I know I have a strong desire to make a difference to the lives of people I know and meet. The older I get, the expectation increases for me to remain healthy to keep hope alive – for others as well as me.

'He who has health, has hope. And he who has hope, has everything.'

I can strongly relate to this proverb. My physical and mental approach has helped me break the shackles of impending doom, to fight harder when all my energy has gone, to be positive when all I wanted was to give in, to take my medication when I want to be carefree, to look to a future rather than an end and to have the courage to keep fighting. I honestly believe that a life with CF can be about more than just existing. Nowadays CFers can make a real difference in society and lead fulfilling lives.

Realistically, my life is still likely to be short so it has to be merry along the way. When the fat lady sings (and she's been warming up her voice up most of my life), I don't want any regrets. Similar to the meanings of Felix's name, I intend to be 'happy-go-lucky' for as long as possible.

To endure is to undergo a hardship without giving in. I use the expression 'pushing on' many times a day and it sums up my obdurate attitude to the daily battle with all that CF and diabetes throw at me.

I try to manage the disease rather than let it manage me. All the medication is just something I need to do at certain times of the day, so that I can get on with my life. That way, CF is not defining who I am. People know me as Tim Wotton, the cheeky chap, who just happens to have CF.

There's a lingering promise of a cure for my CF with some encouraging trials taking place involving gene therapy, where the defective CF gene would be corrected. The bottom line for me is that when that possibility comes knocking at my door, I better be ready and in as good a shape as possible to maximise the level of cure or treatment it could offer me. I've got to keep pushing on until CF stands for 'Cure Found'.

As for my future, I'm blessed with a loving wife, son, family and friends. All my struggles are worth persevering with, to hold onto what I have and what I still intend to do. Against all the odds I'm still alive and kicking. Could reaching 40 be a new start rather than my final hurrah?

For now, heaven can wait. It's too early for goodbyes.